PRAISE FOR
THE BRIDGEBUSTERS

"Want to know the true-life story behind the 57th Bomb Wing where *Catch-22* author Joseph Heller spent the war? Read this thrill ride in the cockpit of a B-25 ... [and learn how] they bombed bridges and destroyed Nazi supply routes to win the war in Italy in World War II."

—Lucian K. Truscott IV, author of *Dress Gray* and *Full Dress Gray* and grandson of the American commander in Italy

"One of Tom Cleaver's trademarks is that he somehow manages to weave mechanical facts into the fabric of a thoroughly human tale in such a way that you come away feeling as if you've just watched a wildly detailed movie. In *The Bridgebusters*, you can almost smell the engine exhaust and hear the empty .50 caliber casings clatter to the fuselage floor under the gunners' feet. He makes the truth read like well-done fiction."

—Budd Davisson, editor of *Flight Journal*

"In *The Bridgebusters*, Thomas Cleaver highlights one the ironies of World War II: seventy years later the public is mostly aware of the Mediterranean Theater of Operations via a fanciful 1961 novel and the 1970 movie. But in addressing author Joseph Heller's wartime service as a B-25 bombardier, Cleaver places much more in context. The little-known Twelfth Air Force fought a long, sanguinary campaign from North Africa to Italy, highlighted by the months-long 'bridge busting' effort in the Alps' Brenner Pass. Flying against lethally proficient anti-aircraft crews, the 57th Bomb Wing paid a steep price for its success. Yet far more is revealed than the 'glamorous' fliers sweating out open-ended combat tours. Cleaver introduces us to long-suffering ground crews who 'kept 'em flying'; careerist officers mostly interested in their next promotion; Italian civilians who suffered in the crossfire; and even *Wehrmacht* leaders and flak gunners. This is rare history—told almost at the last moment as more of those veterans depart the pattern every day."

—Barrett Tillman, author of *Forgotten Fifteenth*

"U.S. Navy vet and lifelong aviation enthusiast Tom Cleaver is making a stunning appearance on the nonfiction book scene as a reliable chronicler of combat military aviation. *The Bridgebusters* goes a long way toward burnishing his sterling reputation for going the extra mile to bring us interesting and unusual detail layered into a heartfelt appreciation of aviators."

—Eric Hammel, aviation historian and author of seventy books, including *War in the Western Pacific* and *Big Week: The Bombing Offensive That Broke the Luftwaffe*

"Cleaver's superb *The Bridgebusters* is the book that finally credits the uniquely brave men of the 57th Bomb Wing with the recognition they so richly deserve. A rigorously researched work, *The Bridgebusters* is nevertheless fast-paced and personal. Cleaver's extraordinary characterization of the men and their actions during one of history's bloodiest air campaigns reads true and compelling, and is enhanced by judicious use of the men's own words, thoughtfully gleaned from contemporaneous letters and diaries. Highly recommended."

—Jay A. Stout, author of *Hell's Angels: The True Story of the 303rd Bomb Group in World War II*

THE BRIDGEBUSTERS

THE
BRIDGEBUSTERS

THE TRUE STORY OF THE *CATCH-22* BOMB WING

THOMAS McKELVEY CLEAVER

REGNERY
HISTORY
Washington, D.C.

Regnery History™ is a trademark of Salem Communications Holding Corporation; Regnery® is a registered trademark and its colophon is a trademark of Salem Communications Holding Corporation

Cataloging-in-Publication data on file with the Library of Congress

ISBN: 978-1-68451-363-5
Library of Congress Control Number: 2016013722

First trade paperback edition published 2022

Published in the United States by
Regnery History
An Imprint of Regnery Publishing
A Division of Salem Media Group
Washington, D.C.
www.RegneryHistory.com

Manufactured in the United States of America

10 9 8 7 6 5 4 3 2 1

Books are available in quantity for promotional or premium use. For information on discounts and terms, please visit our website: www.Regnery.com.

To the men of the 57th Bomb Wing, for their accomplishments

CONTENTS

Meet me over Rovereto
Meet me in the air
There ain't no place
The flak is thicker
No place else but there
We will take evasive action
They will miss us by a fraction
So meet me over Rovereto
Meet me in the air.

—Anonymous (1944)

Cannon to right of them,
Cannon to left of them,
Cannon in front of them
Volley'd and thunder'd;
Storm'd at with shot and shell,
Boldly they rode and well,
Into the jaws of Death,
Into the mouth of Hell
Rode the six hundred.

—Alfred Lord Tennyson,
"The Charge of the Light Brigade"

                    YOSSARIAN
Is Orr crazy?

                    DOC DANEEKA
Of course he is. He has to be crazy
to keep flying after all the close
calls he's had.

                    YOSSARIAN
Why can't you ground him?

                    DOC DANEEKA
I can, but first he has to ask me.

                    YOSSARIAN
That's all he's gotta do to be grounded?

                    DOC DANEEKA
That's all.

                    YOSSARIAN
Then you can ground him?

                    DOC DANEEKA
No. Then I cannot ground him.

                    YOSSARIAN
Aah!

                    DOC DANEEKA
There's a catch.

                    YOSSARIAN
A catch?

DOC DANEEKA
Sure. Catch-22. Anyone who wants
to get out of combat isn't really
crazy, so I can't ground him.

YOSSARIAN
OK, let me see if I've got this
straight. In order to be grounded,
I've got to be crazy. And I must be
crazy to keep flying. But if I ask
to be grounded, that means I'm not
crazy anymore, and I have to keep
flying.

DOC DANEEKA
You got it, that's Catch-22.

YOSSARIAN
Whoo . . . That's some catch, that
Catch-22.

DOC DANEEKA
It's the best there is.

—*Catch-22* screenplay by
Buck Henry adapted from
the novel by Joseph Heller

INTRODUCTION

T his book happened by chance. In 2013, on Veterans Day, I happened to read an account in the Huffington Post of Susan Frymier, whose father, a bomber pilot during the Second World War, had never spoken about his experiences in all the years since. That summer she had discovered the name of his old unit, the 445th Bomb Squadron, and when she googled it she found that they were having their annual convention in a month at the Air Force Museum in Dayton, Ohio. She managed to convince her father to attend with her. As she put it, "Now he can't stop talking." I was hooked. I'm a regular contributor to the magazine *Flight Journal*, which is dedicated to finding these stories that haven't been told and preserving them before they're lost, so I'm always on the lookout for opportunities like this. It took me less than a minute on Google to find her listed as an administrator at the University of Indiana, with an e-mail address. I sent off a query, explaining who I was and what I do as a writer, asking if it would be possible to be introduced to her father. Susan

Frymier was more than happy to make the connection, and thus I met her father, former First Lieutenant Paul Young, whose first mission of the forty-five he flew in the Battle of the Brenner Pass as a member of the 445th Bomb Squadron of the 321st Bomb Group in the 57th Bomb Wing was the first mission flown in that campaign, and whose last was the last mission flown by the squadron before the war's end.

Talking with Paul about his experiences, it was easy to see why someone might not wish to relive what amounted to forty-five charges of the light brigade "into the jaws of hell," each as terrifying as the first.

Paul's story played well with the readership when *Flight Journal* published it in 2014. Later that year, when Jim Hornfischer agreed to take me on as a writing client, we went over my bag of stories to see what might sell. I presented this one and that one, and while he found them interesting, nothing rang the bell. Then I said, "There is the true story of the bomb wing Joseph Heller flew in, that he used for his novel." Bingo! A month of effort resulted in a solid book proposal, which was then promptly turned down everywhere Jim showed it. Fortunately, having spent twenty-five years working as a screenwriter in Hollywood, I long ago learned that all projects are turned down by everyone other than the one person who says "yes." Luckily for me, Alex Novak was that one.

For fifty-five years, ever since *Catch-22* was first published in 1961, the men of the 57th Bomb Wing have lived in the shadow of the novel, with most readers believing the book tells actual historical fact. Heller himself said in many interviews over the years that that was not the case; that while the novel was set in a time and place of his own experience, he had not written a historical novel; and that what he had written in the novel should not be taken as literal history. Still, that happened, with the result that members of the 57th have spent years trying to explain that what they did and what the book says are two different things. When the motion picture came out, Jack Valenti, the president of the Motion Picture Association of America as well as a veteran of fifty-five missions in the 340th Bomb Group, made a point of telling people the movie wasn't history. No one listened. Sadly, no one has ever taken the time to discover the real story in its entirety.

The central facts of the story speak for themselves:

On November 1, 1944, the Allied Fifth and Eighth Armies halted their offensive in northern Italy, unable to break the German defenses on the Gothic Line after sixty continuous days of bloody fighting. That same day, the quartermaster general of the German Army Group C, which manned the Gothic Line with the Tenth and Fourteenth Armies, reported the army was receiving 24,000 tons of supplies daily through the Brenner Pass—600 percent of daily minimum needs—with trains taking eight to twelve hours to travel from Munich and Augsburg in Germany, arriving every 30 minutes at the Bologna marshalling yard, the center of the *Wehrmacht*'s supply system for the Italian front. So long as this level of supply could be maintained, he stated, the armies should be able to hold out indefinitely in the war of attrition they had forced on the Allies in Italy.

On November 6, 1944, the three bomb groups of the 57th Bomb Wing based on the island of Corsica flew their first missions of "Operation Bingo" against the electrical transformers of the rail line that powered the electric trains. Within a week, supplies were reduced to 10,000 tons per day as the Germans diverted coal-fired locomotives to the southern front in an attempt to make up the shortage. Between that day and April 6, 1945, during the coldest European winter in a century, the wing flew approximately 380 missions against bridges, stations, marshalling yards, repair depots, and track, from Bologna in Italy to Innsbruck in Austria. Most were repeat missions against important choke points defended by over 500 deadly anti-aircraft guns, in a struggle to knock things down faster than the German repair crews could build them back up. In fact, 10,267 tons of bombs were dropped on these targets. Forty-six B-25 Mitchell bombers were lost, while 532 were damaged by flak in varying degrees. Over 500 aircrew were killed or wounded. The Germans were not the only enemy; flying in the Alps in winter weather, in unheated airplanes without oxygen, with an ever-increasing number of missions to be survived in order to escape the crucible created a whole other set of problems for the crews.

On March 31, 1945, Army Group C's quartermaster general reported that an average of 1,800 tons of supplies had arrived daily during the previous month, only 45 percent of minimum needs, with each shipment taking four to six days to make the journey through the blasted rail line, which was completely closed for over half those days. On April 9 the final Allied offensive in Italy commenced. Twenty days later, on April 29, 1945, German General von Vietinghoff, who had stymied the Allies from Salerno to Bologna, surrendered Army Group C. The war in Italy was over a week before it ended in the rest of Europe. The Corsica bombers had won the fight by creating the conditions for victory. It was the most successful battlefield interdiction campaign ever carried out by the Air Force, and yet it is largely unknown today.

When I set out to research this book, I was greatly aided by the fact that the 57th Bomb Wing Association has been able to put all their wartime records into a searchable database, which is maintained by Dan Setzer, son of Sergeant Hymie Setzer of the 340th Bomb Group. With the war diaries of each unit available, it is possible to review every mission in detail, including who was aboard each airplane for each mission. The database also includes firsthand accounts by many crewmen, most of whom are no longer available for interviews. Thus I was able both to recount the missions and often to tell the stories that came out of them in the direct words of the participants. Dan went "above and beyond" in making this material available, explaining details, and providing solid criticism of the work in progress. He also put me in touch with Italian historian Roger Juglair, making a connection that was crucial in my ability to tell the story from the point of view of those on the ground and, most important, to learn the facts of the mission of August 23, 1944, the bombing of the Settimo Bridges and the town of Ponte San Martino, which I have come to see as the deciding event of Joseph Heller's time in the unit, the event that would lead to his writing *Catch-22*.

Heller was right to say that *Catch-22* is not serious history; however, the serious history he experienced did heavily influence the book. Using the database, I was able to research Heller's combat record, which has a turning point on August 23, 1944. By that date, he had flown forty missions since his first on May 29, or approximately three to four missions per week, depending on weather, the majority of which could be called "hot" from the mission descriptions in the war diaries. Between August 24 and late January 1945, however, he flew an additional twenty missions, approximately one a week, of which, according to his own statement, the last one that was "hot" was flown September 15, 1944, when he participated in the sinking of the Italian cruiser *Taranto* in La Spezia harbor. When questioned about his wartime service, Heller said he "flew mostly milk runs." Looking at the record, this isn't true. At least half the missions he flew were what the crews termed "Beaucoup" or "Beaucoup-Beaucoup"—involving a high level of danger from the German defenses.

Interestingly, however, nineteen of Heller's final twenty missions were "milk runs"—during a period of operations when the war diarists of all the squadrons made note that relatively safe missions were getting harder to come by: "milk runs are becoming increasingly hard to find and even more difficult to fly." Additionally, when Heller completed his tour in January 1945, he had flown only sixty missions at a time when seventy was the hard-and-fast number that had to be completed for an airman to be sent home. How did this happen?

Enter First Lieutenant Wilbur Blume, a fellow bombardier in the 340th Bomb Group whose pre-war experience as a documentary film maker led to his unofficial appointment as a Group PRO (Public Relations Officer) working directly for group commander Colonel Chapman and responsible for making various documentaries on the group for the Colonel's use in promoting the unit's (and his own) record with Air Force superiors. In September 1944, Blume was given the assignment to do a documentary about the operational training of replacement aircrews in the unit, titled *Training In Combat.* In his diary Blume termed the assignment "the Colonel's boondoggle." The project lasted from late September to just before Christmas 1944. Several aircrews from the group were recruited as "actors" for the film. Among them, playing "Pete, a young bombardier," is none other than Joseph Heller.

I am the first researcher to see the Blume diary, as well as the lieutenant's extensive and never-before-seen photo archive, thanks to his son, William Burton Blume, who discovered both the diary and the collection of over four hundred 4x5 negatives in a box in his father's garage a few years ago, plus the remains of *Training in Combat* when he had the sad duty of going through his father's belongings following his death. Forty-five minutes of the documentary has been restored by the staff of the National Archives. It's my belief that all this—the August 23 mission, which is nearly beat-for-beat used in the most bitter scene in the novel, the controversy over the mission that can be deduced from the after-the-fact explanations for the mission found in the war diaries, and Heller's work with his friend Wilbur Blume on a documentary that effectively removed him from operations—explains the creation of the novel.

My friend Buck Henry advised me at the outset that one should never look for the artist in the work, a principle I by and large agree with, but the circumstantial evidence here is too compelling to a military historian, someone with a background as a writer of fiction, and veteran who understands from my own history the reaction of a creative person to the stifling bureaucracy of the military. It's my belief, based on the evidence, that Joseph Heller wrote *Catch-22* because he said "yes" to the offer he later saw as a moral compromise, the same offer that his alter ego Yossarian said "no" to.

This conclusion comes clear in the story of the 57th Bomb Wing's most important battle, which this book recounts. I am indebted to Sterling Ditchey, George Underwood, Dan Bowling, Paul Young, and Jerry Rosenthal for their memories and for their willingness to read over the manuscript as it progressed to make certain that the story I told is as accurate as possible. I'm also indebted to Michelle Cahill, who published the letters of her late uncle, Tom Cahill, which provided deep insight to the events; also to Lance Bowling, who discovered the manuscript his father Dan wrote immediately after the war recounting his recent experiences with all the emotion attached to them at the time. Many other surviving members of the group also provided memories, which I hope bring this story alive to the reader. It's a story of perseverance and bravery in the most difficult of circumstances, one that should have been told long ago. It's a privilege to be the one who got to tell it.

Thomas McKelvey Cleaver
Los Angeles, California
January 2016

ONE

THE AVIGNON MISSION

The sixty B-25 Mitchell bombers taking off from Alesani Airfield on Corsica at 1520 hours on Tuesday, August 15, 1944, represented the 340th Bombardment Group's five hundredth mission since the unit had begun combat operations in Tunisia sixteen months earlier. Their target was three bridges over the Rhône River outside Avignon, France, a site heavily defended by German guns ranging from the Flak-37 to the dreaded *Abwehrkanone-88*, the famous "88," which could reach the bombers at the altitudes at which they mounted their attacks. "The Dreaded Avignon Bridges," as they were known to the crews, were "the roughest target in the theater" according to Captain James E. Nickerson, intelligence officer of the 445th Bomb Squadron.

The mission's goal was to prevent German reinforcements from arriving on the coast as Operation Dragoon, the Allied invasion of Southern France, hit the beaches of Le Cote d'Azur. More than two thousand aircraft, fighters, and bombers from the Royal Air Force, the French

Armee de l'Air, and the United States Army Air Forces, with support from the U.S. and British navies, provided air cover for the invasion, each unit flying several missions on this day of days. August 15, 1944, would see the 340th group set a record of 1,132 individual aircraft sorties in eleven missions flown from Alesani Airfield in Corsica between 0517 hours that morning and 1900 hours that evening.

The bombardier aboard one of the B-25J Mitchell bombers flying wing in a formation of fifteen "diamond fours" (four B-25s—one in lead, one in trail, one to either side), a twenty-one-year-old kid from Brooklyn flying his thirty-seventh mission since his arrival on Corsica the previous May, looked out of his glass greenhouse in the extreme nose of the B-25 at the lush green summer countryside of southern France below. Suddenly the ship's navigator—a history teacher before the war who was overjoyed whenever a mission took him to places that had figured in his studies—announced over the intercom, "On our right is the city of Orange, ancestral home of the kings of Holland and William III, who ruled England from 1688 to 1702."

"And on our left," replied the worried voice of the Chicago-born radioman-gunner in the rear, "is flak." A glance to the left confirmed that indeed the Germans were ready and waiting for their arrival, as the flak barrage created football field–sized yellow and orange explosions surrounded by ominous black clouds.

The bombers turned on their final approach to the target, and the twenty-one-year-old bombardier from Brooklyn concentrated his attention on the lead Mitchell off to his left ahead in the four-plane formation. When the lead bombardier opened his bomb doors, the twenty-one-year-old operated his controls and the bomb bay behind and below them opened to reveal four olive drab thousand-pound high-explosive bombs hanging from their shackles. The target came closer, closer; it was a matter of moments before "bombs away!"

As bombs began to fall from the lead plane, the young bombardier triggered his own and turned to check the intervalometer that recorded the release of each bomb to insure the bombs were indeed falling as they should. When the fourth light blinked, he hit the door control to close the bomb bays and reported on the intercom, "bombs gone—doors clos-ing." Suddenly the bomber was bracketed by three close bursts of deadly "88" flak, the explosions outside so close and so loud the bombardier could hear them even with his radio headset over his ears and over the roar of the engines. Chunks of deadly shrapnel rattled against the Mitch-ell bomber's thin aluminum skin like a barrage of rocks on a tin roof, penetrating the airplane to strike instruments, gear, and human flesh.

With bombs gone, the pilot commenced immediate evasive action and banked away to the right. At that moment more flak exploded out-side and the right wingtip of the plane was blown off, fluttering away into space. The co-pilot, transfixed in his seat with nothing to do but observe the terrifying moment, gave in to his terror as a voice shrieked over the intercom, "Help me! I'm hit." He reached out, grabbed his control yoke, and whipped it over hard to the right as he pushed forward. The left wing came up at a steep angle as the nose turned down and the plane banked into a wild dive.

"Help him! Help him!" the co-pilot cried into the intercom.

Suddenly the bombardier found himself staring out the front of his greenhouse at the earth below rushing toward him as he was thrown around by the rapid wingover and dive. He was pinned by his head to the bulkhead at the rear of his compartment by the G-force, his feet thrashing the air above the .50 caliber machine gun mounted in the nose. He grabbed at the ammo box to the side and steadied himself, then readied for the pull-out. But there was no pull-out. Over the radio the voice shrieked again, "I'm hit! I'm hit!" just as the bombardier's headset wire was pulled out of its jack by his sudden movement.

In the cockpit, the pilot fought with the co-pilot for control of the airplane. The navigator left his position and tried to restrain the co-pilot, but the man shoved him aside. The pilot took the moment to grab the throttles and pull them back to slow the dive. A lucky punch from the navigator caught the co-pilot on the chin and knocked him back in his seat.

The pilot grabbed the controls and began to pull out of the wild dive, momentarily squashing everyone inside with the G-force of the pullout.

The terrified co-pilot recovered, grabbed his set of controls again, and—in his panic—fought the pilot until the flight engineer threw his arms around him and held him tight. The plane bucked and reared as the pilot fought to prevent a catastrophe.

Finally, several thousand feet below the rest of the formation, the B-25 pulled level, bracketed by light flak as it banked and turned sharply to get away.

With the plane now level, but lower and hence in the midst of more dangerous bursts of flak, the bombardier grabbed hold of the big .50 caliber machine gun in the nose to steady himself and plugged his headset back in. "Help who?"

"Help him! Help the bombardier! He doesn't answer!"

That brought the bombardier up short—had he been hit and not known it? How could the voice know? A quick once-over revealed he was unhurt. "I'm the bombardier! I'm OK! I'm OK!"

"Help him! Help him!" the voice cried.

The bombardier shoved himself through the narrow tunnel that separated him from the rest of the airplane and stood up behind the pilots. The turret gunner and navigator now had the co-pilot restrained as the pilot concentrated on making an escape. Then the bombardier climbed into the narrow space between the roof of the bomb bay and the top of the fuselage and squeezed through to the rear of the plane.

The radioman and the tail gunner were there together—the radioman on the floor with a large oval wound in his thigh; there was a hole in the side of the plane just behind the waist window where the piece of flak that had hit him had entered the plane. Fighting nausea at the sight of the bloody wound, the bombardier tore open the first aid kit, ripped open the package of sulfa, spread it over the wound, then bandaged the leg and gave the radioman a shot of morphine. Then he pulled himself back up into the passageway over the bomb bay and returned to the cockpit.

As they flew back toward Corsica over the deep blue Mediterranean, the co-pilot regained his composure. None of the others thought badly of what he had done or the fear he had given in to. They'd all been there themselves, so terrified they were "all up in the top of my flak helmet," as the bombardier had put it in a letter home, paralyzed by the fear of death. The distance between what each man had experienced himself and what had happened to the co-pilot was so short it couldn't be measured. The entire event, which had seemed to last for hours as their minds entered what other combat veterans have termed "the fifth level of the brain, where time is irrelevant," had actually taken only two or three minutes.

They were minutes the bombardier would never, ever forget.

TWO

WELCOME ABOARD THE "USS CORSICA"

Saturday evening, March 18, 1944, was not freezing, but quiet and cold, with no hint of spring in the chill wind. "Sunny Italy" had not been sunny or warm for the previous six months, as frequent rain and hail storms had affected the course of the war. The twilight sky was partially overcast, promising rain, and the newly risen moon, still just visible through a break in the clouds, glimmered faintly over the high mountain a few kilometers northeast of Pompeii Airfield. There the moonlight cast the shadows of eighty-eight B-25 Mitchell bombers.

A light drizzle began to spatter the twin-tailed, twin-engined aircraft and the sodden ground upon which they stood. Suddenly a distant growling rumble grew in intensity, and the ground shook for a moment. Then it shook again, more strongly. And again. Less than a minute passed before the rumble became a continuous growing roar. Dr. Leander K. Powers, a flight surgeon with the 340th Bomb Group of the Twelfth Air Force's XII Bomber Command, remembered that evening in his diary:

"While we were just finishing supper, someone called to say there were huge red streams of lava flowing down the sides of Mount Vesuvius. It was a sight to behold. Never had we seen such. As we watched the streams, like giant fingers flowing down the sides, we could see a glow in the sky."

The next morning, on the other side of the airfield, First Lieutenant Dana Craig from the 486th Bomb Squadron sat next to the ruin of what had been his barracks and wrote of the damage wrought the previous night in the first eruption of Mount Vesuvius in a hundred and fifty years.

> About midnight, I went out of my billet to answer the call of nature. While outside, in a mild drizzle, I was hit on the head by what I thought was a small rock. Suspecting some sort of joke, I went inside for a flashlight. When I returned, the light revealed a layer of damp cinders on the ground. We began to feel the earth shake as though a bomb had gone off. After each quake, a few minutes would pass before the debris blown out of the crater would start to hit the ground. We quickly understood that Vesuvius was erupting. About daylight, the rear of our building started to cave in. We then began to see the larger rocks coming down. By this time everyone was wearing his steel helmet and heavy sheepskin flying jacket for protection from the falling rocks.

That Sunday morning at the great complex of airfields built around Foggia, ninety kilometers north of Pompeii, men of the 321st Bomb Group—the 340th's sister unit in the 57th Bomb Wing—gaped at the sky. A great cloud rose high far to the south, and within hours, smoke and ash from that column descended on their base, though in niggling amounts compared to what the 340th endured. Nevertheless, by midday the men stationed at Foggia had to use goggles to keep ash out of their eyes.

That evening, Dr. Powers recorded, "All during the night and Sunday there were quakes of the earth with tremendous roars similar to thunder from Vesuvius. The windows rattled, and the entire building vibrated."

March 18, 1944, marked the beginning of a two-week-long series of eruptions. It was not a complete surprise; the mountain had been "acting up" since the beginning of the month. However, most of that activity had been on Vesuvius' northern side. It might as well have been a thousand miles away for all the men on the southeast side of the mountain at Pompeii Airfield knew or cared. None had previously felt the fury of a volcano.

But now rocks as big as grapefruits were falling from the sky and smashing cockpit canopies, plastic gun turrets and bombardier "greenhouses." The damage to the aircraft was worse than what had happened back at Columbia Army Air Base in South Carolina in late 1942 when a winter hail storm had destroyed the 340th's entire fleet of eighteen training aircraft. The bombers were covered with hot ash, which burned away the fabric-covered control surfaces and glazed, melted, or cracked the Plexiglas turrets, canopies, and bombardier's greenhouses. Volcanic ash and tephra seeped through openings and filled the aircraft. The weight tipped them on their tails. Dr. Powers recorded, "The roars became more frequent and grumbled like a lion's roar. Streams of fire were shooting thousands of feet into the air, and the countryside was lit up for miles around. Oft times the entire top of the mountain looked as if it were a blazing inferno. It's really uncanny, yet amazing to look at this phenomenon. The vibrations of the building were truly uncomfortable."

The rain of volcanic ash continued through the following week. On March 22 Dr. Powers reported,

> This morning, we rode down beyond Pompeii. The cinders were so deep that traffic was stopped. Along about noon, the wind changed and the cinders began falling on the town of Torre Annunziato. Everything had a coat of black, just like light snow. We drove up toward Naples on the Autostrade, and, as the wind was blowing toward town, I got a wonderful view of the boiling inferno. Yesterday, I rode into a town that was destroyed by the flowing lava. Apparently the flow was

coming to a stop, but the devastation was terrific. Tonight there is a lot of lightning coming from the clouds around the crater, accompanied by infrequent blasts from within the volcano.

By Friday, March 23, Vesuvius had done more damage to the 340th than the *Luftwaffe* had since they had arrived in the Mediterranean Theater. All eighty-eight B-25s were destroyed, more than the group had lost in the year since it entered combat in Tunisia.

On the evening of March 24, 321st Bomb Group armorers Joe Beresh, Tom Davies, Gil Inman, and Wayne Lash decided to drive down to Salerno to see the volcano up close. Lash had the unit's four-wheel drive weapons carrier, and the four young sergeants decided to use it for the trip. Lash later recalled that they began to encounter the devastation from the eruption as they approached Salerno around midnight. There they found the road covered with up to eight inches of ash that had been turned to mush by the daily rains. "Cars, trucks, motorcycles and carts were stalled at intervals along the way and each held up a line of vehicles."

"Here again," Lash wrote, "I saw the superiority of American equipment. Of all the stalled vehicles, I only saw one American 'six-by-six,' the others were all British or Italian trucks." A few miles further on, the men overtook a stalled truck carrying an orchestra on its way to Salerno to perform *Rigoletto*. They invited several of the musicians aboard and dropped them off at their destination.

They drove on, past the ruins of Roman Pompeii, and decided to go up the mountainside. Finding a rutted trail, they transitioned to four-wheel drive and got about two-thirds of the way before they were stopped by Italian farmers who warned them of approaching lava. The men went forward on foot, finally arriving at a vantage point a mile and a half from the crater. Lash recorded his impressions.

Here, I beheld the most terrible, awesome, spectacular sight of my life, an entire mountain virtually aflame. From the crest of the cone, as the monster belched, a column of smoke, ash, and lava rose several hundred feet, lighting the sky by its incandescence. As the scorching fumes mingled with the cold atmosphere, great bolts of static electricity were released in rapid succession and stabbed the sky in all directions. At a higher elevation, the smoke collected and hung ominously in a huge black cloud that was dispersed by the wind only to be replaced by another. The lightning flashes were filled with a tremendous roar that was accompanied by the lower tones of rumbling. A stream of molten lava flowed from the lips of the crater, and cascaded down the side of the cone to join the avalanche that was crowding its way toward the valley below. Occurring as it did amidst the scarcely-dried blood of another scene of mankind's folly, I wondered if this was not the pains of Mother Earth's groaning for man's inequity.

Sufficiently awed, the four returned to their vehicle and drove down the hillside. A few miles north they were stopped by a British military policeman who wanted to turn the sightseers around. They convinced him they were on their way to a nearby base on official business, and he let them drive on.

Tom Davies remembered, "Without further mishap, we painfully accomplished the fifty-odd miles back to Foggia and arrived at around 0530 hours, tired and cold, but glad for having made the trip." Just as they were about to fall asleep in their cots, the senior armorer came to rouse them. A mission was on, and they had to load bombs in a cold, windy rain.

Unlike in the famous eruption of 79 AD, no lives were lost at Pompeii Airfield; the 340th's only casualties were a sprained wrist and a few cuts. Despite major efforts, however, the damaged aircraft were beyond repair. And for the rest of the month the skies across southern Italy were colored dull gray by ash and smoke. Ash fell as far north as Rome. There was a very real threat of continued volcanic activity, including dangerous lava flows. Moreover, approximately a foot of wet, mushy ash covered the ground. Flight operations were impossible, so the decision was made to evacuate. Between March 23 and 26, the 340th was relocated several kilometers northwest to nearby Gaudo-Paestum Airfield to wait for new aircraft. And American aircraft production at that time was so efficient that the total loss of aircraft in the 340th was made good within a week. New silver B-25Js arrived to replace the battered and war-weary camouflage-blotched B-25C- and D-model bombers left behind at Pompeii. Small formation training missions began within a matter of days, and missions soon after.

The 321st and 340th groups had been flying missions as part of Operation Strangle since being organized under the 57th Bomb Wing in January 1944. They attacked German lines of communication throughout central Italy with the goal of forcing the German Army to retreat from the defensive lines south of Rome. At the same time they supported the Allied forces on the Anzio beachhead and flew missions directly over the battlefield along the Volturno River at Cassino, where the German Army had held off the Allies since the previous December. Their attacks against difficult road and rail bridges were so effective that the 57th Wing had already gained a nickname: "The Bridgebusters."

The eruption of Vesuvius could not have come at a worse time for the Allies. It did more damage to the American air forces in Italy than the Germans had managed to accomplish over the seventeen months since the North African invasion. Twelfth Air Force commanders were now worried that there could be further eruptions and further destruction. The Mitchell squadrons were the heart of XII Tactical Air Force Bomber Command, and any hope of breaking the stalemate on the ground that was the Allied campaign in Italy depended on them. Consequently, during late March 1944 Allied planners considered their options and decided to consolidate the 57th Bomb Wing at a new home far from the volcano and out of the way of the expanding operations of the strategic Fifteenth Air Force at Foggia.

Corsica is the northernmost and smaller of the two large islands west of the Italian Peninsula in the Ligurian Sea; the other is Sardinia. While Sardinia was part of Italy, Corsica had been French since its purchase from the Republic of Genoa in 1764. Following the Franco-German Armistice in June 1940, the island came under the control of the French Vichy regime. Then in November 1942, in the wake of the Allied invasion of French-held North Africa after the German occupation of Vichy France, Italian forces occupied Corsica. By July 1943, there were eighty-five thousand Italian troops there; in early September, in the aftermath of the fall of Mussolini and the Italian surrender, they were reinforced by twelve thousand German troops.

French resistance to the Italian occupation of Corsica began shortly after the Italian soldiers arrived. By early 1943 it was sufficiently organized to request arms deliveries. Free French leader General Charles de Gaulle sent representatives to unite the resistance leadership. The partisans were reinforced, and the movement's morale was boosted by six visits of the elusive Free French submarine *Casabianca*, which brought personnel and arms. Further aerial supply drops by the Free French *Armée de l'Air* allowed the resistance to establish control of more territory in the countryside, outside the major towns.

The tough, small-statured Corsican partisans were called "Maquis" after the tough, small, dense scrub brush on the island. (The name was later applied to the French underground operating in the rugged hinterlands of southwestern mainland France as well.) During June and July 1943 the Italian OVRA Secret Police and Fascist Black Shirt paramilitary groups commenced a largescale crackdown during which 860 Corsicans were jailed and deported to Italy.

The liberation of Corsica began with an uprising on September 9, 1943, when the German troops moved to take control of the Italian forces. While the Italian military leaders were ambivalent in their loyalties, the majority of the soldiers remained loyal to King Victor Emmanuel III, and many fought alongside the partisans during the liberation. While the Allied high command had initially resisted the idea of liberating Corsica through an invasion, in the aftermath of the insurrection it was decided that the reconstituted French I Corps should land on Corsica in late September. One small unit of elite French troops was landed from the *Casabianca* at Arone near the village of Piana in the northwest of Corsica on

September 10. This action prompted the Germans to attack the Italian troops as well as the French. The Corsican partisans and French troops, with the Italian 44th Infantry Division *Cremona* and 20th Infantry Division *Friuli*, engaged in heavy combat with the Waffen-SS troops of the *Sturmbrigade Reichsführer SS* and the *Wehrmacht*'s 90.*Panzergrenadierdivision*. The situation was further confused by the fact that the German units were supported by the Italian 12th Parachute Battalion of the 184th Parachute Regiment, whose troops came from Sardinia and were loyal to the Fascist cause. The Axis force retreated through Corsica from Bonifacio towards the northern harbor of Bastia. On September 13, elements of the Free French 4th Moroccan Mountain Division landed in the port of Ajaccio to block the 30,000 retreating Axis troops. During the night of October 3–4, 1943, the last German units evacuated Bastia, leaving behind 700 dead and 350 prisoners of war.

Shortly after the island was liberated, the French began construction of four airfields that they planned to use for operations by the Free French *Armée de l'Air* over southern France. The USAAF soon offered to assist in developing and expanding these airfields in return for permission to base aircraft on the island. It was obvious that Corsica was a strategic location: targets in southern France and Austria as well as all of northern Italy and even Yugoslavia across the Adriatic Sea would be within range of bombers based there.

During early January 1944, the 5th Fighter Squadron of the American 52nd Fighter Group flew their "Reverse-Lend-Lease" Spitfires from Bari in southern Italy to Borgo Poreta Airfield on Corsica, outside the town of Aghione. By the end of the month the 5th Squadron was joined by the group's 2nd and 4th Squadrons. The Spitfires were soon flying fighter sweeps and patrols over the Anzio beachhead. They were joined in April by the P-38 Lightnings of the 1st Fighter Group assigned to the Fifteenth Air Force, which took advantage of Corsica's location to provide escort to the B-17 Flying Fortresses and B-24 Liberators for their strategic bombing missions against southern Germany, Austria, Hungary, and Romania. In early March, as the Anzio operation stalled, the newly issued P-47 Thunderbolts of the 324th Fighter Group and the weary P-39 Airacobras of the 350th Fighter Group touched down at Ghisonaccia Gare Airfield to join the Spitfires of the Free French *Armée de l'Air Groupes de Chasse GC II/7 "Nice" and GCI/3 "Corse,"* the first French units to be based on free French soil since 1940. Within the week, the veteran 57th Fighter Group that had been the first American fighter unit to enter combat outside the Pacific and had fought across North Africa from El Alamein to Tunisia brought their rugged P-47 Thunderbolt fighter bombers to the island, taking up residence at Alto Airfield near the town of Folleli.

Ghisonaccia Gare was the largest and busiest field on Corsica. In addition to the fighter units, the four squadrons of the 310th Bomb Group, which had been the first B-25 unit to enter combat over North Africa in December 1942, arrived in from their base in Philippeville, Algeria, in late January 1944. Following the invasion of Sicily the previous July, the group—reequipped with B-25G and B-25H attack bombers armed with a 75-millimeter cannon and fourteen .50 caliber machine guns, firepower sufficient to shred a broad range of maritime targets—had become specialists in antishipping operations throughout the Mediterranean.

From temporary bases in Egypt, the 310th's bombers had ranged as far as the Greek islands of the Dodecanese in the Aegean Sea and over the Adriatic Sea along the coasts of Italy and Yugoslavia. Following their movement to Corsica, their initial assignment was to go after enemy shipping in the Ligurian Sea and along the coast of Italy, and they ranged as far west as Toulon and Marseilles in southern France. On March 20, 1944, following the decision to base the B-25s of the 57th Bomb Wing on Corsica, the 310th Group was transferred from XII Fighter Command to become the 57th Wing's third bomb group. In April their war-weary olive drab and gray Mitchell gunships began to be replaced by new silver B-25Js equipped for the medium-altitude bombing role.

The winter weather finally eased as March turned to April; cold rain turned to less-cold rain. At Foggia on Palm Sunday, April 2, 1944, Captain Smith, medical officer of the 445th Bomb Squadron, interrupted a game of baseball between the squadron's officers and enlisted men to pass out "mosquito bars"—soap with quinine—and atabrine tablets, joking that the malaria-carrying mosquitos were "due any hour." The next two weeks saw many missions scrubbed on account of weather and many of those that were flown hampered by bad weather over the target.

The daily missions could be intense, whether one saw combat or not. The experience of 446th Squadron bombardier Second Lieutenant James A. McRae was typical. On April 5 his crew briefed for a mission against the Orvieto railroad bridge at 1040 hours, then went on two-hour standby. They boarded their B-25 at 1315 hours, but just as pilot First Lieutenant Dale Walker was about to start engines it began to rain and the mission was canceled. McRae spent the afternoon sacked out in his tent, exhausted by the wait. After dinner, the squadron operations officer informed him there was a mission the next morning. He stopped by the meteorology section and saw that the morning forecast was scattered showers. That night in bed even *The Maltese Falcon* couldn't hold his interest; he fell asleep in his cot over the open book.

The next morning six bombers got off for a strike on Perugia airdrome, but halfway there the weather turned bad and the mission was aborted. That evening, McRae noted in his diary the psychological frustration of preparing for a mission only to abort—with the knowledge a scrubbed mission didn't count toward the fifty-mission "tour" in XII Bomber Command. As Second Lieutenant Dale Walker wrote to his folks, "Don't believe what they tell you over there about when we can come home because, believe me, they don't know one little thing about it. What you hear is a bunch of bologna."

McRae's mission turned back because of weather, but the 340th's Deputy Group Commander, Lieutenant Colonel Malcolm Bailey, led the six shiny new B-25Js from the 487th Squadron through the clouds to hit Perugia. Just after "bombs away," flak hit the Mitchell bomber flown by Second Lieutenant Gerald Ashmore and set its right engine on fire. Co-pilot Second Lieutenant Hamilton Finney, bombardier Second Lieutenant George Simpson, and radioman Corporal Bernard Burton bailed out and eventually returned to the squadron, but Ashmore's parachute failed to open. Flight engineer–turret gunner Sergeant Julius Iknus and tail gunner Sergeant Jesse Klein were unable to get out and died in the crash south of the target.

On the evening of April 7, 1944, after he finished loading thousand-pound bombs in the six Mitchells set for the next morning's mission, armorer Sergeant Bernard Seegmiller, a dutiful Utah Mormon assigned to the 448th Squadron, sat down and waxed poetic in his diary about the bucolic Italian countryside.

Tonight we have a beautiful full moon that I am sure I won't soon forget. There is something distinctive about spring in Italy that makes it different from anywhere I have been. The fields have been, for the great part, green all winter and the weather, though at times uncomfortable, has seldom reached freezing temperatures. From this state of semi-winter has suddenly dawned a condition of renaissance that cannot be mistaken, even though the trees have not yet put forth their shoots and the mountains, if we could see them for the haze that has covered the valley for several days, are yet splotched with white patches of snow.

This morning as I returned from chow, I stopped to watch the Italian farmer who has a plot of several acres contiguous to our line area plant squash seeds.... The seeds were pre-sprouted and he very painstakingly placed them in a hollow he had dug with his hands and covered them by pulverizing the damp clods. In three days, he said, they will be up.

When Captain Everett B. Thomas heard on April 10 that the 340th would soon be transferred to Corsica, he wrote in the 488th Squadron's war diary, "We're getting ready to move to Corsica, much to everybody's disgust. We're perfectly happy in this nice location in which we have the best and most compact set-up yet."

On April 16, 1944, most of the 340th's ground crews boarded "six-by-six" trucks bound for Naples, where they went aboard an LST (tank landing ship) for the voyage to Corsica. On April 17, two B-25s left

Gaudo-Paestum for a stop in Sardinia before flying on to Corsica with the advance party. They took off in clear weather but ran into a heavy gale over the Ligurian Sea and only just made it to their stop before the severe weather closed in.

That same day an advance party of three Mitchell planes from the 321st Group departed Foggia for Solenzara Airfield on Corsica. Over the next ten days the rest of the bombers made the trip in small groups, accompanied by ground crews to service the B-25s once there, while those left behind flew missions until all had arrived on Corsica by April 30.

On Corsica the 488th was quartered in the Alesani valley, and Captain Thomas found that their living area was filled with heavy underbrush and cork trees but opined that it "looks like it will be a nice set-up once everybody turns to and clears out his individual tent area." He also noted there were fish in the nearby streams and wild boar in the hills above the field.

Corsica was now an unsinkable aircraft carrier that would soon be known to the Americans stationed there as "USS Corsica." But in their location in the central Mediterranean, the crew of that unsinkable aircraft carrier was in dangerous waters. The "bomb line" on the Italian mainland—the point at which Allied bombing posed no danger to Allied troops on the ground—was far south of the island. Meanwhile, German-occupied airfields—at this point the Germans occupied all of France to the north and Italy to the east—were less than thirty minutes' flying time away. The Allied bombers flying from Corsica were in effect operating behind enemy lines. And though missions began quickly, many were scrubbed because of heavy rains over the next ten days. Meanwhile, no one paid attention to Axis Sally's May 1 broadcast greeting the boys of the 340th and promising them a proper welcome.

Around 2200 hours on the night of May 13, Captain Thomas and three friends stopped their bridge game when they heard explosions to the north. They quickly realized it was a "show"—an air raid—but none of them realized that what they were hearing was just the opening act.

Ninety Junkers Ju-88 bombers of the first and second Gruppen of the famous *Lehrgeschwader I,* led by *Oberst* Joachim Helbig, a veteran of 460 missions since September 1939, had crossed out of northern Italy at sea level, thus avoiding Allied radar on Corsica. Their target was Borgo Poreta, home of the 1st, 52nd, and 324th Fighter Groups; their goal was to destroy the fighters. The German bombers dropped fragmentation bombs and incendiaries from six thousand feet. The resultant damage was extensive, with over fifty Spitfires of the 52nd Fighter Group destroyed as well as many P-38s from the 1st Fighter Group and more than half of the P-47s of the 324th.

With the excitement apparently over, the bridge players returned to their game and slipped into their cots shortly after midnight. But Alesani airdrome was roused at 0230 hours by the sounds of explosions on the field. The German bombers had returned to their base, rearmed and refueled, and flown back to do more damage. Again led by Helbig, they had returned to Corsica accompanied by sixty additional Ju-88s of *Kampfgeschwader 76.* Surprise was complete, and the Germans lost no bombers. Twenty-two Americans were killed and another 219 wounded in the attacks on the two airfields. As a pilot of the 488th squadron remembered, "We had all these nice new shiny silver ships, and they reflected the light from the fires so well that the Germans had no trouble spotting where to drop their bombs." These two raids were the last major bombing attacks made by the *Luftwaffe* in the Mediterranean Theater of Operations.

The next morning the survivors surveyed the damage. Sixty-five B-25s had been destroyed, leaving only twenty Mitchells flyable. The 340th had taken a roundhouse punch for the third time in nineteen months. The 487th Bomb Squadron's war diarist wrote, "Picks and shovels were at a premium throughout the area all during the daylight hours while those who didn't have a slit trench dug one and others improved upon theirs." The next day, May 15, in a gesture of defiance, the 340th group mounted an attack against the railroad tunnel at the Italian town of Itri with their surviving airplanes.

Five days later the aircrews and ground crews of the 340th were busy with buckets and brushes, painting the upper surfaces of both the surviving bombers and the new replacement aircraft flown in since the raid with green camouflage paint cadged from the French squadrons at Ghisonaccia Gare. No one noticed the C-47 that landed with supplies and replacement aircrew. The next day, three of the newly arrived second lieutenants, a non-commissioned warrant officer, and three sergeants were assigned to the 488th Bomb Squadron of the 340th Bomb Group. The warrant officer bombardier was Flight Officer Francis Yohannon. And there was another bombardier among the replacements, a skinny Jewish kid from Brooklyn who dreamed of being a writer and had just celebrated his twenty-first birthday on May 1. But Second Lieutenant Joseph Heller hadn't graduated high enough in his navigation school at Santa Ana Army Air Base in southern California to qualify for further training with a specific crew.

A week before his arrival on Corsica, Heller had written in his diary that he was ready to see action. He wanted to see "skies full of flak, and fighters screaming past in life and death duels high in the clouds." Four days after he arrived at the Alesani airbase he flew his first bombing mission. In his tour of duty on Corsica, Heller found all the action he had wished for.

He also found something else. He found there was a catch to it all. Catch-22.

THREE

THE WAR NO ONE WANTED TO FIGHT

D uring the Second World War, the only man who wanted to fight in the Mediterranean was Winston Churchill, who believed such a campaign was a way of getting the Western Allied armies into the Balkans and Eastern Europe ahead of the Soviets. Certainly no American military leader wanted anything to do with combat operations there—since they rightly saw that any effort expended there was a distraction from the main event: the defeat of Hitler's Germany. A campaign in Italy might force the Germans to spread their forces a little thinner and turn some attention away from northwestern Europe, but nothing that happened in the Mediterranean once the Allies secured their lines of communication through the Suez Canal would have any impact on the outcome of the primary confrontation across the old Western Front of the First World War. It was the memory of the First World War that led Churchill to seek alternatives to the bloodletting he had personally experienced as a regimental commander in Flanders after he left the British cabinet in 1915 in the wake of the Gallipoli debacle.

Between the fall of France in 1940 and the entry of the United States into the war in December 1941, Britain stood alone against the Nazis in the west, while events in the east following the Nazi invasion of Russia seemed to presage Soviet defeat. Churchill looked back to the last time Britain had stood alone against a continental tyrant—in the Napoleonic Wars. Napoleon's *Grande Armée* defeated kingdom after kingdom across Europe, but Britain eventually bled him white in Portugal and Spain in the Peninsular Campaign, where the British lack of an army that could stand against the French was compensated for by French inability to bring sufficient force to bear in the Catalan mountains.

More than a century later, in the wake of Nazi triumph on the Continent, North Africa was the one place where Britain had a fighting chance of standing against Hitler's armies as Wellington's had against the French.

War came to the Mediterranean when Mussolini sensed the opportunity to recreate a new Roman *"Mare Nostrum"* in the wake of the Nazi defeat of France and growing British weakness. The Italian dictator longed to recreate the Roman Empire, but his reach exceeded his grasp.

After the Italian army in North Africa suffered a major defeat at the hands of a smaller British army, Hitler reluctantly sent reinforcements. Under the redoubtable General Erwin Rommel the *Afrika Korps* came close to a victory that could have opened the entire Middle East to German domination, resulting in Rommel's promotion to Field Marshal. Rommel was defeated: Churchill stood firm until he found a general who could win, in the person of Field Marshal Bernard Montgomery, supported by American Lend-Lease equipment shipped around Africa to Egypt.

Once the United States got into the war after Pearl Harbor, domestic politics meant that American forces should enter combat as soon as possible. While the British were locked in combat in Egypt, the news from the Pacific went from bad to worse throughout most of the spring of 1942. General George C. Marshall and the U.S. Army leadership believed that the way to relieve the British was an Anglo-American invasion of France. Code-named *Sledgehammer*, the invasion contemplated at that time would not have been massive enough to defeat the Germans in Western Europe decisively. The Americans believed such an invasion could hold territory in western France and force the Germans to divert forces from North Africa and the Eastern Front to resist it.

But inevitably, such a campaign would devolve into a battle of attrition, and a battle of attrition in France was exactly the nightmare Churchill was determined to avoid at all costs. Seeking an expedient alternative he could sell to his new ally, Franklin D. Roosevelt, who was badly in need of good military news, Churchill proposed an Anglo-American invasion of North Africa, which was unoccupied by the Germans and held by a relatively weak Vichy French Army. Such an operation would have an excellent chance of success and could even bring France back into the war on the Allied side. It would extend Allied control of the Mediterranean sea lanes and create a threat in Rommel's rear that he would be forced to turn and face. Additionally, it could satisfy Stalin's demand for an Allied "Second Front" to relieve the Red Army.

Another word for "expediency" is "politics." FDR saw the value of the operation to his political fortunes. Against Marshall's advice, in June 1942 he ordered planning for an American invasion of North Africa to begin as soon as possible.

Meanwhile the failure of Operation Jubilee in August 1942 demonstrated that Operation Sledgehammer was unlikely to succeed. The Germans decisively defeated the large-scale commando raid on the French Channel port of Dieppe that August. The Germans responded so effectively that the Canadian troops who landed in the harbor were forced into premature withdrawal with high casualties, while the *Luftwaffe* attacked the fleet and inflicted defeat on the Royal Air Force units supporting the operation in the largest air battle to occur on the Western front.

Operation Torch, the Allied invasion of North Africa, hit the beaches in French Morocco on Sunday, November 8, 1942, on the heels of the British Eighth Army's offensive at El Alamein (which began on October

23). While there was some initial Vichy opposition to the invasion of North Africa, by November 11 French forces throughout North Africa ceased resistance.

The Germans moved quickly to counter the invasion. *Luftwaffe* units and German troops moved into Tunisia over the following month and taught the U.S. Army Air Forces that the Germans were still superior to the green Americans in combat. Losses of Lockheed P-38 fighters by the 1st and 14th Fighter Groups, which had been diverted from the Eighth Air Force in England, were so high that the P-38–equipped 82nd Fighter Group, recently arrived in England, was sent on to North Africa three weeks after the invasion.

By January 1943 the 78th Fighter Group—the last of the four P-38 groups established to provide long-range fighter escort for the Eighth Air Force B-17s and B-24s over Western Europe—was stripped of its aircraft and pilots (other than flight leaders and command personnel) to make up further losses in North Africa. Marshall's fear that a diversion in the Mediterranean would have an adverse effect on the main effort against Germany had come true. The loss of the P-38s meant that through most of the crucial year of 1943 the Eighth Air Force was forced to make do with P-47 Thunderbolts that did not have the range to protect the bombers, so that a strategic bombing campaign against German industry was delayed.

Rommel struck at Kasserine Pass in Tunisia in February 1943, inflicting severe losses and a crisis of command for the Americans. By March, General George Patton had changed the military equation, replacing leaders who had failed the test with those who had passed. In April the *Afrika Korps* was pushed into northern Tunisia where they held the Mareth Line until their supply lines to Italy were severed by Allied air forces. The Germans surrendered in May 1943, and all of North Africa was liberated.

The 310th Bomb Group brought its B-25 Mitchells to North Africa in December 1942. The 321st Group arrived in Tunisia in February 1943, followed in March by the 340th Group. While the 310th became proficient at sinking German and Italian shipping, the 340th and 321st took part in the June bombing campaign against the island of Pantelleria, which led to the surrender of the Italian garrison without an invasion being necessary. The B-25s next saw action over Sicily and in July flew their first missions against the Italian mainland, culminating in the bombing of Rome on June 19. Both the *Luftwaffe* and the *Regia Aeronautica* intercepted the Mitchells in these combats, but the bombers proved to be stubborn opponents, holding off the German and Italian fighters.

At this point the strategic question became "What next?" Once again the Americans pressed for a cross-Channel invasion in 1943, but it was not feasible because of a landing craft shortage that would not be made up until 1944. Churchill pressed for an invasion of Sicily—ultimately named Operation Husky—which he said would protect the lines of communication through the Mediterranean and put pressure on Italy to quit the war. Again, expediency ruled the day. Sicily was invaded on July 9. After initial hard fighting, German and Italian forces retreated to the Italian mainland by August.

On July 19, a dispirited Mussolini met with Hitler at the latter's insistence at the Ville Feltre in northern Italy, where *Der Führer* lectured *Il Duce* that he must obey the "voice of history" and continue the fight. But that was not to be. On July 23, at the request of King Victor Emmanuel III, who had grown increasingly critical of the conduct of the war over the previous twelve months, former Italian foreign minister Dino Grandi—who in his younger years had been considered the only possible leadership alternative to Mussolini in the Fascist Party—called a meeting of the Fascist Grand Council and moved that they request the King resume leadership of the government. The motion was carried, nineteen to seven with two abstentions.

On July 25 the King summoned Mussolini to a meeting at which he was dismissed as Prime Minister. Upon leaving the meeting he was arrested by Carabinieri and spirited off to the island of Ponza. The King then appointed Marshal Pietro Badoglio to head a new government whose task was to make peace with the Allies—though officially the government reassured the Germans that they remained committed to the war. The Germans were not deceived. As German Admiral Friedrich Ruge wrote, "Mussolini's resignation, accepted without protest anywhere, is the clearest possible proof of the almost total collapse of the Fascist Party."

After the victory in Sicily, U.S. military leaders wanted to withdraw the main American ground forces to England in preparation for the cross-Channel invasion in the spring of 1944. Churchill countered that this would leave the Italians at the mercy of the Germans at a time when there was every likelihood of a full surrender, with Italy joining the Allies. Abandonment of the Allied campaign in southern Europe would also mean that the Germans would have nearly a year's breathing room to prepare for an invasion everyone knew would happen. And without news of continued victories, the lack of fighting would demoralize citizens on the home front. Roosevelt agreed, once Churchill committed himself to complete support of an invasion of northern France in 1944.

Expediency and inter-Allied politics had once again carried the day: by the time the decision to invade Italy was agreed upon there was little more than a month in which to plan and organize it and bring together the necessary forces, a fact that led to many unexpected delays with repercussions throughout the campaign from July 19 to August 17 of 1943.

From the time of Mussolini's arrest on July 25, 1943, the Germans planned to occupy Italy should the government surrender. They were aware of the intense negotiations between Marshal Badoglio's government and the Allies, though the Italians continually professed their loyalty to the Axis cause.

With the Allies in Sicily across the Straits of Messina from Italy, Hitler became convinced that their ultimate goal was to use their Sicilian base to invade Greece and the Balkans. He knew the difficulty his forces would face in defending against such an action because of the poor transportation facilities in the Balkans (which a year later would inspire his only decision to unilaterally withdraw German forces, when Greece and Yugoslavia were evacuated). Hitler understood Churchill's desire to move into Eastern Europe to forestall the Soviets and to take advantage of the fact that Germany's allies in Bulgaria, Romania, and Hungary were not that strongly committed to the Axis cause.

Back in late May, following the Axis surrender in North Africa, Rommel had been sent to Italy to take command of Army Group B, which would be tasked with occupying all of Italy in the event of a surrender. Hitler promised six *infanterie* and *Panzergrenadierdivisions*, two *Panzerdivisions*, two *Luftwaffe Fallschirmjägerdivisions* (paratroops) that would be transferred from France, and two *Panzerdivisions* to be transferred from the Eastern Front. German tank losses in the enormous armored battle at Kursk in July, however, precluded the transfer of the two Eastern Front divisions.

In the face of this loss of force, Rommel had advised Hitler that Italy could not be defended without the assistance of the Italian Army and advocated a retreat to a fortified line south of the Po Valley in the northern Apennine mountains, where the Allies could be held at bay and thus prevented from entering the Reich through the south. On August 1, following Mussolini's arrest, Rommel's forces began infiltrating into northern Italy through southern France, moving across the border in small units so as not to alarm the Italians, who nevertheless became increasingly nervous as the German movement continued over the following days.

Luftwaffe Field Marshal Albert Kesselring—commander-in-chief of German forces in the Mediterranean, known as the Southern Front—had long been making plans to defend southern Italy from the Allied invasion he believed was inevitable using both German units that had been held in Italy on their way to North Africa when the *Afrika Korps* surrendered in May and the Italian Army, which he still believed would be loyal.

When *Luftwaffe Fallschirmjäger* commander General Kurt Student arrived to plan a possible *coup d'etat* in Rome and to arrest the King and Badoglio, Kesselring pressed him about his plans for the defense of southern Italy. Kesselring believed that Rome could be held till the summer of 1944 if the German Army engaged in a campaign of attrition, forcing the Allies to pay in blood for every inch of territory taken in Calabria and Apulia and delaying their approach to the Reich borders as long as possible.

While some German officers believed the Allies might attempt a landing in northern Italy, Kesselring stated flatly they would not invade beyond the range of their air cover on Sicily, which meant that they could not come ashore farther north than Salerno, which he advocated the Germans occupy and fortify against such a move. He pointed out, presciently, that after Rome fell the German Army in Italy could retreat north and hold out "indefinitely" in the Gothic Line of fortifications Rommel had ordered built in the north, so long as sufficient supplies could be secured through the Brenner Pass on Italy's border with Austria, but he advised fighting in the south instead.

Kesselring's argument was strengthened by the successful withdrawal of sixty thousand German troops and their equipment from Sicily across the Straits of Messina, accomplished over the nights of August 15–16 and 16–17 in a massive failure of Allied intelligence: all the Germans' withdrawal plans for Sicily were worked out over the telephone rather than the radio, shielding German communications from being intercepted by Allied radio and decoded through the Ultra program.

Meanwhile, there was much discussion in the Allied command about what exactly to do with Italy once it surrendered. The bolder staffers at headquarters advocated taking advantage of the confusion that would be sure to ensue to disrupt the Germans and give them a real knockout blow in the war—something that would have been difficult to achieve because the Allies did not have accurate information about the size of and plans of Army Group B on account of that army's communications being shielded from Ultra codebreaking. These officers advocated a *coup de main* against Rome itself. They proposed landing the 82nd Airborne at Rome's airport the day the surrender was announced to take control of the city and disrupt the Germans—supported by an Allied landing at Nettuno just west of Rome rather than further south at Salerno. But the idea of a more northerly amphibious landing was abandoned for the very reason German Field Marshal Kesselring had given to his colleague General Kurt Student. It became obvious that there was no way to provide proper air support beyond the range of the Allied air forces in Sicily, as neither the Royal Navy nor the U.S. Navy could provide sufficient aircraft carriers and naval air units to make up the difference. But the idea was not abandoned until General Maxwell Taylor had landed at Anzio in early September and met with the Italians to plan the action in Rome—where it became clear to General Taylor that the Italians could not promise sufficient loyal army units to support the Americans and that Kesselring's forces in the city were far more active than had been expected. There would be no audacity in the coming campaign.

On September 3, 1943, the Armistice of Cassibile was signed by General Walter Bedell Smith, Eisenhower's chief of staff, and by General Giuseppe Castellano for the Italian government, surrendering to the Allies and pledging to join the fight against Germany. That same day the British Eighth Army crossed the Straits of Messina between Sicily and the Italian mainland in Operation Baytown. The Italian government ordered the Italian Army not to resist the Allies, so the British landed without casualties.

The Italian surrender became effective on September 8. The Germans began to hear rumors of it on September 7 and responded with their planned Operation Achse to disarm Italian units and occupy important positions, which lasted from September 7 to September 15. Rommel disarmed all Italian units in the north, while Kesselring ordered those in the south to go home. The Italian Army disappeared overnight.

On September 9, the British landed troops of the First Airborne Division at Taranto in Calabria in Operation Slapstick. If the Allies had only waited until September 12, which was the date the Italians expected the invasion to take place and the date the Germans were using to coordinate plans for their withdrawal to Rome, Hitler's order to evacuate German forces in southern Italy would already have been given—on September 9—and the German Tenth Army would have been in the middle of the withdrawal, which would have made fighting the invading Allies nearly impossible.

On the evening of September 8, Kesselring had bowed to the inevitable and ordered his forces, while holding the positions to which he had moved them, to prepare to evacuate if the order was given. Now, in the face of the Allied landing, with the *Wehrmacht*'s new Tenth Army still in southern Italy, the Germans had the superior force. So they could make a stand, and they stood firm in southern Italy.

The Tenth Army, commanded by General Heinrich von Vietinghoff, had been activated on August 22, and the six divisions of its two subordinate corps were positioned to cover possible landing sites north and south of Naples. *XIV Panzerkorps* was sent to the Salerno plain with the *1.FallschirmjägerPanzerdivision "Hermann Göring." 15.Panzergrenadierdivision* and *16.Panzerdivision* were deployed near Naples, while *LXXVI Panzerkorps' 26.Panzerdivision, 29.Panzergrenadierdivision,* and *4.Fallschirmjägerdivision* were further south. *16.Panzerdivision* held the hills above the Salerno plain.

Operation Avalanche, the amphibious landing at Salerno by the U.S. Fifth Army and elements of the British Eighth Army and the Canadian Army that was the main attack Kesselring anticipated, also took place on September 9. In order to maximize surprise, Fifth Army commander Lieutenant General Mark Clark had decided to forego a traditional preliminary air and naval bombardment. However, his plan backfired, and the Germans were ready and able to respond. As the first wave of the American 36th (Texas) Infantry Division approached shore at Paestum, a loudspeaker in the landing area proclaimed in English, "Come on in and give up. We have you covered." The British 46th and 56th divisions landed alongside the American 36th and had to face the four battle groups of *16.Panzerdivision*. Fortunately, the British divisions were able to fight their way ashore with the support of naval bombardment from Allied warships offshore. By the end of the day, lead elements of the Allied forces could look down on the plain of Naples, but they were hard-pressed to keep their position.

That night the *Hermann Göring* and *15.Panzergrenadier* divisions moved to the battlefield. Fighting was intense over the next three days as Kesselring sent more units from as far north as Rome, as well as the units south of Salerno, into the defense against Operation Avalanche, while Allied reinforcements were constrained by limited transportation and the predetermined build-up schedule based on the planners' anticipation of how the battle would develop.

Kesselring also requested that Rommel send him the two Panzer divisions of Army Group B, but Rommel demurred, saying their loss could not be risked if he was to successfully defend northern Italy after the forces in the south were defeated. After the war, Kesselring told his Allied interrogators that he believed firmly that, had Rommel acceded to his request to allow the two armored divisions to reach him by September 13, he could have defeated the Allies. When one considers just how hard and close the fighting was, it is easy to believe that the addition of two experienced armored divisions might well have tipped the balance in the Germans' favor.

Even without Rommel's armored divisions, the stubborn initial resistance by *16.Panzerdivision* and the German ability to reinforce by land more quickly than the Allies could land by sea or air almost tipped the battle. The Tenth Army came within an ace of defeating the Salerno beachhead. American planners had not anticipated such resistance, a failure of imagination and planning that would repeat itself in the months to come.

The U.S. Fifth Army was short of infantry when the Germans launched their counterattack on September 13. That afternoon two German battle groups overran two battalions of the 36th Infantry Division and nearly wiped them out. The Germans were only stopped by U.S. artillery firing over open sights, naval gunfire, and the fact that a motley crew of artillerymen, drivers, cooks, and clerks stubbornly held a makeshift position. At one point, General Clark and his staff seriously considered an evacuation under fire.

The 82nd Airborne Division, which had been held on Sicily for the possible Rome operation that had been canceled at the last moment, dropped into the beachhead that afternoon to provide the reinforcement necessary to stabilize things. On September 14 German attacks were repulsed with heavy casualties, and that night every Allied bomber in North Africa and Sicily was sent to hit enemy positions in the surrounding hills. The next day the *Hermann Göring* Division attacked on high ground east of the beachhead but was stopped by naval gunfire, including from the 15-inch guns of the battleship HMS *Warspite*. The

B-25s of the 321st and 340th groups flew battlefield attacks against the Germans.

By September 15, Hitler was impressed with the results at Salerno and agreed with Kesselring that a delayed withdrawal was the right thing to do. Kesselring wanted to prepare a defensive line on the Volturno and Rapido rivers north of Naples, which he called the Bernhard Line. Holding this position would allow the German Army to execute a counteroffensive should Allied preparations for an attack against the Balkans result in a withdrawal of forces from the Italian front. This argument probably had considerable impact on Hitler, who was always offensively minded.

On September 16 the *Wehrmacht* went over to the defensive. *Luftwaffe* attacks on the invasion fleet with Fritz-X guided bombs, used for the first time in this battle, damaged the HMS *Warspite* and sank two cargo ships. The English Eighth Army advanced from Messina to provide support at Salerno. Kesselring allowed the Tenth Army's von Vietinghoff to break off contact and commence a fighting withdrawal that would extend over the next month, ending with occupation of the Bernhard defenses, which would stymie further American advances through the end of the year.

On September 19, the Allies attacked toward Naples. On September 22, the newly landed U.S. 3rd Infantry Division under the command of Major General Lucian K. Truscott Jr. took Acerno, followed by Avellino on September 28. On September 27, the Eighth Army took the major airfield complex at Foggia. A rebellion by the people of Naples forced a German withdrawal, and Allied forces entered the port on October 1.

On October 4, Hitler summoned both Kesselring and Rommel to his headquarters to hear their views on the feasibility of a counteroffensive. Rommel's arguments for a northern stand were less dramatic but probably equally valid as Kesselring's advocacy of continuing the fight in the south. Rommel overestimated the amphibious capabilities of the Allies and believed a line too far south was a vulnerability for which he would not want to assume responsibility, though he admitted the Bernhard Line could be held with half the divisions necessary in the northern Apennines. Throughout this period Hitler's advisors were concerned that the Italian invasion was a diversion, that once the airfields at Foggia were occupied the Allies would finally turn their attention to their real objective in the Balkans. Rommel's continued pessimism about fighting in the south convinced Hitler the general was no longer reliable, and he authorized Kesselring to finish the defensive line. A formal order keeping Kesselring and Rommel's separate commands both functioning directly under *Oberkommando der Wehrmacht* (OKW) was signed by Hitler. Because *Der Führer* did not entirely share Kesselring's optimism about holding the Allies away from the northern Apennines for six to nine months, the same order that instructed Kesselring to build up and hold the Bernhard Line instructed Rommel to construct a strong defensive line in the northern Apennines. However, Rommel was ordered to send reinforcements to Kesselring, who had won a major victory in the battle of concepts that would define the rest of the war in Italy.

Finally, there was the question of what would be done with the Germans' former ally Mussolini, who had been rescued by SS commando Otto Skorzeny on September 12. With the former Italian dictator now completely dependent on his German masters—they had moved him to Castel Gandolfo in northern Italy for safekeeping—and the Italian Army disbanded, the Nazis could proceed with the establishment of a Fascist puppet regime, known as the *Repubblica Sociale Italiana*, or RSI. This allowed for the activation of some Italian military units composed of loyal Fascist volunteers, which would include an air force, the *Aviazione dell'RSI*. (Following the evacuation of all *Luftwaffe* fighter units from Italy for the defense of the Reich in the summer of 1944, the Italian aviators would become the sole aerial opposition to the Allied air forces for the remainder of the war.)

The chief of the new Italian army would be Marshal Rodolfo Graziani, who was invited to meet with Hitler on October 9 to discuss the manner in which Italy would again share in the conduct of the war on the German side. During this meeting Hitler and Graziani agreed that German-occupied Italy would be treated as a "friendly" country, with the Fascist government given a measure of independence outside of large areas designated as "zones of operation" where the Germans would control both the fighting and the local population. Since he realized that the loss of Rome would seriously impair the establishment of Mussolini's puppet regime, Hitler concluded that "the intended defense of the [Bernhard] line is of decisive importance to the continuance of a joint struggle."

Between October 4 and November 6 Hitler vacillated in deciding to whom he should give supreme command in Italy, swinging from Kesselring to Rommel and back to Kesselring. Both commanders were again summoned to meet him on November 6. When he was asked whether he thought he could defend the Bernhard Line and hold Rome and central Italy, Rommel replied in the negative. So Hitler appointed Kesselring Commander-in-Chief Southwest (that is, of the Italian Theater) and made him commander of Army Group C. The Fuehrer's order provided detailed instructions for the defense of Italy, affirming that "the Bernhard Line will mark the end of withdrawals." Hitler had made the final decision on which strategy would be followed in the defense of Italy; this judgment determined the manner in which the rest of the war would be fought. On November 21 Rommel was transferred to France to assume responsibility for the defense of the Atlantic Wall against invasion.

Hitler's decision to hold and defend the Bernhard Line set the stage for the bloody battles of the Rapido River and Monte Cassino and the Anzio beachhead over the next six months. Had he not decided to reappraise the strategic defense of Italy, all these places likely would have fallen to the Allies after light skirmishes or perhaps even unopposed.

Thus the bloodbath at Salerno was just a taste of what was to come. By mid-October the Germans were ensconced on the Bernhard Line and the Gustav Line, centering on Cassino further north and blocking the advance to Rome, was near completion. A rainy November and a December full of blizzards and drifting snow saw the Allies held at the Bernhard Line.

It was obvious the easy pickings the Allies had looked forward to in Italy were not easy to pick at all. Allied planners turned their focus on events to come in northern Europe. General Dwight D. Eisenhower, commander of the Allied forces in the Mediterranean Theater since the North African invasion, left for England in January 1944 to become Supreme Commander, Allied Expeditionary Forces for the Normandy invasion. He took with him the 1st Infantry Division, "The Big Red One" that had proven its worth and reputation in North Africa, Sicily, and Italy, as well as the 82nd Airborne Division, the most experienced American paratroop division, with drops at Casablanca, Sicily, and Salerno. For the rest of the war, Allied forces in Italy would find themselves weaker and weaker against their German opponents as men, materiel, and equipment were diverted to operations aimed more directly at German defeat.

The leaders who would ultimately be responsible for winning the war opposed the Italian campaign as a diversion of resources at every juncture. When it was undertaken anyway, it was handicapped by poor Allied military leaders who were consistently out-generaled by their opponent Kesselring until competent leadership was finally appointed a year after the invasion. Between September 1943 and April 1945, nearly 60,000 Allied and 50,000 German soldiers died, with overall Allied casualties approximately 320,000 men, while the Germans and their allies suffered nearly 336,650.

No other campaign in Europe cost more in lives lost and wounds suffered by infantry forces than the bitter small-scale fights at the Bernhard Line, the Gustav Line, Anzio, and the Gothic Line.

FOUR

POINT OF NO RETURN

Twenty-year-old Sterling Ditchey graduated from bombardier flight training at Victorville Army Air Field northeast of Los Angeles in the high California desert on November 13, 1943, and was commissioned a second lieutenant in the United States Army Air Forces (USAAF). At the school Ditchey had sat next to a tall skinny cadet who was so quiet that it wasn't until he read *Catch-22* thirty years later that he managed to remember his fellow student's name: Joe Heller. Ditchey had spent the previous summer attending cadet training at Santa Ana Army Air Base in southern California, which he thought was fine duty since his family lived just fifteen miles away in the town of Orange and he could spend his weekend furloughs at home.

On November 20, 1943, both Second Lieutenant Ditchey and Second Lieutenant Thomas D. Cahill arrived at Columbia Army Air Field outside Columbia, South Carolina, the home of advanced training for B-25 Mitchell crews. Tom was a southern California transplant from New

Hampshire who was also a recent graduate from bombardier training. The fact that Ditchey and Cahill had attended training at Santa Ana Army Air Base at the same time, would spend the same time in training at Columbia, and would be transferred to the Mediterranean Theater on the same transfer order and even fly in the same formation as far as Natal, yet would never meet, was an indication of just how big the USAAF was by then. Cahill, a prolific letter writer and an Irish story-teller, described Columbia in a letter home: "There are sixteen of us Sassy Seconds living in a long low structure, divided into four rooms, with the walls, ceiling and floor beautifully covered with charming black tar paper. We have in each room one potbellied stove and one locker just about big enough to hang a change of underwear in. The latrine is com-munistic, an affair nestled about 75 chilly yards from the door. And, when it rains, the water rushes down the sides of the gully in rollicking rivulets which form a delta right around the entrance."

By this point in the war, pilots arriving at Columbia were all gradu-ates of multi-engine flight training schools, which made their transition to the North American B-25 less of an ordeal than many of their prede-cessors had faced. The first stop for all was ground school, where pilots, bombardiers, radiomen, and gunners all learned the various systems in the B-25. Each man then learned the specifics of his position in the bomber: radios, gunnery systems, and bomb release mechanisms were covered in detail.

Captain Joe Carver, one of the original pilots in the 310th Bomb Group, recalled the way crews were formed:

> After our transition training was completed, my co-pilot and I waited for a crew to be assigned. It was a simple process, they just went down the list and picked them out. Nobody interviewed prospective members, there were no questions about personalities or likes and dislikes. A guy showed up and announced he was your gunner, bombardier, engineer or radio operator. You shook hands and that was that. It never occurred to us to wonder if we would like a guy or not—we

just did because he was in the crew. Eventually we became familiar with each other's personal life. We knew everybody's hometown, his girl's name, his folks, where he had gone to school, what he liked and what he wanted to do when the war was over. We knew these things just as if we were his family, which I suppose in a way we were.

Sterling Ditchey's crew was a little different from the standard B-25 crew, though, since they were assigned to fly the cannon-armed B-25G attack bomber. "We didn't have a co-pilot, and the crew didn't require a bombardier, so I had to take a crash course in dead-reckoning naviga-tion. I was the Limited Co-pilot, Navigator and Cannoneer. After the 270 hours we spent in training, I could probably have put the plane on the ground more or less in one piece from the basic training our pilot Chuck Akins gave me." Soon the full crew had been assigned. The "old man" was their twenty-four-year-old pilot, Second Lieutenant Charles Akins. Sergeants Robert Semm, William Morgan, and Francis Gough were assigned as flight engineer–top turret gunner, radioman–waist gunner, and tail gunner respectively. "They didn't waste any time once we were all there," said Ditchey. "We started flying the airplanes on December 5. Our training consisted of a variety of flights including cross-country and over-water navigational flights to the Bahamas and Miami Beach."

Cahill, who also trained on the B-25G, described his new job in a letter: "Whether we ride astride the cannon or side-saddle, nobody seems to know, but already we are trying to find a new name for our trade. 'Cannoneer' had a brief spurt of popularity. 'Bazooka Boys' is coming up fast. 'Cannigator' is a dark horse, but most popular of all is one I cannot repeat to you, my mother. We are designing a new pair of wings with crossed 75-mm shells rampant on a field of dividers and protractors."

In early February, the B-25G was phased out in favor of the B-25H, whose "Sunday punch" was a stripped-down 75-millimeter pack how-itzer that was fitted in what in a standard B-25 was the crawlway tunnel through which the bombardier reached the "greenhouse" in the nose.

For those assigned to the B-25H, the most impressive part of the training was actually firing the cannon:

> The cannon had tremendous recoil normally, and to lessen that they had modified the breech so that some of the gases escaped when it fired. What that meant was it shot flame out the back. As the cannoneer, it was my job to load each round. I slammed that round into the breech and closed it, and then jumped back up on the flight deck as fast as I could to avoid that fire coming out. The top turret gunner's position was almost directly behind and a bit above that thing, and he would either turn to the right side away from the gun or crowd up on the flight deck beside me. Even with the modification, when we fired it, it felt like the airplane slammed into a brick wall from the force of the recoil.

With the breech modification, the cannon had a shorter range. Ditchey remembered they never hit the target during practice: "They had mock-up ships at Myrtle Beach south of Charleston, and we could come in low from out at sea and get off a shot or two each run, but I don't remember anyone ever hitting anything."

In addition to the cannon the B-25H had two .50 caliber machine guns in streamlined pods on each side below the cockpit and four in the nose above the cannon. The top turret just behind the pilot's cockpit held two more, while one pointed out the waist to either side behind the wing and there were two more in the tail position. Firing all eight forward-firing weapons at once was memorable: "They made one hell of a racket and the whole airplane rattled and shook. Anything that wasn't tied down would go flying around inside the airplane."

When Ditchey's crew completed their training a few days ahead of the others in late March 1944, they were ordered to take their airplane and get in as much cross-country flying time as possible. A long weekend pass was thrown in, good for March 24–27. Pilot Chuck Akins suggested they fly up to Cleveland, Ohio, which the rest thought was a good idea.

He then suggested to Ditchey that the two of them take the Greyhound bus to his hometown of Warren, Ohio, where his family would put them up for the weekend. A weekend home with family before heading off to war sounded good.

Once in Cleveland, the two young lieutenants hitched a ride into town. While waiting for the bus, Sterling Ditchey had what he would see in retrospect as a life-changing encounter. "There was a young woman who was also from Warren, waiting for the bus. She and I chatted and I learned her name was Cleola Green. We sat together on the bus and talked some more, then said our good-byes in Warren." The two officers were supposed to catch the bus back to Cleveland that Sunday afternoon. "We managed to miss the bus we were supposed to take, and had to wait for the next one. Lo and behold, who turned up to return to Cleveland but Cleola." The two once again spent the bus ride talking and again said good-bye in the bus depot. "It was too late to fly back that night, so we called Columbia and told them we'd fly back in the morning." The next morning they arrived at the field to find it socked in by bad weather. "All I knew about what Cleola did was she worked for a government housing authority. It took several phone calls, but I managed to finally call the right office. She agreed to set up one of her friends for a date with Chuck, and we all went to dinner that night." When Ditchey dropped Cleola off at her apartment, he asked if he might write Cleola while he was overseas. "I ended up writing just about every day I was overseas. When I returned the next March, I met her family and she came out to visit mine in California. On March 23, 1945, I asked her to marry me and she said yes." The two have been together ever since.

All that was in the future. Upon the crew's return to Columbia, everything changed when they learned they would be flying to Africa to join a group in the Mediterranean—without the B-25H they had trained in. Only two bomb groups were now using the cannon-armed B-25, both in the Pacific. The 310th Bomb Group was at that time in the process of being assigned to the 57th Bomb Wing in the Mediterranean Theater of Operations, with their mission changed from maritime attack to medium bombardment, though this fact was unknown to a crew as junior as

Ditchey's. "We left our B-25H there at Columbia and went down to Savannah, where we picked up a brand-new B-25J with orders to ferry it to West Palm Beach. Past that, we knew nothing of the coming trip, since they only gave us orders from one stopping point to the next." The crew spent three days at Savannah, slow-timing the engines and calibrating the instruments on B-25J-1-NA, serial number 43-4050, the airplane they picked up, one of the last B-25s to come out of the factory with camouflage paint, a coat of olive drab on her upper surfaces and neutral gray on her belly and under the wings and tail.

The "southern route" to the Mediterranean involved crossing the South Atlantic at its narrowest point, between Brazil and West Africa. Before 1939, very few had flown the route, which was the province of aerial adventurers like French aristocrat, poet, writer, and aviator Antoine Marie Jean-Baptiste Roger, Comte de Saint Exupéry. He was known to the book-reading public as Antoine de Saint-Exupéry, 1939 National Book Award winner and author of *The Little Prince* and *Wind, Sand and Stars*, a book that recounted his adventures flying over the South Atlantic and across South America and would be read by many of the young Americans who followed his trail only a few years after he and his comrades pioneered it.

The North Atlantic presented severe challenges for fliers because of weather and the long distance with few stopping points. The South Atlantic was a natural alternative aerial route to Europe, as the distance between Brazil and West Africa is only a bit more than one-third of the distance from North America to Britain. The first solo crossing of the South Atlantic happened five weeks before Lindbergh's famous flight from New York to Paris, when Portuguese aviator José Manuel Sarmento de Beires flew from Portuguese Guinea to Brazil the night of April 16–17, 1927. About ten days later, on April 28, 1927, Brazilian pilot João Ribeiro de Barros, with co-pilot João Negrão, navigator Newton Braga, and mechanic Vasco Cinquini, flew from Cabo Verde in Portuguese Guinea to Fernando de Noronha, Brazil in the hydroplane *Jahú*, as one leg of a flight that originated in Genoa, Italy, and terminated at São Paulo. Nineteen-twenty-seven would continue to be a busy year for flying the

South Atlantic. French aviators Dieudonne Costes and Joseph le Brix (who in 1932 would make the first Paris–New York flight flying a highly modified Breguet 19 named *Pointe d'Interrogation*) flew from Dakar, Senegal, to Brazil on October 14–15.

The French *Aéropostale*, which was already involved in developing air mail service in South America, made the first commercial flight carrying official air mail across the South Atlantic when Jean Mermoz (who would be immortalized by his friend and fellow aviator Saint-Exupéry in *Wind, Sand and Stars* for surviving a crash in the Andes) with co-pilot Jean Dabry and radioman Léopold Gimié, left St. Louis, near Dakar, Senegal, on May 12, 1930. The 1,600 mile flight to Natal, in northern Brazil, took twenty-one hours in a single-engine Latécoère 28 floatplane, and there the mail was offloaded and flown on to Rio de Janeiro and then Buenos Aires by Raymond Vanier in a Latécoère 25, arriving in the Argentine capital on May 13.

On December 17, 1930, Italian Air Marshal Italo Balbo led the first of his famous long distance formation flights with twelve *Savoia-Marchetti S.55* flying boats leaving Orbetello, Italy, to arrive in Rio de Janeiro, Brazil, on January 15, 1931.

In the summer of 1931 the German airline DELAG introduced regular scheduled passenger service from Frankfurt and Friedrichshafen, Germany, to Rio de Janeiro and Recife, Brazil, using the southern route in the famous airship *Graf Zeppelin*, which made the crossing 136 times between 1931 and 1937. *Deutsche Lufthansa* airline maintained twice-weekly airmail service between Bathurst, Gambia, and Natal, Brazil, from February 1934 to August 1939. In December 1935, Air France opened a regular weekly airmail route between Dakar and Natal, with service on to Rio de Janeiro and Buenos Aires.

All of this ended with the outbreak of war in September 1939. Some 1,500 people, all told, had participated in these adventures. Five years later, three times that number would make the trip every day.

At the August 1941 Atlantic Conference, Winston Churchill pressed Franklin D. Roosevelt for aid to support the Commonwealth forces engaged against the German *Afrika Korps*. The "southern route" would ultimately play an important role in that aid. Churchill's request came at a good time. In the 1930s the United States had been faced with South American nations ruled by nondemocratic governments that had established strong ties to Germany. Every South American nation and even some in Central America had received arms supplies from the Third Reich. There were large German immigrant populations in the major South American countries, many of whose members were prominent in local economic and political affairs. Entire regions in Brazil were dominated by expatriate Germans, giving rise to fears Germany might establish secret military facilities there. Additionally, there were large Italian immigrant populations in Brazil, Uruguay, and Argentina. Through strenuous diplomatic efforts that involved both inducements and threats, however, the United States had been able to forestall further military cooperation between the Latin American countries and the Axis powers—but only by providing the military supplies the countries would have received from Germany.

Through Roosevelt's "Good Neighbor Policy," the United States had undertaken to provide economic assistance to Brazil to develop a number of civil airports and port facilities in the northeastern part of the country, using funds from the 1940 Airport Development Program (ADP). The American goal was to develop a network of airfields from which reconnaissance and patrol flights could be made throughout the Caribbean and South America. Survey teams from the United States were sent to assess the condition of the existing facilities, and *Panair do Brasil*, a subsidiary of the U.S. company Pan American Airways, used funds from the ADP to develop facilities at Belém and Natal for use as major ferry and transport bases on the South Atlantic route.

The talks between Churchill and Roosevelt ultimately set in motion a series of events that eventually created an American-pioneered, American-supplied, and American-maintained trans-Atlantic air route between the United States and Africa—extending on through the Middle East to India and over the Himalayas to China. The 1940 "Destroyers for Bases" agreement had already given the U.S. access to facilities in British-controlled territory at Trinidad and British Guiana, and both became major stopping points on the two-thousand-mile flight separating Puerto Rico from Belém, the northernmost Brazilian airfield capable of handling heavy traffic. On the other side of the Atlantic, bases were established in British colonies in Central Africa en route to the Middle East. Liberia, with its long relationship with the United States, made several airports and port facilities available, and its capital of Monrovia became a key staging point for American flights.

The month before the Allied leaders' meeting in 1941, Atlantic Airways Ltd., another Pan American subsidiary, had initiated limited service utilizing trans-Caribbean and South American air routes, with an extension from Natal to West Africa, in order to ferry aircraft on an alternative to the North Atlantic route, which was at the mercy of bad weather so much of the time. After the United States entered the war in December, the operation would be expanded into a series of connecting air routes that were used to ferry aircraft and transport equipment and personnel from the United States to points throughout the Eurasian and African continents. These flights were memorialized by Ernest K. Gann, one of the pilots who flew the route, in his classic of aviation writing, *Fate Is the Hunter.*

The most important link in Pan American Airways' ferrying and transport services was the operation across Central Africa. By providing a transport service and maintaining bases, Pan American Airways–Africa supported movement across the continent of aircraft arriving from both the United States and Great Britain. In Africa Pan Am cooperated with the British Imperial Airways, which during the 1930s had pioneered routes across the continent and established operating bases that allowed the air service to be extended to Cairo and on across the Middle East to India.

By April 1944, when Sterling Ditchey and his crew set out on their odyssey, Parnamirim Army Air Field at Natal, with twin airstrips, was the busiest American air base in the world, handling a landing every three minutes day and night, as troops and cargo were flown across the South Atlantic to feed campaigns in Italy, Africa, Russia, Burma, and China— and the looming invasion of Normandy. The surrounding base had become an American military city, with barracks and tents for 6,600 soldiers, a weekly newspaper, and the largest Post Exchange outside the United States, supplied by South America's first Coca-Cola bottling plant.

Upon taking off from Savannah Army Air Field in the brand-new B-25J, Chuck Akins set course for Morrison Field, Florida, which had opened in 1940 as a Third Air Force fighter base before being reassigned to the Army Air Forces Ferrying Command on January 19, 1942, at which point the field became the initial point of departure for aircraft flying the southern route.

Ditchey remembered how he was equipped to do the navigation for the journey:

> When we set out to fly the mission, the ultimate destination of which was unknown to us, I had a set of charts, a protractor, a ruler, two pencils and a watch, which were all on a clipboard on my lap as I sat in the co-pilot's seat. We knew nothing of the route until we received a briefing at West Palm Beach, where we learned it was a long, circuitous route, supported with only the most meager of radio and other navigational aids. Chuck could listen to the radio beacons on his headset, while Bill Morgan made the radio frequency changes I gave him as we flew along. The flight depended almost entirely on dead reckoning navigation—visual sighting of landmarks via computation of airspeed, wind direction and speed, ground speed and compass headings. No ground controllers monitored the flights, except on landings and takeoffs at the airstrips themselves.

The southern journey began on Easter Sunday, April 9, with a departure from Morrison Field shortly after dawn. Ditchey and his crew were part of a formation with several other B-25s, in one of which was Second Lieutenant Tom Cahill with his crew. They were headed for Borinquen Field, Puerto Rico, 976 miles south-southeast of Morrison. It was a prewar base established in 1936 and now used as a refueling station and service depot for aircraft of all types flying to the war theaters. Depending on circumstances, crews had the option of stopping in Cuba or one of the other islands. After refueling and servicing at Borinquen, Ditchey's formation continued on for 1,021 miles across the sparkling deep blue Caribbean to Atkinson Field in British Guiana outside the capital of Georgetown, which was the South American terminus of the Air Transport Command Caribbean Wing. The field at Borinquen had been constructed after the United States obtained basing rights in British Guiana as part of the 1940 Destroyers for Bases agreement with Britain.

In the morning, after being briefed on the next leg of the trip, the American fliers headed on across the Amazon jungle 868 miles to Val de Caes Field, Belém, Brazil, the primary refueling and servicing stop en route south to Natal. The runways here were all-weather, five thousand feet long, and made of concrete and asphalt to accommodate the heavy traffic. Outside of the base at Natal, Val de Caes Field was one of the largest and best equipped Army Airfields in the world. When Ditchey's crew checked in with the tower at Belém, however, they learned the field was low on gas and were queried as to whether they had enough fuel to make it to Sao Luiz de Maranhao, Brazil. Replying that they did, they flew on over Belém to Sao Luiz. Flying over the Amazon jungles was an experience Ditchey remembered ever after. "It was such a brilliant green that it looked as though there were floodlights shining up through the foliage."

The next day they flew on to Natal, Brazil. Problems surfaced on the flight to Parnamirim Army Air Field there when they lost a supercharger in the right engine. Ground crews checked the problem and declared that they did not possess the necessary parts to replace the broken supercharger and that it would take at least ten days for the necessary spares to be flown down from the United States. Fortunately, Ditchey stopped by the on-base USO office, where he discovered that an old friend from high school in California was in charge. He and the rest of the crew were able to avoid ten days in the transient barracks when his friend offered to put them up at his home in town. Tom Cahill and the other B-25s flew on across the South Atlantic two days after they all arrived in Natal.

"The trip to Ascension Island was the first real test of my navigation skills," Ditchey remembered. Ascension Island is 1,438 miles from Natal:

> The briefing we got for the trip was the first time I ever heard the term "point of no return," the last position where you have the fuel to turn around and return to your starting point. This was a maximum-range flight for a B-25, and Ascension Island was only four miles wide by five miles long, which made it a veritable dot in the middle of the South Atlantic. I did my homework before I climbed aboard for this flight. Over those seas roll swift-gathering storms. In them abide schools of ravening sharks. We were aware of our chances of rescue if we were forced to ditch in these waters. It was a real thrill to see the island, seemingly, all of a sudden, rise out of the ocean after seven hours of flying over open sea.

Ascension had been a prewar British cable station. An airfield there, located in the South Atlantic approximately midway between the Brazilian and the African Atlantic coasts, made it possible for twin-engine aircraft like the B-25 to cross the South Atlantic in two fairly easy jumps with a normal gas load. The American construction crews that built the airfield had arrived in March 1942; construction got underway by April 13. Less than three months later, on July 10, 1942, the six-thousand-foot runway at Wideawake Air Field was open for traffic. The field was named after the bird colony on the island. Sooty terns, also known as "wideawake birds," were a constant source of menace to plane and pilot, since every time an airplane started down the runway for takeoff the roar of the engines would bring a huge flock of birds into the air right in its path.

After spending the night at Ascension, Ditchey's plane lifted off the field in the morning without incurring a bird strike, and the crew were on their way to Africa, headed for Roberts Air Field outside Monrovia, Liberia. This part was easy, even though the distance was 1,250 miles, since "Africa was pretty hard to miss." Roberts Field, initially established by Pan Am in the late 1930s as a terminal for trans-Atlantic flights, was by the spring of 1944 used only by twin-engine aircraft, with longer-ranged four-engine aircraft flying directly from Ascension to Dakar in Senegal.

After an overnight stay at Roberts Field, Ditchey and his crew lifted off the next morning and headed for Mallard Air Field—the Vichy French airport at Eknes Field that the Americans had begun using in September 1942—outside the port of Dakar, Senegal. Mallard Field had been built to accommodate B-17 Flying Fortresses and B-24 Liberators on their way to England; those planes made the 1,876 miles from Natal, Brazil, to Mallard Field non-stop. Once Ditchey's crew arrived there, the weather closed in for two days.

The next leg was also daunting. At the pre-flight briefing, Ditchey learned he would be flying more than 1,000 miles over the forbidding Sahara Desert to arrive at Menara Airport outside Marrakech, French Morocco. "En route to Marrakech from Dakar, we flew through a storm that at times was so violent that we were encountering sand at 11,000 feet flying altitude. The leading edges of our wings and tailplane were sandblasted clean, down to the bare aluminum underneath." They arrived over Tindouf in southern Algeria, where they received radio clearance to fly on to Marrakech. "The trick, though, was to get through the Atlas Mountains—they were too high for us to fly over. We had good maps and pretty good photographs, but there was only one pass—all other entrance canyons were dead ends. We flew up one, turned around, and found the right one on the second try. Then it was easy on to Marrakech." There was a surprise waiting when they arrived. "We thought we were big stuff in our B-25 medium bombers, but on the field, landing just ahead of us, were several squadrons of B-29 super bombers, enroute to India. They were so big that we could park B-25s under their wings. It had taken us 16 days to reach Marrakech. They had flown in overnight, direct from Wichita, Kansas." Ditchey's crew remained in Marrakech for two days because of the Sahara scirocco wind before taking off for Telergma, Algeria. Weather forced a diversion to Maison Blanche, where they were grounded for five days while waiting for the skies to clear for the last leg of the trip. On May 1, 1944, they finally made the one-hour flight to Telergma, Algeria, where they delivered their aircraft.

Eleven days later Ditchey and his crew were issued a combat-modified B-25J, serial number 43-27642, which they decided to name "Puss and Boots."

On May 13, 1944, "Puss and Boots" left Telergma at dawn and headed north across the Mediterranean. At midday they touched down at Ghisonnaccia Air Field on Corsica, the home of the 310th Bomb Group. Sterling Ditchey and his crew had flown thirteen thousand miles to get to their war. Along the way, at Natal, Ditchey had turned twenty-one. By the end of the day of their arrival, they had been assigned to the 380th Bomb Squadron and provided quarters in a building in the town of Ghisonnaccia. That same day, May 13, Tom Cahill and his crew landed at Alesani Field, home of the 340th Bomb Group, and by the end of the day, he was a member of the 486th Bomb Squadron.

That night, Ditchey was awakened by the sound of bombs exploding in the distance. Once out of his bunk, he could see the fires burning twenty miles south on Alesani Airfield, where the *Luftwaffe* had just struck the 340th Bomb Group. Tom Cahill was right in the middle of it.

Several hundred other new members of the 57th Bomb Wing would follow Ditchey and Cahill across the South Atlantic over the next ten months.

FIVE

THE CRUCIAL MONTH

The night of May 11, 1944, Captain William J. Nickerson, the intelligence officer (S-2) for the 321st Bomb Group's 445th Bomb Squadron and the best of the 57th Wing's war diarists, wrote in the squadron war diary that "Tonight [Group Commander] Colonel Smith called a meeting of the crew members and S-2 officers for the purpose of discussing the major push contemplated by the Fifth and Eighth Armies on the Italian front. He discussed the plan generally, beginning with the 1,400-gun barrage of ours which was to start at 2300 hours. Captain Abbott, the Air Liaison Officer, covered the plan in detail, going over the assignments of each division involved. The 321st was scheduled for air support for the Fifth Army and a busy few days ahead was ardently promised." Operation Diadem, the final offensive to break through the Gustav Line at Cassino, was on. The month of May 1944 would see all three groups of the 57th Wing stretched to the maximum.

The 321st Bomb Group first arrived in the Mediterranean Theater in February 1943, commanded by Colonel Robert D. Knapp, a man with a lifelong involvement in aviation. Born in Georgia but raised in Auburn, Alabama, he had met the Wright Brothers at age ten when they stayed with his family for ten days in 1907. Commissioned in March 1918 as a second lieutenant in the U.S. Army Air Service and serving as a bomber pilot, he held U.S. Pilot License Number 187 and had been flying for longer than most of his young aircrews had been alive. Knapp served in the Air Corps throughout the interwar period, serving with future USAAF leaders Hap Arnold and Ira Eaker in 1919 on the U.S.-Mexico border. In 1923 he pioneered the southern airmail route from Montgomery, Alabama, to New Orleans. Promoted to chief of primary flight training at Randolph and Kelly Fields in 1929, he was responsible for all Air Corps flight training. In 1937, he led a ninety-eight-plane formation of Advanced Flight Training graduates on a national tour to recruit ROTC students at land-grant colleges into aviation.

When war preparations began in 1941, Colonel Knapp was placed in charge of organizing the first six B-25 bomb groups and training three of them: the 310th, 321st and 340th. After much politicking on his part, he was named commander of the 321st group when they were ordered overseas despite being considered "too old for direct combat duty." Knapp used his position to get several of the surviving pilots and crews from the Doolittle Raid assigned to the three groups he was responsible for training at the time they were formed, giving the new aircrews experienced role models as they trained for combat, since Knapp had organized and trained the Doolittle Raid crews themselves in the 17th Bombardment Group (Medium), the first group to equip with the B-25. At age forty-five, he led the 321st in combat throughout the North African campaign, the Sicilian campaign, and the Balkans campaign, flying forty tough missions that included the first mission to bomb Rome in 1943 and a successful unescorted raid on an Axis convoy protected by German and Italian fighters, for which he was awarded the Silver Star. Knapp led the Athens mission for which the group received its first Presidential Unit Citation. Under his leadership the 321st was the first bomb group to be based in Italy, starting a month after the invasion. By the time the winter weather closed in, the 321st had flown missions as far afield as Athens, Greece, and Sofia, Bulgaria.

When the 57th Bomb Wing was formed in January 1944, Knapp was promoted to brigadier general and placed in command. He is the man caricatured as "General Dreedle" in Joseph Heller's *Catch-22*, but he was remembered by those who originally trained and served under him as Dreedle's polar opposite: tough and demanding but never asking a man to do something he had not done first himself. He made every effort to ensure treatment of his crews that was as good as the situation would allow. The B-25s traveled throughout the Mediterranean on his authority to obtain good food and drink and bring them back to Corsica.

Following Knapp's promotion to command the 57th Wing, the new replacements who arrived in 1944 did not know him as the leader who climbed into the left seat for "the tough ones"; those who knew him that way were mostly gone that summer, their tours over. Knapp became a distant figure—just "the general"—to most of his young fliers, who viewed him as the hard taskmaster who required them to fly mission after mission. They had no idea of his persistent efforts on their behalf when he had to compete with units "fighting the real war." Unfortunately, whenever there was a shortage of replacements, Knapp had to raise the number of total missions the veteran crews had to fly to complete a combat tour. While the men benefitted from his largesse at the dinner table, it wasn't widely known that he facilitated the deals for top-quality food from Naples to Cairo to Tunis and Casablanca. He wasn't one to "toot his horn," and generals do not usually inform lieutenants of such activities.

The 321st arrived in Corsica in late April 1944, just in time to take part in an offensive Allied military leaders believed could end the war in Italy. The 340th Bomb Group had been forced by circumstance to completely re-equip with new B-25J Mitchells in March and April after the sacrifice of all their old airplanes to Vulcan in the eruption of Vesuvius, and the 310th Bomb Group had traded in their B-25G and B-25H gunships for B-25Js in late April when their assignment changed from maritime attack to medium bombing. The 321st, however, last in line for new airplanes, had flown from Foggia to Solenzara Airfield on Corsica in their weary old B-25C and B-25D Mitchells. Some of these airplanes had crossed the South Atlantic when the group originally moved to North Africa, and all wore sun-faded camouflage and were careworn and oil-streaked, their skins covered with patches over the holes punched in them by German flak during missions over the Mareth Line in Tunisia, Sicily, Greece, Yugoslavia, and Italy during the fifteen months the group had been engaged in combat.

Beginning in early May of 1944, the crews of the 321st started flying the old airplanes down to Telergma Field outside Algiers, where they exchanged their old mounts for shiny new silver B-25Js. On May 11, armorer Sergeant Bernard H. Seegmiller recorded in his diary: "Just now our Group is in process of being equipped with new airplanes, bright new B-25Js. They look sleek and shiny with their silver skins, but soon they will be beaten up and patched just like the ones we are turning in. Already we have begun stripping off guns and excess equipment in the amount of many thousands of dollars, equipment that just as well have never been sent to this theater of operation. I have been assigned one of the new planes and today it flew its first mission. Everything went off OK." The "stripping" Seegmiller referred to included removing the four "package" guns mounted two on each side of the nose below the cockpit of the B-25J as a factory "improvement"; since these bombers, unlike their counterparts in the Pacific, would not be taking part in any ground attack strafing missions, the weight saved allowed a heavier fuel load and a longer range.

A few of the older B-25s had been present from the beginning, having somehow avoided the untimely ends that the multitude of aircraft produced for the war were subject to. One of these was B-25C 41-13061, known throughout the 310th group as "Little Joe," which had joined the 380th Bomb Squadron in September 1942. First Lieutenant Robert Thorndike had taken delivery at Westover Field, Massachusetts, and with Thorndike in the left seat "Little Joe" had flown the North Atlantic via Labrador, Greenland, and Iceland to Britain in November 1942 as Allied troops stormed ashore in North Africa. Then it was on to Tafaroui, Algeria, on December 7, 1942, when the war was a year old for Americans. In the seventeen months prior to May 17, 1944, when the airplane returned to Ghisonaccia Airfield from a mission to bomb a railroad tunnel at Itri, "Little Joe" had tallied 128 missions without one mechanical abort. After mission 128 it was decided that "Little Joe" would fly back to the United States for a war bond tour with one of the veteran crews now being relieved by the arrival of Sterling Ditchey's crew and the other new and very welcome replacements.

The ground crews in the twelve squadrons of all three bomb groups could look forward to unrelenting work during the coming offensive. Combat took a heavy toll on aircraft, and considerable time and effort was required to keep the Mitchells operational. On Corsica the crews faced one task they hadn't had to deal with much in Africa: changing tires. To insure they could be used in all weathers, the Corsican runways were constructed using pierced-steel planking. The mats were frequently bound together with wire, which could come loose or break, allowing the planking to separate and creating runway surfaces that "ate tires morning, noon, and night," as Sergeant Frank Dean recalled.

The Gustav Line had stopped the Allied ground advance north toward Rome from Salerno and Naples by the time the winter blizzards arrived at the end of December 1943. From early January of the next year, the western half of the Gustav Line was anchored by German positions in the Rapido, Liri, and Garigliano valleys and the surrounding peaks and ridges. The position had been chosen with care and was an attacker's nightmare.

The Germans had flooded the Pontine Marshes, limiting the lines of advance that Allied ground forces could use. The fast-flowing Rapido River ran down from the central Apennine mountains through the town of Cassino and across the entrance to the Liri valley where the Liri River joined it to form the Garigliano River, which continued on to the sea. Thus assault anywhere along the line to the north involved a river crossing under fire, one of the most difficult military maneuvers. With heavily fortified mountain defense lines, difficult river crossings, and a flooded valley, Cassino was the linchpin of the formidable line of *Wehrmacht* defensive positions stretched across Central Italy.

The U.S. Fifth Army only reached the Gustav Line on January 15, after six weeks of heavy fighting to break through the Bernhardt Line positions north of Naples, during which they took sixteen thousand casualties. Kesselring's strategy of making the Allies pay in blood for every foot of Italy they took was bearing fruit.

Desperate to find a way around the Gustav Line, Churchill advised Lieutenant General Mark Clark to make a flanking amphibious attack at Anzio, less than thirty miles from Rome. With surprise and quick movement, Rome could be taken and the Gustav Line cut off from the rear. Third Division's commander Major General Lucian K. Truscott Jr., the most successful division commander in VI Corps, pointed out that a successful landing in a basin surrounded by mountains depended completely on surprise and swift movement; if there were any delay the defenders could occupy the mountains and entrap the invaders. At the same time VI Corps landed on the Anzio beaches on January 22, 1944, the British X Corps attacked at the Garigliano River on the Gustav Line in an attempt to draw German forces south, away from Anzio. After hard fighting, X Corps was successful in establishing a bridgehead across the Garigliano which they were able to hold despite German counterattacks.

The three divisions of VI Corps achieved surprise at Anzio. A jeep reconnaissance patrol made it to the outskirts of Rome two hours after the troops were ashore. Corps Commander General John Lucas had orders to "1. Seize and secure a beachhead in the vicinity of Anzio 2. Advance and secure Colli Laziali [the Alban Hills] 3. Be prepared to advance on Rome." Unfortunately, rather than speed his forces out of the beachhead Lucas established defensive positions against a counterattack. His caution was due to the bloody experience at Salerno and the fact that he had never before held a battlefield command. The delay was fatal; it allowed Kesselring to pull forces from the Gustav Line and take control of the surrounding hills, giving the Germans the ability to keep VI Corps surrounded in the beachhead until the end of May.

The flanking attack over the Garigliano was intended as a diversion, but the main American attack against the Gustav Line had already begun two days earlier, on January 20. Lack of time to prepare the assault properly meant that the highly technical business of an opposed river crossing lacked the necessary planning and rehearsal. After several days the attack ended in failure, with heavy casualties. The final assault took place on January 24, when the U.S. II Corps and the French Expeditionary Corps attacked the northern part of the German line. Difficult fighting raged for three weeks, after which the fought-out French and American units were withdrawn from combat. The battle was a win for the German strategy in Italy: blocking the Allied advance as long as possible while inflicting maximum casualties.

The Second Battle of Cassino was noteworthy for the bombing of the historic abbey of Monte Cassino on February 15, 1944. Allied commanders believed that the commanding heights on which the ancient abbey was situated were being used by the Germans to observe the entire region. The bombing, which is still controversial, destroyed the ninth-century Benedictine abbey more completely than had invading Arab armies in the tenth century, and the ruins only became a perfect defensive position for the German paratroopers, who had not used the position before.

The B-25s of the 321st and 340th Bomb Groups were among the air units that participated in this assault. Earlier bombing by the B-17s and B-24s of the Fifteenth Air Force had been imprecise, with only 10 percent of the bombs dropped hitting the target, while the rest hit both German and Allied infantry positions. Sixteen five-hundred-pound bombs hit the United States Fifth Army command compound at Presenzano, seventeen miles from Monte Cassino, exploding only a few yards away from the trailer in which Fifth Army commander Lieutenant General Mark Clark was doing paperwork at his desk. The bombs dropped from the Mitchells, in contrast, were all "on target."

Over the next several days, Indian and New Zealand divisions attempted to take the abbey and the German positions around it. Winter rains made movement next to impossible on the steep slopes and limited air support from Allied fighter bombers. The Indians and New Zealanders were withdrawn after a week, fought out with heavy casualties.

For the Third Battle of Cassino, Allied commanders decided to launch twin attacks from the north along the Rapido valley, one towards the fortified town of Cassino and the other towards Monastery Hill, with the goal of clearing the path through the bottleneck between these two features to allow movement into the Liri valley. No one was happy with the plan, but it was hoped that a never-before-attempted preliminary bombing by Fifteenth Air Force heavy bombers would clear the way. Three days of good weather were required. The assault was postponed for twenty-one days in succession as troops waited in their freezing, wet positions for a favorable weather forecast.

The first bombers were finally overhead at 0830 hours on March 15, and the last departed three and a half hours later. Seven hundred and fifty tons of thousand-pound bombs were dropped, many with delayed-action fuses. At the conclusion of the preliminary bombing, the New Zealand Division, now back in the fight, advanced behind a creeping artillery barrage from 746 artillery pieces. Success depended on the attackers' taking advantage of the paralyzing effect of the bombing. But once again bombing by the Fifteenth was proving to be wildly inaccurate; only 50 percent of the bombs dropped landed within a mile of the target point and only 8 percent within a thousand yards. Still, between the bombing and the shelling, half of the three hundred defending German paratroopers were killed. The survivors, however, rallied faster than expected, while Allied armor was held up by the bomb craters. By the time a follow-up assault on the left was ordered that evening it was too late. The German defenses had reorganized. Worse, the rain had begun again, contrary to the forecast. Torrents flooded the bomb craters, creating huge lakes, and turned rubble into a muddy morass, and communications were wrecked since the radio sets could not survive the constant immersion. On March 18 a final attack by Commonwealth units holding positions around the abbey was ordered for the next day. But early that morning the German *1.Fallschirmjägerdivision* launched a surprise and fiercely pressed counterattack from the monastery that disrupted any possibility of an assault. The Allied tanks, lacking infantry support, were all knocked out by mid-afternoon by Germans equipped with the new *Panzerfaust* anti-tank rocket. The New Zealanders rallied, and small attacks were attempted over the next several days, but the battle came to an end on March 22 when the exhausted British and Indian units were withdrawn, with the Germans still in control. The German defenders had also paid a heavy price: the XIV Corps war diary for March 23 noted that the battalions in the front line had strengths varying between 40 and 120 men, between one-third and one-fifth their authorized strength.

The Allies waited for the end of the winter rains before making a fourth attempt to break the German defenses. With Operation Overlord, the invasion of Normandy set to take place in less than a month, Operation Diadem had two objectives. British Field Marshal Sir Harold Alexander, who had become Allied Supreme Commander in the Mediterranean in Eisenhower's place in January, notified Allied commanders that his strategy was "to force the enemy to commit the maximum number of divisions in Italy at the time the cross-channel invasion is launched." He also planned, once the Gustav Line was broken, to block the retreat of the German Army in Italy by a breakout from the Anzio beachhead by a reinforced VI Corps, now doubled in size to six divisions and under the command of General Truscott. The six divisions would push across the major roads south of Rome and link up with elements of the British Eighth Army, which would attack west across the Apennines. If everything went according to plan, there was an excellent chance of blocking the retreat and capturing the bulk of the German Army. Such a military defeat for the Germans could result in a retreat from Italy by their remaining forces in the north, ending the war in the Italian peninsula.

On May 10, First Lieutenant Arthur J. Tarmichael and his aircrew left Solenzara in one of the old B-25Ds, destination Telergma. There they turned in their old mount and were issued B-25J 43-4050, the very same airplane Sterling Ditchey and his crew had flown across the South Atlantic. After test-flying it on May 11, they took off the next morning and flew across the Tyrhennian Sea to Solenzara. Two days before Tarmichael and his crew had picked up their new airplane, First Lieutenant Warren Annear and his had picked up B-25J 43-4026, the Mitchell that Tom Cahill had flown across the Atlantic. While Tarmichael's Mitchell was droning across the Mediterranean, Lieutenant Annear and his crew were landing theirs at Solenzara at the conclusion of their first mission.

May 12 was a red-letter day for the 321st, with the group flying four "hot" missions against German airfields, road junctions, and gun emplacements north of the Gustav Line, with flak on all missions recorded by Captain Nickerson as "heavy, intense and accurate."

With the bombers operating over the battle zone, it was crucially important that they know the exact positions of Allied ground units to avoid mistakes—dropping their bombs on the Allied side of the "bomb" line—with terrible consequences. Thus the job of the Air Liaison Officer (ALO) assigned from the ground forces was to keep up to date a large map showing Allied positions, to brief crews on what was going on in the land battle so they would understand the value of their missions and the reason for the choice of target, and to debrief crews regarding what they had seen, such as heavy traffic on roads. Royal Army Captain Dan Gurney had arrived at Solenzara in early May to become ALO for the 321st group. Gurney could personally vouch for the need for such knowledge on the part of the airmen: "In April 1943, shortly after the capture of Tunis, the armored division in which I was serving as brigade intelligence officer was pulled back to rest some fifteen miles from the front. Between us and the front was a large flat lake, an unmistakable landmark one would think. In clear sunshine one morning, we received the full bomb load of a squadron of B-25s onto our innocent heads!" Gurney hit it off quickly with the intelligence officers at Solenzara: "As a British officer, I was entitled to a monthly ration of Scotch from the British NAAFI (PX). As I didn't go for Scotch myself, I used to trade this for Hershey bars, for which there was no shortage of takers!" He forged a lifelong friendship with Hollywood actor Jeffrey Lynn, the junior intelligence officer of the 445th squadron.

As the Fourth Battle of Cassino commenced, the four squadrons of the 321st Group, along with the eight squadrons of the other two groups, began flying two missions a day, every day that the weather allowed. The three groups followed an operational profile in which two squadrons launched twelve planes each for the morning mission, while the other two squadrons were jointly responsible for the afternoon mission. During the battle, there were some days when as many as four missions were flown by each squadron, but such "maximum efforts" were difficult to sustain since, despite the herculean efforts of the ground crews, as many as half the aircraft of any squadron might be unavailable for a mission while damage from flak hits was being repaired or engines and wheels were changed. Some of the bombers might fly every day, while others seemed to require more maintenance and might only get in two or three missions in a week. Mitchell 43-4026 was one of those airplanes that was always ready, while 43-4050 (in which Sterling Ditchey crossed the Atlantic) had blown a supercharger at Natal on its delivery flight and turned into a "maintenance hog" for the rest of its operational life.

The plan of attack was for U.S. II Corps on the left to attack up the Ligurian coast along Route 7 towards Rome. To their right, the French Expeditionary Corps would attack from the bridgehead across the Garigliano originally created by X Corps in the First Battle of Cassino in January—into the Aurunci Mountains that formed a barrier between the coastal plain and the Liri Valley. In the center, to the right of the French, British XIII Corps would attack along the Liri valley. On the right the 3rd and 5th Divisions of the Polish II Corps, newly arrived that spring from Iran after being formed from Polish prisoners of war held in the Soviet Union after the simultaneous Russian and German invasion of Poland in September 1939, would attack. The Polish troops, who ultimately proved to be the toughest fighters in the Italian campaign, would attempt the task that had defeated the 4th Indian Division in February: to take Monte Cassino and push into the Liri valley to link with XIII Corps and cut off the Cassino position. Pinching maneuvers by the Polish and British Corps were the key to success. Improved weather, ground conditions, and supply would be important factors. The Canadian I Corps would be held in reserve, ready to exploit the expected breakthrough. Once the German Tenth Army had begun to withdraw, VI Corps would break out of the Anzio beachhead to cut off the line of retreat in the Alban Hills.

The final battle of Cassino opened at 2300 hours on May 11, 1944. A massive Allied artillery bombardment involved 1,060 artillery pieces on the Eighth Army front and 600 on the Fifth Army front. Within ninety minutes the offensive was in motion in all sectors. By dawn the U.S. II Corps had made little progress, but the French Expeditionary Corps had captured their objectives and had moved into the Aurunci Mountains, which were considered impassable and were therefore unde-fended. The French were led by Moroccan tribesmen from the Atlas Mountains who were mountain warriors with a fearsome two-thousand-year reputation.

A crucial requirement for Allied success was that the German Tenth Army be cut off from supply and reinforcement to the maximum extent possible. The three bomb groups of the 57th Bomb Wing were tasked with destroying as many bridges as possible between Cassino and Rome.

In the days leading up to the attack, the weather was "iffy" for the bombers; it only began to clear on May 11. On May 12, the 321st Bomb Group flew a maximum effort of five missions between dawn and dusk, recording 114 individual sorties and establishing a new group record. The morning mission, number 279 in the squadron record, saw First Lieutenant Tarmichael and his crew—co-pilot First Lieutenant Charles R. Knapp, bombardier Second Lieutenant Daniel Galindo, flight engineer Sergeant Andrew Marinucci, radioman Staff Sergeant Sam Rossi, and tail gunner Sergeant Leslie Lemke—fly B-25J 43-4026 on her second mission while 43-4050, the B-25J they had delivered the day before, was still being stripped of extraneous equipment. But their old plane would fly missions that day, too, with Lieutenant Annear and his crew taking her out once in the morning and again at midday on a mission that ended in a weather abort. In a good indication of how heavy operations were this first day of the Fourth Battle of Cassino, in the late afternoon Annear and his crew flew another mission in another plane, B-25D 41-30125.

Clouds in the morning hindered several missions. At 0630 hours, bomber B-25D 41-30327, flown by Second Lieutenant Erle G. "Swanny" Swanson of the 448th Bomb Squadron, took off on Mission 280 to bomb the German command center in Pico. The sky was cloudy and the target was obscured, but the bombers were visible to the gunners below. The veteran B-25 was hit by flak before bombardier Second Lieutenant Anthony Quartuccio could drop his bombs. An "88" scored a direct hit in the right wing behind the engine, severing the hydraulic lines so that the main gear dropped and the bomb-bay doors remained open, while a near-miss sprayed the left engine with shrapnel. Swanny left the formation in order to salvo the bombs, but bombardier Quartuccio was only able to release six of the 500-pounders successfully. Meanwhile gasoline from a severed gas line in the right wing sprayed into the rear of the plane. As the crew left the Italian coast behind, Swanson found he had to feather the left engine. Without enough power to maintain level flight, the B-25 was now rapidly losing altitude, and the crew lightened ship by throwing all equipment overboard. Because of the gasoline leak, the right engine began to sputter as it ran out of fuel and finally died with Corsica in sight on the horizon.

Swanson called the crew to their ditching stations and set up for a water landing twelve miles off the coast. He made an expert landing, holding the plane in the air until it stalled and dropped it vertically into the water at the moment it ran out of flying speed so that the lowered landing gear would not flip it over upon touching the water. The men had two and a half minutes to get out and deploy their life rafts before the Mitchell sank beneath the waves. Fifteen minutes later, two P-39s from the 350th Fighter Group on their way back to Corsica spotted the survivors and circled until a PT boat from Bastia arrived to pick them up at 1230 hours. After spending the night in the hospital at Bastia, the men returned to Solenzara the next morning and flew another mission that afternoon.

Of the twenty-four aircraft on the mission when Swanny's Mitchell was hit, all twenty-three that made it back to Solenzara were "holed" by flak, a term that could mean anything from a few small holes to parts of wings and stabilizers knocked off and engines damaged. Flying at bombing altitudes of 8,000 to 14,000 feet, the Mitchells were within range of every German anti-aircraft gun from the Flak-37 to the *Abwehrkanone-88*, the dreaded "88." On the other missions that day, the flak was accurate enough to hole at least a third of the Mitchells, including B-25J 42-64667, "Wet Dreams," in which Lieutenant Tarmichael and his crew flew their second mission of the day. That night crews relaxed by watching Kay Kyser in *Swing Fever.*

On the Eighth Army front that day, XIII Corps made two crossings of the Rapido, meeting strong resistance. Crucially, the engineers of the 8th Indian Division succeeded in bridging the river by late morning, allowing the tanks of the 1st Canadian Armored Brigade to get across and provide vital support to beat off the inevitable counterattacks that were made by German armor.

The Poles assaulted the aptly named Mount Calvary but were forced to pull back when German paratroops counterattacked. The Polish infantry divisions met devastating mortar, artillery, and small-arms fire, which all but wiped out the leading units. The battle see-sawed from May 12 to 15, with Polish attacks and German counterattacks creating heavy losses. The Poles lost 281 officers and 3,503 enlisted in battle with *4/4.Fallschirm-jägeregiment*, which was reduced from an authorized strength of over two thousand to only eight hundred men capable of fighting. Witnesses said the mountain had been turned into a "miniature Verdun."

By the afternoon of May 12, the bridgeheads across the Rapido had been expanded despite furious counterattacks.

That night, the men of the 321st and 310th bomb groups were awakened by the explosions that echoed across Corsica as the *Luftwaffe* paid its visit to the 340th Bomb Group at Alesani. The next morning the 445th's Sergeant Seegmiller wrote in his diary,

> The weather is good again and for the last two days we have been going all out to support the 8th and 5th Army push against the Gustav line. Yesterday our planes were badly shot up. Two of the new Js were sent to the Service Group [the major

engineering overhaul unit]. No one was injured in our squadron. This morning about 0400 Jerry bombed the 340th Group,
which is situated some distance up the coast. I did not go out,
but the boys who did say it was quite a show. Today we learned
that fourteen persons, including the Group CO, were killed,
81 wounded and only 28 planes of about 90 were left service-
able. We half expected them to return again, perhaps to this
field, their results last night being so good. Our planes make a
perfect target on account of as yet the dispersal area is not
complete and they are all bunched along one taxi strip.

Later on May 13, camouflage nets were hauled out and draped over
the silver B-25s at dusk. 445th Bomb Squadron diarist Captain Nickerson recorded that men were complaining about a shortage of shovels and
pickaxes as slit trenches were extended and turned into bomb shelters.

While those not flying missions attended to strengthening the airfield
defenses, the 445th Bomb Squadron sent nine B-25s to take part in Mission 284 against the German fortifications, and seven Mitchells bombed
a railroad tunnel in Mission 285, in which B-25J 43-4026, flown by
Second Lieutenant Vernon Dossey, made her fifth mission of the offensive.

That day the German right wing at Cassino began to give way under
Allied pressure. The French Expeditionary Corps captured Monte Maio
and were now in position to give flank assistance to the Eighth Army in
the Liri valley. Field Marshal Kesselring ordered the German Tenth Army
to put in every available reserve as he sought to buy time in which to
move troops to the second prepared defensive position, the Hitler Line,
eight miles to the rear.

Also that same day, on a mission to bomb a railroad tunnel guarded
by "88s" that were manned by gunners of the *Hermann Göring* Division,
twenty-four Mitchells of the 310th's 380th and 381st Bomb Squadrons
encountered flak that was "heavy, intense and accurate." As he knelt over
his Norden bombsight, bombardier Fred Nelson of the 381st Squadron
was startled by four salvos so close he had no trouble hearing them even
with his ears covered by his headset. "I called 'Bombs Away' and watched

the light on the intervalometer record each drop. I called 'bomb doors coming closed!' We whipped over in a near-vertical bank and dived after our leader, Lieutenant McLaughlin, who was in close to a vertical dive. When the airspeed indicator hit 350, I stopped looking, I didn't want to see any more. I looked back to see how the others were doing and the sky was black with flak bursts. Six of our planes were hit so bad they turned for a base in Italy knowing they couldn't make it back."

After they recovered from the wild dive, crossed the coast, and headed across the sea toward Corsica, Nelson went back to check the bomb bay: "Even though I had every indication the bombs had dropped, I went to check anyway." He squirmed into the tight space between the roof of the bomb bay and the top of the fuselage and unscrewed the "manhole cover" that would allow him to make a visual check: "I was dumbfounded to find none had dropped. We had gone through all that for nothing!"

Second Lieutenant Clifton Campbell of the 380th squadron was flying one of the B-25s that got hit. As his formation approached their target, an intense flak barrage was laid in front of them. A direct hit by an "88" in the right engine nacelle of Campbell's B-25 severed the oil lines to the right engine and cut the right aileron cable, damaged the engine, and punched holes in the wing gas tank. Campbell managed to hold formation long enough for his bombardier to drop the bombs, but then on withdrawal the Mitchell took a second hit in the fuselage that destroyed the instrument panel and showered Campbell and his co-pilot with shards from the instrument faces. Somehow Campbell managed to keep the tough bomber airborne. Lacking all instruments and with only one engine, he flew home across 250 miles of ocean and landed successfully at Ghisonaccia Gare, where the airplane was immediately pushed aside to become a source of spare parts. For the feat of getting his crew back alive, twenty-one-year-old Clifton F. Campbell was awarded the Distinguished Flying Cross.

On the next day, Sunday, May 14, the 321st Group flew missions against the Castiglione Florentine and Castiglione Del Lago railroad bridges, cutting the tracks and damaging the south end of the latter bridge. Crews were glad to report a lack of anti-aircraft fire over the targets. B-25J 43-4026, which had been flown by Tarmichael on May 12, was flown by 445th Squadron commander Major Percy D. Register in the second mission that day. That bomber was finally joined by Sterling Ditchey's 43-4050, which was flying her first mission of the campaign with none other than Lieutenant Tarmichael in the left seat. The other three squadrons of the 321st also flew missions against the bridges. Back at base, Captain Nickerson noted that the effort to camouflage the airfield had borne fruit: "Ingenious foxholes and slit trenches have appeared from nowhere. Some sport twigs, branches and boarding, some tin covering, while others closely resemble the I.R.T. and B.M.T. Subway entrances in New York City."

That day, Moroccan Goumier tribal mountain warriors, moving over the mountains parallel to the Liri valley (undefended territory because the Germans thought it was impossible to traverse such difficult terrain), led three battalions of the French Expeditionary Corps to outflank the German defenses in the rear of Monte Cassino.

On May 15, the British 78th Division passed through the bridgehead divisions and executed the turn that would isolate Cassino from the Liri Valley.

That was one of the bloodiest days the 321st Bomb Group would experience. Ten B-25s each from the 445th and 447th squadrons flew against the Porto Ferraio docks on the island of Elba, while nine from the 446th and ten from the 448th bombed an alternate target, the Orvieto South railroad bridge. The 446th squadron lost four of nine B-25s to the heavy, intense, and accurate flak over the bridge. B-25J 43-27499, flown by First Lieutenant Rolland R. Othick, and B-25J 43-27697, "Miss Margie," flown by First Lieutenant Allan Sampson, were hit just past the target. Heading for the open sea, Sampson gave the order to bail out; after making sure everyone else was out, Sampson jumped only moments before the plane exploded in mid-air. An Air-Sea Rescue OA-10 Catalina flying boat was able to land and pick up all the men. Othick made a wheels-up landing on the German-held island of Pianosa, south of Elba, where he and his crew became prisoners of war.

Back at Solenzara, B-25J 42-32446 "Mascot," flown by Second Lieutenant Richard E. Hodge, was lost when the brakes failed during landing. The plane careened across the PSP runway and crashed into a ditch, where the landing gear collapsed. But Hodge and his crew were safe. Moments later, First Lieutenant R. W. Walsh touched down and discovered he had no brakes. When his plane, saturated with gasoline from fuel line leaks, hit bumps in the PSP runway, it exploded and burned. No one got out.

The next day the 321st flew a four-squadron mission against the Foligno railroad bridge and completely demolished it, dropping ninety-eight thousand-pound bombs from an altitude of ten thousand feet.

On May 17, the day the Poles launched their second attack on Monte Cassino, the 321st made a low-level bombing mission against a German fighter airfield at Viterbo, blanketing the field with fragmentation bombs that knocked out six Bf-109s.

On the heights of Monte Cassino, the fight was fierce and at times hand to hand as the Poles advanced with little natural cover under constant artillery and mortar fire from the strongly fortified German positions. The survivors of the second offensive on the Cassino heights were so battered it was hard to find men who had enough strength to climb the few hundred yards to the summit. Finally, a patrol from the 12th Podolian Cavalry Regiment made it to the top and raised a large Polish national flag over the ruins. In taking Monte Cassino, the Poles had opened the road to Rome.

With their line of supply now threatened by the Allied advance in the Liri valley and the destruction of several bridges, the Germans began to withdraw from the Cassino heights back to the Hitler Line. The next day, the British 78th Division and Polish II Corps linked up in the Liri Valley two miles west of Cassino town.

Having broken the German lines at Formia, units of the Eighth Army now advanced up the Liri valley while the Fifth Army moved up the coast to the Hitler Line—renamed the Senger Line at Hitler's insistence, to minimize the significance if it were penetrated. An immediate follow-up assault against the position failed. Getting twenty thousand vehicles and two thousand tanks through the ruins of the Gustav Line took several days; now it was the Allies who had to deal with the blasted bridges and roadblocks created by their own bombers.

Beginning on May 20, the weather began to change with spreading rain showers limiting the missions that could be flown from Corsica. On May 21 rain kept the B-25s on the ground, and on May 22 the famous Corsica gales began to blow, and some men discovered to their chagrin, as they were awakened by a collapsing tent, that they had not set their shelters up properly.

The weather continued to be inclement on May 23, when the Polish II Corps attacked Piedimonte San Germano, which was defended by the veteran *1.Fallschirmjägerdivision*. The 1st Canadian Division began an attack on the Hitler Line and breached the German defenses the next day, and the 5th Canadian Armored Division poured through the gap.

As the Canadians and Poles launched their attack on May 23, VI Corps commander General Truscott launched an attack using three American and two British divisions of the seven divisions in the Anzio beachhead. The German Fourteenth Army in the hills surrounding the beachhead had no armored support since the Panzer divisions had been ordered south to help Tenth Army at Cassino. *26.Panzerdivision* was in transit from north of Rome, where it had been held in anticipation of the non-existent seaborne landing the Allies had faked, but its movement was halted by the bridges blown by the Corsica bombers.

Skies were clear on May 24, and the aircrews were able to take advantage of the better weather to support the battle. The losses to the 340th Group from the *Luftwaffe*'s raid on May 13 had been made up by about half, allowing them to join the other two groups to go after the German communications. The German defenders were active, and flak at all targets was reported as "heavy, intense and accurate"; nineteen B-25s of the 445th squadron returned to Solenzara with varying degrees of damage after they hit the Rignano Rail Bridge.

May 25, the day victory could be declared at Cassino, saw the Twelfth Air Force's most active day yet in the war; fighter bombers attacked retreating German units while the bombers hit every crossroads.

The 321st had their best bombing mission to date when twenty-five Mitchells scored 100 percent hits against the Todi Road bridge, dropping it into the river below. By dusk, the Poles had taken Piedimonte, and resistance by the Tenth Army had collapsed. There was nothing blocking the Allied advance to Rome and beyond.

The German Tenth Army was now in full retreat. The Allied VI Corps drove east out of the Anzio beachhead to cut them off and would have been in position to block the line of retreat and trap the Germans with all their reserves against the Canadian I Corps had they continued that advance. But, astonishingly, General Clark ordered Truscott to change the line of attack from a northeasterly one toward Valmontone on Route 6 to a northwesterly one directly towards Rome. Controversy has surrounded the decision ever since. Most historians point to Clark's ambition to be the first to arrive in Rome as the reason for the order: he had formally requested of General Eisenhower that the invasion of Normandy be delayed so that the liberation of Rome could be "properly celebrated." His request was not honored.

Truscott was shocked by Clark's order, writing later,

> I was dumbfounded. This was no time to drive to the northwest where the enemy was still strong; we should pour our maximum power into the Valmontone Gap to insure the destruction of the retreating German Army. I would not comply with the order without first talking to General Clark in person.... [However] he was not on the beachhead and could not be reached even by radio.... [S]uch was the order that turned the main effort of the beachhead forces from the Valmontone Gap and prevented destruction of Tenth Army. There has never been any doubt in my mind that had General Clark held loyally to General Alexander's instructions, had he not changed the direction of my attack to the northwest on May 26, the strategic objectives of Anzio would have been accomplished in full. To be first in Rome was a poor compensation for this lost opportunity.

Had VI Corps continued its attack to Valmontone, where the Germans would have been pinched between the Americans and the Canadians, there would have been no alternative for the Germans but surrender. The Italian campaign would have been over.

On May 26, the bombers maintained their campaign against communications lines to block the German retreat. The two afternoon missions flown by the 321st ran into heavy flak that forced them to miss the Incisa Aqueduct and the nearby bridge. The 445th and 446th squadrons also sent bombers against the aqueduct: twenty-five planes including both 43-4026, which had flown every mission in the previous week, and Ditchey's old 43-4050, which had been in a morning mission aborted by weather—its first mission since May 18. "050," as it was known in the squadron, was flown by Second Lieutenant Sheldon R. Groh, with Second Lieutenant Charles F. Spencer in the right seat and Second Lieutenant Earl E. Rehrig as bombardier. Sergeants Marinucci, Rossi and Lemke, who had been with "050" since they had picked it up in Algeria, were accompanied in the rear by group photographer Sergeant Jack M. Cotter, there to record the results of the bombing.

Major Hunter, the executive officer of the 446th, was hit by the "heavy, intense and accurate" flak as he led the formation toward the viaduct; the flight scattered with the result that only six planes were able to drop on the aqueduct, with poor results. Hunter's Mitchell was last seen by the leader of the RAF Spitfire escort heading southeast past Arezzo. Co-pilot Second Lieutenant Walter Brickner, navigator Second Lieutenant John Kinney, bombardier Second Lieutenant Laverne Reynolds, flight engineer Sergeant John Denny, radioman Tech Sergeant Alfred Todd, and tail gunner Sergeant William Lanza successfully bailed out while Hunter held the plane steady for them to make their escape. Hunter was unable to get out of the stricken B-25, which went out of control as he left the cockpit.

First Lieutenant Frank L. Lonsdorf, flying the rearmost Mitchell of the diamond formation Hunter was leading, reported seeing Hunter's B-25 explode on impact with the ground. Bombardier Reynolds and engineer Denny were captured soon after they bailed out and survived to be liberated from prison camp on May 26, 1945, while Brickner, Kinney, Todd, and Lanza managed to evade capture and contact Italian partisans. They were liberated by advancing Allied troops in July.

When he returned to Corsica, navigator Kinney was able to fill in the details of what had happened, reporting,

> On the bomb run, about 35 seconds before bombs away, our ship was hit by enemy flak. The nose was hit first and then the right wing suffered two hits. The Major rang for all crew members to abandon ship. Two men in the rear jumped almost immediately. The engineer gunner and the bombardier then bailed out, and I was about to jump when the co-pilot called me back. An attempt was made to trim the aircraft, but it proved impossible to hold altitude. I jumped at about 4000 feet; the altitude of the country below was 3000 feet, and I did not, therefore, have much time to observe the stricken aircraft. I do remember seeing one other chute, which I believe to have been that of the co-pilot. I hit the ground with some violence and was knocked unconscious. When I came to, a deathly quiet was broken by a number of pistol shots from the valley below. I evaded capture by Fascists. Later on, reliable partisans stated that a man had been found dead in our plane. He had worn a golden oak leaf, as well as a shoulder holster and a .45 revolver and .38 pistol. Major Hunter had always carried two guns, and had worn a shoulder holster; I am therefore positive of the fact of death in his case. I know nothing of the eventual fate of the remaining crew members, although the partisans did say that one man had been killed by Fascists, one man had been killed when his chute failed to open, and one man had been taken POW by the Germans.

Hunter's bomber wasn't the only one hit. Sheldon Groh's 43-4050 took a direct hit from an "88" that knocked off the right rudder and a section of the right stabilizer as the right elevator went fluttering in the slipstream. A B-25 was almost uncontrollable in such a situation, but Lieutenant Groh performed what was recorded in the war diary as "a miracle of flying to bring the plane back," fighting the controls all the way to Corsica. Unable to land, Groh ordered the crew to bail out once they were over Ghisonaccia Gare Airfield and held the plane in a circle under control long enough for them to get out.

Below on the field, Sergeant Frank Dean of the 310th witnessed what happened.

> The plane circled our field and dropped out everybody except the pilot. He flew the plane out to sea on the north side of Ghisonaccia Ville, maybe a quarter mile offshore. The plane rolled over on its back and the pilot dropped out the top escape hatch. When we saw it, we thought this was an intentional maneuver, but I heard later that the plane rolled over when the pilot let go the controls. The pilotless aircraft then righted itself, flew around a bit, then entered a dive.
>
> In practically every village in Corsica there was a small grassy area that contained a monument to the boys of the town who had been killed in World War I. There was such a plot about 65 feet across in the very small village of Ghisonaccia Ville, and the M.P.s had erected a tent nearby. This stricken bomber chose that plot to land on. Most of the fuel must have been used up for there was little fire, although it did destroy the M.P. tent. I visited the site after the plane had been removed. There was a new tent up and a sign in front: OFF-LIMITS TO AIRPLANES!

Lieutenant Groh broke his leg bailing out of 43-4050 when it rolled on him. He was taken to the 310th's hospital, where his first words upon leaving the ambulance were "How's the rest of the crew?" Everyone else had escaped without injury.

Just over three weeks since Sterling Ditchey and his crew had delivered 43-4050 to the replacement field at Telergma, the bomber was a pile of parts in the 310th's boneyard. Ditchey, who had been with the 310th for a bit over two weeks himself, never forgot the strange feeling that came over him when he saw the left rudder and recognized the serial number of the junked bomber.

The rest of the planes on this mission bombed the Cecina road bridge on the way home. Captain Nickerson recorded in the war diary that "Photos showed that bridge too added to the growing list of bridges knocked out during the month of May. Lieutenent Cormier made a fine single engine landing. Lieutenant Conover's eye was slightly cut from flying Plexiglass. Sergeant Reddy received a mean flak wound in his arm. All in all, the 445th can consider itself proud and fortunate."

That night, 445th armorer Sergeant Seegmiller wrote in his diary,

> Considerable activity. Today we are sending a total of 26 ships on two missions. The 8th and the 5th Armies in Italy joined forces yesterday. The kitchen has moved into the club house and food and feeding conditions are generally good. There are loud explosions taking place hourly. They are due to an engineer outfit using German mines to blast gun pits, latrines, etc. Today is pretty, though for two days we had a strong miserable wind. Margaret's letters are most satisfactory. We have no time off but I don't mind that because we are busy towards winning the war. We have had several alerts, but no bombs have been dropped on us. The squadron bombing lately has been pretty good.

Around the same time Seegmiller was writing in his diary, 445th squadron pilot Second Lieutenant Charles Frederick Ritger Jr. wrote a letter home to his family in Newark, New Jersey:

> Hello Folks,
> I guess I am a bit early with this letter but I just have to do something. One of my best pals went down today and it

hit me as hard as a thing like that could. Lieutenant Laverne Reynolds, the best damn bombardier in the world, was knocked down while on a mission over Italy. I have become pretty much used to such things but he was such a swell fellow it is mighty hard to see him go. Enough for that now because I can't express what I feel.

I haven't received any more packages lately but I did get the Diary and the pack of Edgeworth (excuse me I mean Briggs). I also got a couple of pictures of Marilyn [Ritger] that were mighty fine. Pop [Ritger] will have to teach me when I get home. And that family photo, that was the kind of thing I go for. Please keep them coming.

I don't remember whether I ever told you about the plane I am flying now. It is painted olive drab, all except the nose section which is bright red. On the sides in large white letters is printed "Red Nosed Beckie"! I guess it's the old McCaddin Irish but that ship has been darned lucky.

I am applying for an absentee ballot for the coming elections and I would like some dope about the caliber of the candidates in the local area. Open up Pop and let's hear what you think about the guys.

I don't feel like writing much tonight so I will hit the sack.
I will write again soon.
Love to all,
FC Jr.

The offensive continued, as did the missions. On May 27, Captain Nickerson recorded, "Continuing the accelerated pace, four missions, totaling over a hundred sorties, were flown this date and five bridges knocked out. 445th Squadron bombing the North Massa road bridge on the last mission of the day placed 96 500-pounders directly in the target area, chalking up another hundred percent bombing accuracy mark for this Group. The 447th put ninety percent of their bombs on the Massa South bridge, making the total effort for the complete mission highly successful. Three other bridges smothered by our bombs were the Orvieto North and South bridges and the Massa Railroad bridge."

The crews were getting good enough that even when something or someone intervened they could pick things up and continue:

> Mission 313: On the second mission today, against the Vado Viaduct, nine aircraft failed to rendezvous but the other sixteen continued and laid a devastating pattern through and around the target. Photo interpretation showed that once again the 321st had bombed the target with one hundred percent accuracy. The one hundred percent total was tougher to attain this time since the flight had to fly through several minutes of heavy, intense, accurate flak which tended to scatter the formation. The fact that they stayed in there all the way is a tribute to the high degree of tenacity and skill maintained by the combat members of this group, which at present is "hotter" than during any other period in its history.

Older airplanes continued to provide solid performance: "This mission was led by Lieutenant Russell in old reliable *Idaho Lassie* (41-13202)."

The Germans were getting better, too—at opposing the bombers: "The unfortunate choice of axis on this target was due to the majority of these gun positions having been unreported from any source and were [sic] therefore unknown to us prior to this attack." As the Germans learned to keep their "88s" mobile, aircrews could find themselves under attack at any point in a mission after crossing the bomb line. The flak on this mission took another B-25, blowing off the wing of Second Lieutenant Denham's airplane. No parachutes were spotted as the Mitchell went down.

On May 29, the 321st knocked out the Viareggio railroad bridge with several direct hits. More important to everyone at Solenzara,

Captain Nickerson reported, "The Squadron latrines have been placed in the surrounding woods and completely screened in. There are footpaths leading to them that are not unlike the winding pioneer trails. These are the best latrines we have had since arriving overseas."

On May 30, as the Canadian I Corps continued its pursuit of the retreating Tenth Army, the 321st Group launched two missions of twenty-six aircraft each. Weather prevented proper target identification, and both formations diverted to their alternate targets: good bombing concentrations were reported at the Rosignano rail and road bridges and at the Tarquinia road bridge, with photos showing that both targets were smashed.

The last day of May saw sixty-nine 321st B-25s smash bridges and roads at Cave, Subiaco, and Civitella Roveta, losing one plane when it crash-landed at a friendly base in Italy: the reliable 43-4026—previously flown by Cahill and Tarmichael, but on this mission by Second Lieutenant Gerald W. Wagner—which received a direct flak hit in the tail that blew the tail gunner out of the rear and caused two other crewmen to bail out approximately two miles south of the target.

Second Lieutenant Daniel Galindo, aboard the plane at the time, recalled,

> The target was attacked from an altitude of 9,500 feet on an axis of 200 degrees. After the bombs were released, a hard right turn was made and the formation flew over Valmontone. During violent evasive action over the city, our bomber received its first flak hit in the tail section. The plane immediately began to go downward. Fifteen seconds later the plane received more flak hits. An 88-mm shell went through the right wing and gas tank. Another hit holed the fuselage and wing. The gasoline line in the bomb bay was cut and gasoline began to gush out. Before fifteen seconds more had elapsed, the bombardier bailed out. He was followed by the turret gunner whose vest-type parachute caught in the escape exit

on the way out and left him dangling. I made an attempt to pull him in to the plane but his weight was too great. I lifted him forward enough to permit his chute to slide out. The aircraft recovered at 6,500 feet.

Second Lieutenant Wagner reported,

Meager, distant and inaccurate flak was encountered on the last of the bomb run. After the hard break to the right during violent evasive action, the plane received the first direct burst of flak in the tail section. The plane started downward nose first. A check on the instrument panel revealed that the ball on the flight indicator was on the extreme left. I tried to trim the plane to prevent a possible spin. The elevator gave very little response and the aircraft continued downward. The other crew members were immediately notified to be ready to bail out. Several seconds later the plane leveled out with the aid of more power on the engines and I called out that everything was OK. The second hit, believed to be an 88-mm, went through the right front main gas tank. A few seconds later, the navigator informed me that Lieutenant Werrlein and Sergeant Eiff had left the plane, disregarding the suggestion to ask the pilot first. Another burst came, hitting the wing, fuselage and the gas line in the bomb bay. I tried to call the tail gunner. The radio operator came forward and told me that he was blown out when the first burst hit the tail. I notified the flight leader to slow up so that I could join the formation. Upon checking the bomb bay, the navigator discovered gasoline gushing out of a broken line. The doors were opened to air out the bomb bay. I notified the flight leader that I would land near Anzio. The landing was more of a three-pointed landing because of the crippled elevator. Fuel and ignition were out on the approach and we rolled to a stop with the engines off.

Radioman Staff Sergeant James E. Kintly was the unfortunate witness to what happened to the tail gunner:

> We broke away to the right after dropping the bombs out and the first hit blew me from my seat. While I was in mid-air—which to me seemed an eternity—I saw the tail gunner blown out of the plane. When the pilot got the plane under control, I fell on my back. As I got up, I heard the pilot calling the tail gunner. I notified him that he was blown out of the plane. The pilot notified me to stand by. We received another hit that shook the plane very badly. Somewhere along here I saw a chute open through the opening in the tail. Being under the impression that no one had bailed out, I called over the interphone to the pilot and told him that the tail gunner's chute had opened. It was only later that I discovered that his chute was still in the tail of the plane.

In the B-25 immediately behind "026," pilot First Lieutenant Damon McLain saw the entire incident: "On the turn off the target, I had just regained my position behind Lieutenant Wagner's plane when it seemed to explode and flare out. Quite a bit of debris came out of the tail with the tail gunner. He was spread eagled with his face and chest facing the sky as he went by, passing about ten feet below our left propeller. I did not see a parachute on his chest as he went by and I don't believe that he was wearing one. His clothes seemed to be badly torn and smoking. It was my impression that he was not conscious."

The reliable B-25J 43-4026 had lasted a whole twenty-one days from when the airplane first touched down at Solenzara.

At 2200 hours that night, Sergeant Seegmiller had a moment to sit down after a very busy day and wrote,

> Just came from loading bombs. I stopped in the Mess Hall and Inman, who was on guard there, gave me a wonderful bread and apple jelly sandwich with butter. We flew two missions

today. From the first one, my ship returned with the bomb bay doors badly damaged. During violent action caused by "prop wash" two of the 1,000 pound bombs had come off the racks and dropped through the doors. A third hung by one lug of the shackle until the shackle pulled apart. Luckily they all got away without blowing up. We changed both doors. On the late afternoon mission one ship was shot up so badly it had to land at Anzio. The tail gunner named Callister was blown or bailed out over the target without a chute. The radio man also bailed out and his chute was seen to open. The day before, I went on an interesting practice mission off the northern tip of Corsica. A green pilot struck a rock on the edge of the taxi strip and completely wrecked one of our newest planes. Got paid today. Should get rations soon. It's amazing how one's week can come to revolve around a package of chewing gum and a candy bar. The dream of going home is what keeps a man going.

May 1944 had seen the bombers of the 321st take their heaviest losses of aircraft suffered in any one month since the unit had arrived in the Mediterranean, with fourteen bombers lost from all causes, although most of the crews managed to get out.

Sterling Ditchey had flown his first mission on May 19, seven days after arrival at Ghisonaccia Gare and the same day that Joe Heller arrived at Alesani. The next day, Tom Cahill, who had arrived on Corsica the same day as Ditchey, flew his first mission, "which had me all up in my helmet, I was so scared." On May 23, both Ditchey and Cahill flew their fifth missions while Heller went out on his first, a mission to bomb the railroad bridge at Poggibonsi. As he later wrote, "Poor little Poggibonsi. Its only crime was that it happened to lie outside Florence along one of the few passageways running south through the Appenine Mountains to Rome.... as a wing bombardier, my job was to keep my eyes on the first plane in our formation, which contained the lead bombardier. When I saw his bomb-bay doors open, I was to open mine. The instant I saw his bombs begin to fall, I would press a button to release my own. That was the theory." But distracted by what he saw below, Heller didn't react immediately to the bombs falling from the lead Mitchell and was a few moments late dropping his load, which blasted a hole in a mountain several miles from the bridge. Four days later, Cahill wrote home that he had five missions under his belt and "now I feel like a ringside spectator."

On June 4, 1944, two days before the Normandy Invasion that General Eisenhower had refused to delay for General Clark's celebration, the American Fifth Army entered Rome, which the Germans had evacuated and left as an "open city." As the victory parade was held and the troops marched past the ruins of Imperial Rome, the German Tenth Army retreated around the Eternal City to the east and north and broke out of the trap with the Canadians still in pursuit. The Eighth Army would continue the pursuit up the Italian peninsula for the next six weeks, harrying the retreating Tenth Army for some 225 miles towards Perugia, where seven of the German divisions managed to make their way to the Trasimene Line to link up with the Fourteenth Army and make a fighting withdrawal to the formidable Gothic Line.

The war in Italy would grind on for another eleven months because of General Mark Clark's ego. Joe Heller, Sterling Ditchey, Tom Cahill, and everyone else in the 57th Wing would get to know the imposing and dangerous country of Alpine Italy well—and see more war than any of them had expected.

SIX

THE WORST DAY

The fall of Rome on June 4, 1944, created a feeling of euphoria, a sense that the war might be over soon, among the exhausted men of the Fifth Army and Twelfth Air Force. None of the young men riding in tanks, or trudging alongside the roads with a rifle on their shoulder, or climbing into bombers for dawn missions were privy to knowledge of the strategic mistake that had taken place when VI Corps stopped its drive to cut off the Tenth Army and instead turned to liberate the open city of Rome. Two days later, on June 6, came the news of the successful landings in Normandy. Surely, the men thought, the Germans can't keep on in the face of success like this. But it was soon clear that the Germans had not received the message to quit.

With eleven of the fourteen bridges over the Tiber River undamaged, on June 5 the infantry and armored divisions of VI Corps had left the celebration of liberation to others and crossed the river, headed north in pursuit of the escaping Germans. By June 9, the Roman port of

Civitavecchia was in Allied hands. North of the port, Fifth Army units ran into stiff German resistance at Grosseto, which was not overcome until June 16. By June 19, after four days of battle, the island of Elba—once the prison of Napoleon—had fallen. In the meantime, the French Expeditionary Corps, the Polish II Corps, VI Corps, and the Canadian I Corps kept close on the heels of the *Wehrmacht*'s Tenth and Fourteenth Armies. By June 27, following a house-to-house battle over four days, the ruined city of San Vicenzo was in Allied hands while the French pushed forward west of Lake Trasimene. By the end of the month, the French were five miles from Siena.

The Germans had kept to their strategy of forcing the Allies to pay dearly for every advance. Their fighting retreat saw the leading units enter the forts of the Gothic Line in early July. Based on the supply center at Bologna, the southern terminus of the railroad that brought supplies down from Munich through the Brenner Pass in eight hours, the troops manned the pillboxes with their interlocking fields of fire on the heavily forested, steep mountainsides of the Apennines and wheeled their artillery into the prepared positions.

Throughout this period, the three groups of the 57th Bomb Wing kept flying missions against road and rail bridges to slow and block the German retreat. They fell into a rhythm of two missions a day, with most aircrews getting a day off between missions. Still, the pace was fast. By the end of June, Tom Cahill, now a veteran of sixteen missions, could write home and tell his mother a bit more about the kind of flying he was doing.

> I found out yesterday that I can write about flak and fighters, though give no specific instances. No doubt you have been wondering about them. Missions are generally classified as "milk runs," "beaucoup," and "beaucoup-beaucoup." Beaucoup means, in our parlance, flak. Flak can generally be evaded if you see it coming—one—two—three and don't be around for four. The colonel says it's just a "harassing agent," but when I'm the guy being harassed it makes the cheese decidedly more binding.... The fact that Jerry is on the run

helps considerably, but as their positions keep moving, a flak-free target yesterday may be Hitler's hideout today.... For my money, any trip you come back from is a milk run, so don't worry about that stuff anymore. A real milk run comes frequently enough so that you don't get the idea you are personally getting the whole German artillery thrown at you.

Staff Sergeant George B. Underwood had arrived as a replacement gunner-armorer in the 381st Bomb Squadron of the 310th Bomb Group in November 1943, while the group was still in Algeria. Underwood had grown up in Hollywood, California, after his parents moved there from New York when he was six months old. In the '20s and '30s, much of the Movie Capital of the World was still open lots, though there was lots of residential construction going on. George and his friends played soldiers in the vacant lots and backyards, taking cover in the piles of lumber and bricks. At the time there were fifty-five airfields in Los Angeles County, and he looked up every time he heard an airplane fly overhead. In 1932, when he was nine, his father took him to the National Air Races at Mines Field, where he saw daredevil race pilot Roscoe Turner flash over the finish line to set a transcontinental speed record from New York City in the Bendix Trophy Race—and later be disqualified from taking first place for cutting a pylon in a turn. Movie theaters were everywhere, and George came of age on such films as *The Dawn Patrol*, *Helldivers of the Navy*, *Test Pilot*, and *Dive Bomber*. At Fairfax High School, he enrolled in the Junior Reserve Officer Training Corps: "The fact they had a rifle team, of which I became a leading member, was the one thing that kept me in school till graduation." George graduated in February 1941, enrolled at Los Angeles City College, and took a job at Lockheed Aircraft, over the Cahuenga Pass from Hollywood in Burbank, working in Canteen Food Services as war work expanded employment for everyone. "Every chance I had to get outside, I was out there looking at those P-38s as they came off the line."

Six months later, war came to America. "We had driven home from the Hollywood Methodist Church on that clear blue Southern California winter Sunday, and were sitting out at our picnic table in the backyard, eating hamburgers Dad had just grilled." George's father, a teacher of history and civics at Fairfax High, was a news junkie and had put speakers in the backyard trees so they could hear the radio that sat in the living room. "We were listening to KNX on the radio, when suddenly John Daly made that never-to-be-forgotten announcement, 'We interrupt this program to bring you this news bulletin.... Japan has bombed Pearl Harbor in Hawaii.'" Nothing would ever be the same again.

The job at Lockheed, no matter how lowly, deferred the draft, but George could only be restrained from enlisting by his mother's demand that he first pay for a recent operation on his nose, which he had broken in a basketball game. Once he had paid her the hundred dollars she had spent on the doctor, he was free to join up. "I had just had a visit from a high school chum who had enlisted and was going through P-38 training. I wanted to fly one of those P-38s we made out in Burbank, but when I went to the Army enlistment office in Hollywood, the sergeant told me they weren't accepting anyone for pilot training at the time, but he assured me I would be first on the list when it opened up after joining the Air Corps. I was anxious to get to the war and signed up anyway."

George's experience as an ROTC marksman stood him in good stead, and the Army made him an aerial gunner and then an armorer, the man responsible for keeping the guns in good operating condition. But he wasn't satisfied to stay on the ground and clean the weapons—he wanted to be the one in the airplane shooting them. In the summer of 1943, shortly after his nineteenth birthday, Sergeant Underwood reported to Columbia, South Carolina, for training as an aerial gunner in the B-25 Mitchell. His crew was among the first to be trained to fly and fight in the new B-25G gunship. "Around Greenville, it was the practice for the pine trees to be cut back from the highways. This allowed our aircraft just enough room for our hot pilot, Storey Larkin, to fly on the deck, lifting up over cars to the surprise and ire of the motorists." The crew was issued the new plane in October. "We had about 30 hours on the new plane when we went out on another low-level training mission. We thought we were pretty hot, and got a little too low. They didn't like those telephone wires they found trailing from the right wing when we got back to Columbia." As a result of this incident, the crew would not be able to fly their plane off to war. "I suspect they wanted us out of there quickly, to avoid any further questions about that flight." So Underwood and his crew crossed the South Atlantic via Air Transport Command.

The C-46 they departed in developed engine troubles and had to make an unscheduled stop at Fortaleza, Brazil. "We spent an enjoyable few days there. You could get a complete T-bone steak dinner in town for 45 cents, and a chicken dinner for a whopping 35 cents." Underwood also bought himself a set of handmade leather boots. Arriving at the Brazilian city Natal in a C-47, they were treated to a USO show by Joe E. Brown before climbing aboard a C-87, the transport version of the B-24 bomber, for the flight across the Atlantic. "Our first exposure to enemy fire came from a surfaced German submarine, which took a couple shots at us. Thankfully, they missed, but it added some spice to a long and otherwise boring flight." From Dakar, Senegal, they flew on across the Sahara in another C-47. When they finally arrived in Algeria, they spent several cold weeks at the "repple depple" (replacement depot) at Telergma Airfield before finally being sent on to the 310th Bomb Group at Philippeville, where they were assigned to the 381st Bomb Squadron. "Storey Larkin and our bombardier, Lieutenant Art Vlahon, were assigned to other crews and we crew were assigned to Lieutenant Leonard Heller, a pilot with 20 missions, and Staff Sergeant Harold W. Smith, our cannoneer, who had six missions. We were ready for action."

The 381st specialized in anti-shipping strikes known as sea sweeps, using their big 75-mm cannon and .50 caliber machine guns to go after Axis vessels along the coast of Italy. In February 1944, the group moved to Corsica and went after ships along the Ligurian coast of Italy and across the Tyrrhenian Sea to the coast of Southern France, but in late April they reluctantly turned in their gunships for B-25J bombers.

By June 22, 1944, the longest day of the year, Staff Sergeant Underwood was a veteran of fifty-seven missions and victor over a German Do-24 flying boat he'd shot up on a sea sweep at low altitude north of Sardinia back in March.

It had been cloudy that morning, with a hint of rain, and it seemed at first that flying for the day might be canceled. But shortly after lunch Underwood and the others were told to stand by for a mission that afternoon. The weather continued to be "iffy," and the men spent the afternoon playing card games, reading books, and attempting to sleep. The weather cleared sufficiently for a "nickeling" mission of three B-25s tasked with dropping leaflets urging surrender over the German lines to take off around 1400 hours. Finally, at 1600 hours, most of the crews—but not Underwood's—were called for a briefing. He took that as a sign they likely wouldn't fly at all, but they still had to hang around in "ready" condition.

At the briefing the crews were told the 380th and 381st squadrons would each put up two twelve-plane formations, each joined by six B-25s from the 379th squadron, to make up an eighteen-plane mission for each squadron. The targets were the rail bridges north and south of the town of Vernio, which was east of Florence near Viareggio on the west coast of the Italian peninsula. The bomb loads would be heavier than usual, six thousand-pound high explosive bombs per plane rather than the usual four, which would make the Mitchells "mushy" and noticeably slower at the bombing altitude of twelve thousand feet. The bridges were a known "beaucoup" flak target, but no one was particularly worried. They had been there before on June 15, and the "window" (aluminum foil strips) they'd dropped had thoroughly confused the radar-directed guns.

Takeoff was delayed until a bit before 1700 hours, but the bombers were all airborne and on their way by 1720 hours, with the target approximately ninety minutes' flying time distant. Fred Nelson of the 381st remembered the takeoff: "Almost from the first, we knew we had a ship that didn't like the extra weight. We must have used up most of the runway getting off, and the pilot, Lieutenant Robert F. Killian, had one heck of a time controlling the plane. Forming up, we nearly collided with the leader as we misjudged our rate of closure. Finally we settled into our right position, number eight on the right wing." Within minutes they met up with the twelve RAF Spitfires that would provide escort. A takeoff this late was cutting things close, since it meant they would return right before sunset.

Just as the B-25s of the second Vernio mission were lining up for takeoff, word came that the Germans in the port of Leghorn had been spotted by aerial reconnaissance preparing to tow four gutted hulks out to the southern harbor entrance, where they would be sunk to block Allied use of the harbor when it fell. The Germans had already sunk several hulks in the northern entrance, and it was necessary to prevent them from completely blocking the port because the fall of Leghorn was expected in a few weeks. A "quickie" mission was laid on, with three B-25s of the 380th, three from the 381st, and twelve from the 428th squadron charged with sinking the hulks before the Germans could pull them out to a position where they could block the entrance of the harbor. Underwood's crew was among those assigned the mission: pilot First Lieutenant C. W. Prasse, co-pilot Second Lieutenant H. D. Collins, and Underwood's flying buddies—togglier Staff Sargeant Harry Smith—who was responsible for dropping the bombs in the absence of a bombardier—radioman tech Sergeant Jim Heaney and tail gunner Sergeant Herb Campbell. Underwood and the other three sergeants had flown almost all their missions together, but the pilot and co-pilot were new for the mission. For once, the crew was assigned to fly "their" B-25J, 43-27507, the one with their names on it. She was known as "507" in the squadron, having arrived in Corsica a week earlier and not having even been named.

Veteran pilot First Lieutenant Glenn T. Black of the 381st was assigned to lead the mission. As he later recalled, "On this special mission, I was to lead three from our squadron, three from the 380th and twelve from the 428th. I didn't like the arrangement, for we had our best missions when the whole mission was made up of crews from one squadron. We all knew each other and were able to work together better. Although I didn't like the arrangement, I expect the second element lead crew liked it much less." That second element lead crew—pilot First Lieutenant Peterson, co-pilot First Lieutenant Lightsey, bombardier Staff Sergeant Hunt, gunner Sergeant Ptach, and tail gunner Sergeant Pizzimenti—had joined the 380th squadron in the fall of 1943 and just completed their tour of seventy missions. At the last minute, radioman Staff Sergeant Morgan from Sterling Ditchey's crew was assigned to fly with them. The men had already been given their orders to return to the states the next day, and their B-4 bags were packed in their tents in anticipation of the event. When Peterson's crew was detailed for the mission, all the other 380th crews said quietly to each other that they shouldn't be put on such a mission. No one made any direct complaint, however, and all went out to man their aircraft. Twenty minutes after the last of the earlier flights had disappeared over the horizon, the B-25s lead by Black began taking off. After circling the field for join-up, the eighteen planes set off over the Tyrrhenian Sea toward Leghorn.

As the bombers neared the port, the formation was scattered by clouds. Glenn Black's formation of six, which included George Underwood's "507," was to bomb from 12,500 feet and to the left of the other two flights that were bombing at 8,500 and 10,000 feet, all flying at 200 mph. Having had the experience of looking up at the open bomb bays of other American bombers that had overrun him and praying not to be hit by their falling bombs, Black elected to turn wider over the Initial Point (IP), placing his flight well behind the others. He was aiming for a three-minute bomb run (the most dangerous part of the flight, in which the target was sighted and the bombs were dropped) long enough for his bombardier to line up on the hulks below, while hopefully not enough time for the German gunners to get their range—though from the black puffs of 88-mm shell explosions around the formations ahead it was certain the Germans were ready and waiting. Since his B-25 was not equipped with an autopilot connected to the bombsight, Black lowered his seat so he could concentrate on the PDI (Pilot Direction Indicator), which moved right or left as the bombardier lined up on the target. Black wasn't aware that his wide turn had added about ninety crucial seconds to their run.

In the distance ahead, flak burst all around the second formation as their bombs fell away. Suddenly the lead B-25 erupted in flame when her right wing caught fire. The plane fell away in a steep dive toward the harbor as the fire spread to the engine nacelle and then to the fuselage.

Black's heart was in his mouth as he watched, silently screaming "Jump! Jump!" The second formation bomber was now headed straight down. At the last moment a body came out of the rear escape hatch and the parachute began to stream. It was too late, and whoever it was fell all the way to the harbor below with a half-deployed parachute. The Mitchell exploded on impact with the water's surface. Lieutenant Peterson and his crew wouldn't be catching that flight home in the morning. As if that wasn't bad enough, the second plane in the formation ahead of Black also took a hit in the bomb bay that set the oil system for the right engine afire and caused other heavy damage. The pilot, Lieutenant Quitta, nosed over in a dive to try and put out the flames and headed out to sea away from the exploding sky over the harbor. As he did so, the lower rear hatch flew open and a crewmember believed to be tail gunner Sergeant W. F. Watkins, hurtled out. His parachute was seen to open, but nothing else was ever heard of him.

From his turret behind the cockpit of "507," George Underwood scanned the skies for enemy fighters and glanced over his shoulder at the other planes in the formation as they entered the bomb run. This was the moment of maximum danger—the bombers had to hold straight and steady for accuracy. The other planes moved closer into as tight a formation as possible to insure a good concentration when they released their bombs on the leader's drop. The German gunners below opened up with their deadly "88s", and the bombers were quickly surrounded with bursts from exploding shells, some so close that the explosions could be heard over the roaring engines—and felt, as they sent a jolt through the airframe in addition to shrapnel.

In the lead ship, Black got the feeling the run was taking longer than it should. "A few days before, we'd had intercom problems, and I wondered if we were having further intercom problems. When 4,000 pounds of bombs, spaced to hit 50 feet apart, leave a B-25, there is a sudden sensation of rising. But vertical air currents or flak bursting fairly close beneath can cause the same sensation. Two or three times, I felt such sensations, but I heard no call of 'bombs away!' from my bombardier."

In Underwood's Mitchell, Sergeant Smith crouched in the nose, his attention on Black's airplane ahead and his hand on the panel to toggle the release of his bombs. Underwood glanced impatiently over his shoulder in time to see the lead ship's bomb bay doors come open and heard Smith's call on the intercom, "Bomb doors open." A moment later he saw the bombs began falling from the lead plane and felt the bumps as their own bombs fell clear. "Bombs Away! Bomb doors closing," Smith announced. "Let's get the hell out of here!"

Black now realized that his formation was too far from the other twelve to join up for evasive action. He decided to alter his plan: "Originally I had planned to turn left and climb as soon as the bombs were released, since that would put us on a heading out to sea, away from the target and above the altitude the Germans had their shells set to explode at more quickly. I had noticed before that the Germans had come to expect this maneuver, since they would fire to our left we dropped our bombs. Since we were so far back, I elected to turn right and dive, since they wouldn't expect us to turn toward them."

As the other five airplanes in his formation maneuvered to follow Black, the Germans got the range in a series of lucky shots.

"We took a close burst just ahead of the right wing outboard of the engine, and it was very quickly apparent the engine had taken the worst of the hit when smoke poured out of the cooling flaps," Underwood later remembered. In the lead ship ahead, Black felt his whole plane seem to stand still and shudder in midair as several shells exploded close by.

I looked down at my right hand, which had been on the throttles—it lay limp in my lap. I looked down at my right arm and could see the jagged end of the lower part of my bone in my upper arm and the jagged ends of the bones in the lower part of my arm. My elbow was no more. My lower arm reminded me of the drumstick of a freshly-butchered chicken. The only connecting flesh I could see holding my lower arm looked like raw meat. I turned the controls over to my co-pilot, but he pulled up straight and level so I took over again and did evasive action one-handed that was probably more violent than was necessary. After we were out of range of the flak, I turned the controls back over to him and called for Nick [the bombardier] to give me first aid.

Out to sea, the dire situation in Lieutenant Quitta's B-25 seemed resolved when the oil system burned itself out and whatever was afire in the bomb bay departed the aircraft. With the right engine feathered but still smoking, with the potential for fire to burst out at any moment, Quitta turned on a heading for Corsica as the sun dipped towards the western horizon.

In "507," Lieutenant Prasse broke left out of the formation and dove for the open sea when the bomber was hit in the right engine. As he turned away, a second "88" burst near the left wing. Prasse feathered the right engine and headed for Corsica. Underwood kept his eyes on the left "good" engine as white smoke from burning oil appeared out of the cowling flaps.

Co-pilot Jerry Gerg managed to get Black's B-25 headed out to sea, but when he tried to apply power to climb to a safer altitude for crossing the sea, he discovered that the control cable from the right prop pitch control lever was severed and he could not change the propeller RPM and add power, since increasing the manifold pressure without increasing the propeller RPMs would blow the engine. "We had cruise RPM on that engine," Black explained, "and could not increase it to maintain altitude." Black ordered the crew to get rid of the guns and everything else that could be thrown overboard to lighten the plane in hopes they could make it to Corsica. Ahead, the sun was just above the western Mediterranean horizon, creating a kaleidoscope of light through the badly fractured windshield in front of Gerg. Throughout the long flight back, Black had to tell Gerg what was out front as they flew on into the setting sun. Hydraulic fluid sloshed in the bottom of the plane. "There was a neat hole through the center of our artificial horizon, and the normally-horizontal bar was straight up. The hydraulic pressure gauge registered zero, which meant we couldn't lower the flaps or gear."

Back at Ghisonaccia Airfield, those waiting on the ground heard the approaching roar of the B-25s returning from the Vernio missions. Sunset light glinted off canopies and bombardier greenhouses and turrets as Mitchells came overhead and broke for landing. Red flares shot out from several planes, indicating wounded aboard. The ambulance drivers started their engines. Shaken crews emerged from the planes with reports of heavy, accurate, "beaucoup-beaucoup" flak in the target area, with continuous flak bursts among the formations. Everyone marveled at the seemingly miraculous fact that no one had been killed except in the one crew lost over the south target. When a Mitchell named "The Little King" landed, 380th maintenance sergeant Frank Dean examined the airplane for new flak holes. "A small hole was found right beneath the bombardier's compartment, where it had been stopped by an extra piece of armor plate we had installed for just such purpose. Had it not been in place, there could have been a fatality. Most of the other aircraft bore mute evidence of the accuracy of the German gunners."

Underwood's original pilot, First Lieutenant Storey D. Larkin, remembered, "We took the worst pasting of our lives in one of the bloodiest battles we were ever in. The minute we started the bomb run, their accuracy was deadly. Just as the lead ship dropped, they got hit in their left engine and the pilot had to feather it. They got back. The Germans concentrated on us and got in some excellent shots but we got off with just one hole in the gas tank. At the south target one ship went in head first, as well as one of the escorting Spitfires. Nobody saw any 'chutes. We managed to overfly a flak position on the way home and they opened up on us. Our element drew the brunt of their fire. The plane on the right got it in the left engine. He seemed OK for a few minutes and then the main wheels dropped and the bomb bay came open which meant they had no hydraulics. The engine caught fire and he continued to lose altitude as we crossed the coast. We stuck with him and at 2,000 feet a 'chute came out the rear. He circled back over land and another five 'chutes came out. Then the plane went out of control, dove to tree top height, pulled out and went into a stall and flat spin. Another crew saw the pilot's chute at the last minute when it stalled. When we got back to Ghisonaccia, we orbited while planes with wounded landed ahead of us."

Still over the Tyrrhenian Sea in the fading light, Lieutenants Quitta, Black, and Prasse nursed their crippled B-25s home from the Leghorn mission. Quitta looked ahead and saw the dark shape of Corsica on the horizon, perhaps twenty miles distant. Just as the men began to think they'd made it, the fire in the bomb bay caught again and spread rapidly. The gas tanks soon caught fire. Quitta managed to pancake the bomber onto the sea surface, but it went under before anyone but co-pilot W. B. Helgeson could climb out the upper escape hatch. He managed to drag the badly injured Quitta with him. A rescue boat was on the scene quickly and pulled both from the sea. But Quitta was already dead, and Helgeson died a few hours later. The other four men went down with the plane.

Aboard "507," Underwood thought they might make it when Sergeant Smith's voice came over the intercom, "Corsica dead ahead." Soon they were over Ghisonaccia, with a green flare for landing. But when Prasse tried to lower the gear, it wouldn't come down. Underwood and radioman Jim Heany handcranked the wheels down. Not knowing what else might be wrong with the airplane, Prasse elected to land in the dirt beside the PSP runway, so as not to damage it. The Mitchell touched down nose high on its main gear. As the nose came down and the nosewheel touched the ground, it collapsed from what was later determined to be flak damage. "We got thrown around inside from that fast stop." Tail gunner Campbell wrenched his back when he stepped out of the open rear hatch—its cover having been ejected by the screeching halt—only to discover he was twenty feet in the air. "We counted 200 flak holes, including one 88-mm hole in the left wing where a shell had passed through without exploding." Mitchell "507" had lasted only a week before it was dragged off to the boneyard to be dismantled for spare parts.

Flying at cruising speed, George Black's B-25 was the last one back.

We had been steadily descending on the way home, and I worried that the mountains of Corsica rise to about 8,500 feet. I was worried about descending below the clouds and running into one of them. However, we broke out of the clouds north of Corsica and as soon as I saw the island I knew right where we were.

The closest airfields were fighter fields with short strips. The only base hospital was on the south end of the island, a ways from Ghisonaccia. The 340th's base at Alesani was the closest to the hospital, so that's where I decided we'd land.

Co-pilot Jerry Gerg called the Alesani tower and was cleared straight in. Black signaled bombardier Nick Paul to start pumping the emergency hydraulic system to lower the gear, but it was useless. Paul looked for the crank to get the gear down manually, but it was missing. "We were then too low to give the crew the opportunity to bail out, and we couldn't climb back up. A belly landing was our only alternative. Hydraulic fluid and 100-octane fuel was sloshing around in the lower fuselage. When I looked in the navigator's compartment, I saw a fog of fumes. There was a great possibility of fire and explosion in our crash landing."

Black took the controls with his left hand, with Gerg holding his yoke too. As they set up to land, Paul stood behind the pilots and called out the airspeed so that Black could keep his attention on the landscape below. Black recalled, "I had a thick yellow cushion placed vertically on my lap. If I was thrown forward on landing, hopefully it might protect my chest and face."

At two hundred feet, he retarded his single throttle on the right engine. Paul called out 135 miles per hour airspeed, then moved to take position for the crash. "As we flared over the runway, Jerry started to pull back, but I said let's get this on the ground and he pushed forward with me. The tail touched and we slid on the ground so smoothly that we didn't feel anything but the rapid deceleration."

Once they came to a stop, they needed to get out fast. Tailgunner Sergeant Morris and radioman Sergeant Katairules in back pushed open the rear escape hatch on the right side of the fuselage and quickly crawled out while navigator Paul pushed open the cockpit escape hatch and climbed up and out onto the nose, followed by turret gunner Sergeant Blentz. "I had never considered my crew an eager-beaver crew, but they did move quickly that day!" Black released his straps and tried to stand up but discovered the parachute's right leg strap was still fastened. He couldn't get it loose with his shattered arm. Co-pilot Gerg reached over and unstrapped him, at which point Black realized his co-pilot had been badly hurt, too, with a deep flesh wound in his left hip. Gerg pushed Black out the escape hatch and followed him.

"Men were swarming toward us from all directions. Some of my crewmembers shouted at those approaching with lighted cigarettes to get out of there since the plane was full of gas. Fortunately, our plane did not explode or burn. I was later told by the 340th's engineering officer that we did very little damage on landing, but when they had to get it out of the way for other emergency landings, they dragged it over boulders and damaged it beyond repair."

George Black spent the next two years in Army hospitals, undergoing surgery and therapy to regain some use of his right arm. Jerry Gerg returned to flight status a week after the mission.

On the Leghorn mission the 380th squadron had lost two B-25s of three sent out, with all aboard killed, and the 381st two B-25s of three, but with no fatalities. The mission had succeeded; the hulks were sunk away from the harbor entrance. At Vernio, the 381st lost a plane while the 380th had no losses, and the approaches to both bridges were listed as "heavily damaged." The "lucky" 428th came back with one plane holed over Vernio, while the 379th's Mitchells had no damage. Of the total aircraft sent out, three were lost, two were so badly damaged they never flew again, and thirty-eight had varying degrees of flak damage. Two crewmen were killed and five wounded. The dead were buried at the American cemetery at Bastia. The crashed aircraft were mined for valuable parts and their carcasses dragged away. All the surviving crewmen were recommended for the Air Medal. June 22, 1944, was the worst day the 310th Bomb Group would experience during the war.

After a two-day stand-down, the 310th went back to war, flying seven more missions by the end of the month. All the crews returned with big smiles. "No flak. No fighters." Sergeant Dean recorded in his diary, "We had no explanation as to how this could happen."

George Underwood flew his sixty-eighth mission against the Borgo-forta railroad bridge on June 28. On August 1 he took off for mission sixty-nine. There was a weather abort, and the mission didn't count. On August 2, he took off on mission sixty-nine a second time; this time the B-25 aborted for mechanical problems. The next morning, after a night spent tossing and turning through nightmares, he went to the flight surgeon and told him he couldn't fly again, because he knew he'd never get past number sixty-nine of the seventy he needed to go home. A week later he had orders back to the states, one of the few men in the 57th Bomb Wing to find a way around *Catch-22*.

SEVEN

SHOT DOWN

I t took only a moment for chance to take an airman from the ordinary
fear involved in every tough mission to the abject terror felt by the crew
of a burning shot-up bomber. Then, after the shock of throwing himself
into the vastness of space to rely for survival on a parachute, a flier could
land in enemy territory, subject to capture by German troops and Italian
Fascist paramilitaries, dependent on "the kindness of strangers"—the
people of Italy—for survival if he was not immediately taken prisoner.
Any Italian who hid an Allied flier took a step whose possible outcome
included death not only for himself but for his family at the hands of the
occupying Germans and their Italian stooges. There was a civil war in
Italy, between the Germans and the Italian Fascists on the one hand and
the partisans of the resistance on the other. The common people were
caught in the middle.

The plane that Storey Larkin, with horrified eyes, had watched crash following the attack against the Vernio railroad bridges on June 22, 1944, was 43-4087, the B-25J that bombardier Fred Nelson was in.

There had been trouble from the start for what was Nelson's fifty-second mission. From the takeoff, the additional load of two extra thousand-pound bombs made the airplane's performance "mushy." "When we reached the coast of Italy just above Viareggio, on went the flak jacket and helmet. I gave the helmet strap an extra tug just to make sure it stayed put. We had some difficulty locating the IP but finally turned on the bomb run."

As the formation turned and headed for the bridges, Nelson's eyes were glued on the lead ship, waiting for its bomb doors to open so he could open his, but they remained shut even as the target got closer. "As I puzzled this, the first burst of flak exploded right in front of the ship on our left wing." Nelson watched with horror as the flak burst caused the B-25 to bounce upward violently, while hydraulic fluid and oil streamed from the left engine. More flak burst around the formation, with several explosions just off the right wing of Nelson's Mitchell. Pilot Robert Killian banked left into a steep turn, a violent evasive action to shake free of the gunners' aim, but the bomber was completely bracketed. "Shells exploded on each side above and below, sending chunks of steel through the side of the ship that sounded like large size hail." Finally they cleared the blizzard of flak. Nelson glanced at the bomb panel and realized that the bombs were still aboard; when they turned over Florence to run for home, Nelson called Killian on the intercom and asked if he could drop his bombs on the Florence airport as they flew over it. But before Killian could reply, "Flak exploded in such numbers and intensity that it made the other barrage seem mild." The lead bomber in the formation twisted and turned to get away from the bursting flak, but the German gunners below held the formation in a death grip. The path of the six planes as the bombers sought to escape could be followed through the sky along a black highway of flak bursts.

"Then the gunners switched over to our plane as four shells struck us. The first one went into the side of the left nacelle and out the top of the wing without exploding, setting fire to the outboard wing tank. Immediately in front of my glass cage, three coal black bursts with flaming red centers appeared simultaneously. They were so close I could almost taste the cordite. Someone shouted 'Fire in the left engine!'" Nelson looked out at the twisting formation of B-25s seeking safety from the pummeling they were getting. Three of the bombers trailed smoke from their left engines. Nelson screamed, "Whose left engine?!"

The answer was quick, "Ours!"

"That was all I needed to drive me into action. I opened the bomb doors and salvoed the bombs, then dived for the crawlway and reached the pilot's compartment in record time." In the cockpit Nelson stood up and glanced out at the left engine but could see nothing wrong. Then the turret gunner, Sergeant Jerry Jared, dropped out of his turret and started strapping on his parachute. Nelson crowded past the gunner and climbed into the turret to get a look outside. "What I saw horrified me. There was a hole about a foot wide completely across the nacelle and metal was peeled back. Sparks and fire shot out all the way beyond the trailing edge of the wing." Nelson suddenly realized he had left the bomb doors open. Fearful that the airplane would take a hit while he was unable to escape, he nevertheless retraced his route back into the nose, closed the doors and returned to the cockpit as quickly as he could. Killian had his hands full, trying to keep the plane level as they were jolted by more explosions outside. He glanced over at Nelson and yelled "I'm going to try and make Elba!"

More flak explosions burst outside as the German gunners kept 43-4087 in their sights. Suddenly, a terrific jolt shook the entire airplane. Nelson's terror increased when he looked out the cockpit window. "I saw that the entire rear of the left nacelle had been blown off. Either the tire had exploded or the auxiliary gas tank had blown up." Nelson turned to Killian and screamed "Feather the engine!" Killian feathered the prop, but the fire continued. "I'm going to try to blow it out!" he shouted at the co-pilot, Second Lieutenant Halvorsen.

Killian turned the yoke to the right and pushed forward on the controls. The bomber pushed over in a dive, but the fire only grew stronger.

Killian pulled back on the yoke to bring the bomber level. "Bail out! Bail out before we lose the wing!" he ordered. For Nelson it was one of those moments where time seemed to stand still, though only seconds passed. Sergeant Jared kicked out the lower hatch and threw himself through the opening head first. Nelson snapped on his chest pack parachute and removed his glasses, tucking them in his jacket. "Facing the rear, I dropped through the open hatch feet first and the slip stream caught me in a giant hand that tore me away from the ship. I yanked on the rip cord but nothing happened. I clawed the pack open, pulled the silk loose and gave it a heave into the wind." The canopy opened with a swinging jerk. As he steadied himself, Nelson saw his airplane still streaming sparks and fire. He spotted Jared's chute below and north of him as they drifted toward the coast.

Later, back at Ghisonaccia, First Lieutenant Robert L. Johnson wrote a Missing Aircraft Report about what he had seen of the last minutes of B-25J 43-4087:

> We followed our element leader down to assist in what I thought would be a water landing. As we crossed the beach, rapid anti-aircraft fire came up at us and beat on our sides and I saw two parachutes come open and drift over the beach. The stricken aircraft made a left turn about half a mile out to sea. I saw a third parachute open and drift back to the shore. After re-crossing the beach, I saw a fourth and fifth chute open, the last being a delayed action jump. The airplane stayed in a left turn, skidding and diving violently. Then its nose dropped vertically and headed for the ground. At approximately 20 to 50 feet, it pulled out, leaving vapor trails and climbed almost straight up, then stalled at about fifteen-hundred feet. At this time a sixth chute appeared. The plane then went into a flat spin and crashed in flames.

In fact, the crew of 43-4087 bailed out in the following sequence: radio operator Staff Sergeant John Close went first out the lower rear hatch, followed quickly by tail gunner Sergeant Walter Kwiecien as the bomber crossed the beach out to sea. Turret gunner Sergeant Jared was next, drifting back toward the shore. Bombardier Fred Nelson's was the one described as a "delayed action jump" because he had to claw his parachute pack open. At the same time Nelson went out the lower hatch, co-pilot Halvorsen pushed open the top hatch and climbed out, while Killian held the Mitchell as steady as possible to allow the crew to escape. Killian then fought the bomber through its death throes till he could throw himself out the top hatch when the B-25 fell over into its final dive.

For Fred Nelson and his crew, the troubles were only beginning.

As he drifted toward the ground under his parachute, Nelson heard something go past like giant bees. "I heard gunfire and looked off to my right where the dirty Kraut bastards were shooting at me! Green tracers whipped by at a terrific speed and made a popping sound as they passed through my 'chute." Nelson yanked on the risers to make himself as difficult a target as possible. Just before he touched down, he saw his airplane strike the ground and catch fire. "I landed in a small clearing close to some woods. The impact was worse than I expected and it knocked the wind out of me. When I could breathe again, I got up, unbuckled the 'chute and dragged it over a small rise, then covered it with some leaves and brush." He stuffed his inflatable Mae West life preserver and parachute harness in a hollow tree stump, then took off through the woods, headed south toward the front lines.

A short while later Nelson came across a path that led toward some farmhouses. He approached them cautiously but was spotted by a peasant farmer. In tolerable English, the farmer told Nelson to follow him into his vineyard, where he hid the American flier and went off to his home. A few minutes later he returned with some civilian clothes, a bottle of water, and two loaves of bread. Nelson quickly doffed his uniform, which the farmer hid, and turned himself into an Italian peasant.

Nelson had been very lucky. While most Italians would be glad to see the Fascists defeated and hated the Germans who occupied their country, the majority did not want to become involved with any downed Allied fliers. Both the *Wehrmacht* and the Italian Fascist paramilitary groups of the *Repubblica Sociale Italiana* (RSI)—Mussolini's Italian Social Republic puppet state that had been proclaimed the previous September 24 after his rescue from the Gran Sasso by SS commando Otto Skorzeny—had a policy of immediate execution for any Italian found helping a downed Allied airman. The farmer had most likely not taken Nelson into his house in order to keep the encounter secret from the rest of his family so that no one might betray them later with a thoughtless word. Had Nelson been discovered in the house by either a *Wehrmacht* patrol or the RSI authorities, the entire family would have been subject to execution and the farm burned.

Nelson set off again in the general direction of the Allied lines. "After I had a rest, I started out for the nearby hills. The sun was setting by this time and when I came to the main road, some little voice told me not to walk on the surface, so I started south, paralleling the highway, keeping a row of grapevines between me and the road." He hadn't gone a hundred yards when he heard the "clomp" of hobnailed boots on the road. Slowing to a shuffle and pulling his hat low over his eyes, Nelson glanced over to see two black-uniformed Waffen-SS troopers, each armed with an MP-40 submachine gun. When one of them shouted at him, Nelson feigned tipsiness and waved his bottle at them. "One of them laughed, then they picked up their pace and moved away down the road to disappear in the darkening twilight." Several German trucks sped past, dark shapes without their headlights in the shadows cast over the hills by the setting sun.

Once he was sure the road was clear, Nelson crossed it and followed a path that led into a field. After several minutes of walking, he came to a section where the path was hedged on both sides. It soon came to an abrupt end at a closed wooden door set in a wall. Nelson tried the handle and found it unlocked. He opened the door and stepped into an enclosed patio. After he took several steps, he suddenly realized that a man and woman eating dinner on the patio were very surprised by his appearance. "They stared at me as I walked past, hoping there was a rear exit. Neither spoke as I found the door and closed it behind me."

Heart pounding from the close encounter, Nelson walked until he found some woods, where he sat down and rested a few minutes before setting off again down the road in the last light of day. "I got careless, and just before it was completely dark I walked up to a German jeep with four soldiers in it. I walked slowly past as they stared at me." After walking a few hundred yards in the gathering gloom, Nelson heard a shouted "Amerikaner!" followed by a burst of machine gun fire. He kept going. Hours later, in the middle of the night, he discovered an abandoned farmer's hay wagon and climbed in to sleep.

Awakened by the rising sun, Nelson kept on moving. A few hours later he found a spring in a copse and decided to hole up for the rest of the day. That night he continued on, until it began to rain. He took cover under a large tree and fell asleep. At dawn he started moving again.

Suddenly an Italian peasant armed with a British Sten gun stepped out from behind cover and took aim! Nelson raised his hands as the man checked him over. Nelson pulled his dog tags out from inside his shirt and showed them to the man. Satisfied that that Nelson was an American, the man motioned for him to follow as he headed into the woods. They soon arrived at the hidden camp of the local partisans, where Nelson was glad to discover Killian and Halvorsen. The good news was tempered by Killian's news about radioman Close and tail gunner Kwiecien. The partisans had found their bodies; both men had been shot in their parachutes.

The three Americans now found themselves in the confusing situation that was wartime Italy. While Mussolini's Fascists had controlled the country since 1922, they had not succeeded in completely repressing their leftist opposition, which had gone underground in the years before the war. With the arrival of the Allies in 1943 and the subsequent Italian surrender and change of sides, the anti-Fascist opposition groups resurfaced. In the fall of 1943, the *Comitato di Liberazione Nazionale* (Committee of National Liberation, or CLN) had been formed by the *Partito Communista Italiana* (the Communist Party), the *Partito Socialista* (the Socialist Party), and the *Partito d'Azione* (a republican liberal party). The

Democrazia Cristiana (Christian Democrats) took bureaucratic control of the movement as its public leaders, in alliance with King Victor Emmanuel III's government and the Allies. The CLN organized resistance in German-controlled northern Italy and had the support of most anti-Fascist groups in the region, which mostly belonged to the Communists, the Socialists or the *Partito d'Azione*. The armed partisan guerrilla groups were the Communist *Garibaldi Brigades*, the *Giustizia e Libertà* [*Justice and Freedom*] *Brigades* of the *Partito d'Azione*, and the socialist *Matteotti Brigades*.

By the summer of 1944, there were actually several wars going on in Italy. There was the war between the German and Allied armies, the war between the Germans and the resistance, and a civil war between the anti-Fascists and the surviving Fascists. There were also ideological and political differences among the various political groups in the CLN, which on some occasions broke out into armed fighting. As they had done in Yugoslavia, the British dropped Special Operations Executive (SOE) teams into northern Italy to work with the major resistance groups and take responsibility for gathering up and returning Allied aircrew.

Americans who were captured by the Germans were generally transported north to Germany proper, where they were imprisoned in POW camps, but by 1945 transportation to Germany had become difficult and POW camps were organized in northern Italy. Those who were captured by the RSI paramilitaries had a higher likelihood of being shot than if they were captured by the Germans; if they made it into captivity, they were then turned over to the Germans. Escape and evasion for downed airmen was easier in Italy than if they were shot down over Germany, since their targets were only a hundred miles or so beyond the front lines, so that they had a good chance of getting back to Allied territory if they were picked up by partisans.

A partisan unit such as the one Nelson and the two pilots had stumbled across was usually composed of around twenty to fifty members, the numbers governed by the degree of local support and the group's ability to arm, clothe, and feed its members. The largest groups operated in the Alps and the Apennine mountains, where they ambushed and harassed the Germans and their Italian puppets in the RSI. The *Wehrmacht* attempted to separate the guerrillas from their peasant supporters by instituting a policy of killing ten Italians for any German or RSI man killed, but the result was an increase in the peasant support for the partisans, who came from the peasant communities.

Partisan leaders informed the three Americans that they would be taken south in a few days to contact the advancing American Army. While the airmen were in the camp, the partisans got into a fight with a fifty-man German patrol that stumbled upon them. Though there was no clear winner, the Germans retreated and the partisans captured three of the soldiers, but then they had to break camp and move to a different location in the mountains before the Germans could report their presence and send reinforcements to attack them. The next day scouts announced that American troops had arrived nearby. The three fliers set out the day after that to contact the Army. They spent the day avoiding German patrols and at night took shelter in an abandoned farmhouse. The next morning, a jeep recon patrol from the 34th Division rolled into the farmyard. The GIs were initially suspicious of the fliers, but they were able to prove their identities. As they rode back to the division headquarters in the jeeps, they came upon the burned-out remains of 43-4087 in a ditch three miles north of San Vicenzo. Once at the division HQ, they were given transportation to Rome, where they arrived that night at 2000 hours.

Sergeant Jared had a very different experience.

Bailing out just ahead of Nelson, Jared was also shot at by *Wehrmacht* soldiers. He landed in a wooded area, where his parachute got caught and hung up in a tree, leaving him dangling some fifteen feet in the air. Desperate not to be caught like this, he cut his harness straps and fell to the ground, where he landed hard on his lower back. When he tried to scramble away, the pain from the fall was so intense that he dropped to his knees and crawled into the bushes, where he decided to stay for the night in hopes of feeling better in the morning.

The next morning he did feel better and set off south toward the Allied lines. That evening, after nearly walking into a German bivouac that he avoided only when he heard voices, Jared settled in a cornfield, where he pulled down corn stalks to sleep on and set his clothes out to dry overnight. The next day he continued his travel. Hungry after two days, he found a farmhouse where a young woman his age was gardening. When he told her he was an American, she took him inside. The young woman's parents were cautious about having an American in the house but gave him food and some civilian clothing. He stayed with them for several days, until some soldiers stopped by. Warned by the father, he climbed out a back window and ran from the house. The only hiding place Jared could find was an olive tree, which wasn't much cover, but fortunately the two soldiers who searched for him came within ten feet of the tree and didn't look up before they moved on.

He left the farm the next day with a local youth as his guide, in hopes of getting to the American lines. But that afternoon they spotted a German patrol and the guide abandoned him. Back on his own, he hid for the night in some woods. The next day he came across another farm. This time the Italian couple were reluctant to help him but did allow him to sleep the night in their house. The man woke him the next morning and told him that three German soldiers had just been there and he must leave. Not sure where to go, Jared hid in the woods nearby. A few hours later, he heard the sound of engines, and then the man came out and motioned for him to come inside.

Once he was there, the man told him an American Army patrol had arrived. When Jared stepped out to meet the GIs, they were wary, not believing his story at first. A captain in a jeep drove into the yard, and Jared told the officer who he was and how he came to be there. Then he was taken to the company headquarters in a village a few miles to the south, where a call to the 310th on Corsica confirmed his identity.

All four crewmen arrived back on Corsica the same day. Their mission had taken nine days to complete. They were happy to be told that since they had managed to evade capture they would now all be returned to the United States. This was standard Air Force policy, to ensure that a man who had evaded capture was not put at risk of being shot down again and ending up in captivity, where the Germans might force information from him about those who had helped him.

As part of the program to build public support and a sense of personal involvement in the war, shortly after the United States entered the war the Treasury Department created a money-raising program called "Buy a Bomber." Any group or organization which raised $175,000 through War Bond sales could "buy a bomber" that would be named after them. Soon after the program was announced, the twelve hundred students attending McKinley Junior High School in Muncie, Indiana, decided to take up the challenge. By April 1943 they had raised over $200,000.

So in June 1944 a B-25J named "McKinley Junior High School" was delivered to Corsica and prepped for combat. As with many of the Mitchells on Corsica, her combat life was not long. In July, on her thirteenth mission, "McKinley Junior High" was shot down over the Gricigliana Railroad Bridge.

Almost the instant after "bombs away," the airplane took a direct flak hit that blasted the left engine. Moments later another burst, amidships, sent shrapnel flying through the rear compartment at the radioman's position. The airplane shook as though trying to tear itself apart. Co-pilot Second Lieutenant Harry George realized that the plane had caught fire. When he glanced to his left, he was shocked to see that his lead pilot, First Lieutenant Thomas V. Casey, had been hit in several places by shrapnel. Part of Casey's skull was missing and his blood was splattered all over the inside of the windshield and instrument panel. "I didn't see how a man could lose that much of his head and be alive." The fuel lines had been shredded by flak, and it was a matter of moments before the fuel tanks in the wings would explode. The hydraulic lines had also been hit. The right engine sputtered and coughed. In another instant, the prop started running away; this was a pilot's worst nightmare since at some point the propeller speed would become too great for the blades, which would then fly off the hub directly into the cockpit a foot away from their spinning tips.

Harry George took control of the B-25 and issued the order to jump over the interphone. Without any hydraulic assist, it was all he could do to keep the plane level. "Keeping the plane under control took every ounce of strength my arms had. I tried to kill the right engine, but those controls were gone." He hung onto the controls with a death grip to give the rest of the crew a chance to get out.

The hydraulic and fuel lines crossed amidships; both spewed their highly flammable fluids into the plane. The fire was directly behind the cockpit in front of the bomb bay. The flames soared out through the top turret, which had melted away in the heat, creating a chimney effect.

The fire was so big that flames shooting out the rear of the plane danced on the nose of the B-25 a hundred feet behind "McKinley Junior High." Slowly, the stricken bomber fell from the formation as Harry George fought desperately to avoid colliding with other planes.

Sergeant George Obravatz, the tail gunner, called over the interphone that Sergeant Paul Kaplan, the radioman-gunner, was dead. Then he kicked open the rear escape hatch and threw himself out of the blazing inferno. He was never seen again.

Sergeant Russell Ahlstrom, the top turret gunner, was in the middle of the fire. His harness was on, but his parachute lay on the floor by the forward escape hatch, which had become engulfed in flame. Ahlstrom jumped down into the fire to retrieve his parachute and open the forward escape hatch. His clothing caught fire as he desperately kicked at the stubborn hatch, which remained closed.

The ammunition in the top turret started going off as the fire spread. George was grazed on his nose and left shoulder by .50 caliber bullets flying through the cockpit.

Second Lieutenant Ed Dombrowski, the bombardier, crawled back through the crawlway under the cockpit into a wall of fire. A two-hundred-pounder who was "strong as an ox," he threw Ahlstrom aside and went at the hatch, which he finally forced open. By then Ahlstrom was completely on fire. As the hatch fell open, Ahlstrom jumped, engulfed in flames. No one in the other B-25s saw the parachute ever open, though all could see the human torch as it fell toward the ground below. Dombrowski clipped on his chest pack parachute and dived out the hatch.

Harry George wasn't sure he could let go and throw himself out without the bomber going out of control. Despite his best efforts, the Mitchell had nosed down and was gaining speed in its final dive. "I looked over at Casey and figured him for dead. Just then, he turned his eyes toward me and said, in one last act of heroism, 'For God's sake, Harry, get out!' and died. I climbed out of my seat, stood there for a second or two at the most, then went down through the fire and out the hatch."

Harry George managed to make it to the ground safely. Eventually he was taken in by a local farmer named Beppe, who fed and protected him. Members of the three families who lived in the large farmhouse and worked the land made him feel he was almost a member of their families. At night he hid out in a nearby cave since the Germans were aware that American crewmen had bailed out and were hiding in the area. They were on the hunt throughout the region.

After a few days, he began to think he was safe. But he still slept at night in the cave. One morning, shortly after waking and making his way to the farmhouse, he heard a roar of motors in the farmyard. A dozen German soldiers leaped from their Opel Blitz truck, weapons at the ready. An officer climbed out of the sidecar of the BMW motorcycle that was in the lead.

The families were ordered out of the house and the troops searched it quickly. Finding no one inside, they gathered all the families together outside for questioning, including the children. The commander, who spoke Italian, demanded to know where the American was, but no one responded. He ordered his men to line the people up against the side of the house. The troops then lined up opposite them as the commander stood to the side and ordered his men to raise their weapons and they snapped their rifles into position. He told the three families that if they didn't tell them where the American was they would all be shot.

Beppe stepped forward. "We know nothing." He stepped back and everyone knew they were to remain silent. After a long tense moment, the German commander elected not to shoot but warned them they would be closely watched as he climbed back into the sidecar and left.

Harry George eventually made it back to Allied lines a few weeks later, and from there he was sent back to his unit on Corsica. He was immediately sent back to the States not knowing the fate of his fellow crewmen. The last he had seen of Dombrowski when he jumped, the bombardier's clothes had been on fire. It was assumed he was dead.

In fact, Dombrowski had survived the bailout but been captured by the Germans shortly after he landed. A week later he was put in a column of other Allied fliers, to march north through the Brenner Pass to a POW camp. A day into the march, the column was attacked by Allied fighter planes and Dombrowski escaped. He was found by a group of partisans and ended up fighting with them for fifty days until advancing American troops liberated him.

Ed Dombrowski and Harry George were finally reunited only when Dombrowski came to the 1976 reunion of the 57th Bomb Wing and asked to register for the event. The woman who took his registration read its first line, then jumped up and threw her arms around a very surprised Dombrowski, kissing and hugging him. Harry George's wife had immediately recognized the name of the man who got the hatch open and saved her husband's life.

During the winter of 1945, the Corsica Mitchells were at the forefront of the Battle of the Brenner Pass. By February, the Germans had over four hundred 88-mm anti-aircraft cannons located throughout the pass, with hundreds of other light AA weapons ranging from 20-mm to 37-mm ringing every target along the rail line that stretched from Verona to Innsbruck in Austria.

On February 27, 1945, Larry Pisoni, then a 7-year-old Italian farm boy, watched a drama play out in the skies above his native village of Vezzano in the Italian Tyrol, a region now known as Trentino-Alto Adige. "The sky was full of planes, fire, smoke and explosions from the heavy German flak. I vividly remember seeing the airmen bailing out of a hit plane just before it crashed into a mountain."

The airplane was B-25J 43-36228, "Miss Bobby." Flown by Second Lieutenant Jay DeBoer of the 445th squadron, she was one of three Mitchells assigned to go after the flak gunners, dropping white phosphorus on the gun positions. At 1157 hours DeBoer turned onto the bomb run. Flight Officer William Brooks, the bombardier, waited to catch sight of their target, gun positions south of the town of Lavis. In the narrow valley, German gun positions located high on the mountainsides could almost fire straight at the Mitchells. Neither DeBoer, bombardier Brooks, co-pilot Second Lieutenant Lucian Crutchfield, navigator Second Lieutenant Robert Cravey, nor Sergeants Robert Hitchell, Charles Reagin, or Carl Swinson saw any gunfire till suddenly an 88-mm shell exploded in the right engine, which burst into flame that quickly spread toward the fuel tanks in the wing. Brooks quickly salvoed the white phosphorus bomb load to save them from blowing up in a crash while DeBoer fought with the controls as the B-25 left the formation, headed toward the ground below. With the ship barely controllable, he turned west to put as much distance as possible between them and the Germans they had just showered with deadly white phosphorus.

As the fire spread, DeBoer ordered his crew to prepare to bail out and radioed to the rest of the formation that they were getting out. He paid no attention to the small Italian mountain village in the distance ahead. The men opened the front and rear hatches and began exiting the bomber as it nosed down, headed directly toward a craggy peak. As he dived through the forward hatch, co-pilot Crutchfield hit his ankle against the edge of the opening. The pain was intense as he pulled the D-ring on his parachute minutes later and the canopy opened above him.

On the snow-covered wooded hillside below, twenty-two-year-old Giovanni Cainelli and thirty-six-year-old Vigilio Paissan and six other men looked up from their work chopping trees and watched the crew bail out some six thousand feet overhead. "It seemed like they took about twenty minutes to come down and that gave us enough time to get to where they landed at about the same time they did," Cainelli recalled. "We had to hurry because the Germans were coming up the mountain with dogs. We knew that the partisans were also headed our way." Only later would navigator Bob Cravey and tail gunner Carl Swinson learn how lucky they were to have been found by Cainelli. The baying dogs that led the Germans up the hillside could be heard coming closer as several partisans, led by forty-year-old Roberto "Berto" Peterlanna, appeared out of the woods. Cravey turned to the burly partisan.

"Do any of you speak English?" he asked hopefully.

Peterlanna laughed. "Sure," he replied, "I spent fifteen years in New Jersey." He ordered Cainelli and the others to get out of there before the Germans found them, and he led the two Americans into the woods.

On his way down from the plane in his parachute, pilot Jay DeBoer looked at the forest below him, hoping to find an opening in the trees, but there was none. In an instant he had his hands over his face as he crashed through the pines. He was brought up sharp as his parachute canopy snagged in a treetop. The snowy hillside was six feet below him. For a long moment he hung there; then the canopy began to rip above him, he fell into a snow bank, and the parachute covered him. Struggling to his feet in the deep snow, DeBoer managed to shuck his harness and push on to where the snow wasn't waist deep. In the distance he heard the baying hounds. An involuntary shiver of cold and fear went through him.

Co-pilot Lucian Crutchfield cried out when he landed in a clearing further down the mountainside from where Cravey and Swinson had been found by the partisans. He managed to get out of his parachute, but he couldn't walk on his ankle. As he looked for something to splint it, he was knocked over by the dog that landed atop him, pinning him as the animal slavered in his face. A moment later he stared up at the black uniform of a Waffen-SS trooper who pointed an MP-34 submachine gun at him. Crutchfield raised his hands in surrender.

Not far from where Crutchfield had come down, bombardier Bill Brooks landed in a grove of trees, where his parachute hung up so that he dangled several feet above the snow. The baying of the hounds was close by. As he reached for his knife to cut himself free, he heard the dogs below and looked down to see two of the big German Shepherds at the base of the tree. A moment later, two Waffen-SS troopers appeared out of the woods. Brooks raised his hands in surrender as they raised their MP-34s and took aim at him.

Jay DeBoer, meanwhile, struggled through the snowy woods, trying to be as quiet as possible as he heard the dogs seemingly all around him. He found an empty animal den in a ravine and crawled into it to hide. The cold wind was bone-chilling, and he curled into a ball to stay warm.

The sun had already gone behind the tall Alpine hills to the west when the SS men and their two American captives appeared in Vezzano. Larry Pisoni, the boy who had seen the airmen bail out, wanted to see what was happening, but his mother kept him inside and closed the doors and windows of their home. Later he would learn that the Germans had gone to the police station, which was manned by men of the RSI paramilitary police, and put two Americans in a cell for the night.

The next day, DeBoer was cold and stiff when he crawled out of the den. Soon he heard the dogs again and knew the Germans were still on the hunt. He cut branches from a bush to cover the opening of the den and crawled back inside, hungry and thirsty. After eating half an emergency ration candy bar, he scraped snow off a rock and ate it.

Swinson and Cravey were awakened by the rising sun in the old stone barn in which they had been hidden. A bit later, Berto Peterlanna, who spoke German as well as English, came out from the farmhouse and took them in for breakfast.

Later that morning, Larry Pisoni saw Crutchfield and Brooks when they were taken out of the jail. "It was the first time I had ever seen Americans. I will never forget the tall, handsome young men with clean open faces, so unlike the monsters described to us children in Nazi-Fascist propaganda." The Germans marched them out of the village toward the village of Arco, which was twelve miles away. Aided by Brookes, Crutchfield managed to stumble downhill about a kilometer before he tripped and fell, crying out in agony. Brooks turned back to help his friend. As he did, one of the SS troopers yelled at him. There was a burst of machine gun fire from the Waffen-SS sergeant in charge and both Brooks and Crutchfield fell into a ditch at the side of the road.

DeBoer had ventured out of his hiding hole and heard the gunfire nearby. He peered down the hillside from behind a stand of trees and saw the Germans examine the bodies of his two crewmen in the ditch. It was obvious they were dead. The SS men moved on down the road, leaving Crutchfield and Brooks where they had fallen. DeBoer retreated back into the forest.

After that first night at the farm, Berto's partisan group took Cravey and Swinson to the hometown of partisans Vigilio, Mario, and Angelo Paissan, in a village of three hundred people three miles from Vezzano named Cadine, where Mario and Angelo hid them in the home where Mama Paissan, the family matriarch, Angelo with his wife and two children, and Mario with his wife and four daughters lived. As Vigilio recalled years later, "The whole town knew where the Americans were, but nobody talked. They were lucky they met good people because everybody knew the penalty for harboring Americans was death. They were hidden in a secret, tiny room in the basement of my brothers' house, but to get to it you had to come down through a hole in the floor of the attic. I lived in another house with my family, but I would go to my brothers' house every day."

Cravey and Swinson remained in Cadine until the village was liberated by troops of the Tenth Mountain Division at the end of April 1945.

After hiding in the woods for a week, DeBoer was so cold and hungry that he no longer cared if he was captured or not. He came across a peasant's hut and determined he would knock on the door; whatever happened would happen. As luck would have it, he had stumbled on a house being used by partisans for their base. He was taken in and spent a week there regaining his strength. The partisans took DeBoer, disguised as a Trappist Monk—so that he wouldn't have to talk and betray the fact that he was an American—to the rail line, where he traveled the route his comrades were bombing, and then he was guided by other partisans across the border into Switzerland in late March 1945. He returned to the 321st at their new base in Italy in May of that year after the end of the war in Europe.

Radioman Tech Sergeant Charles T. Reagin and turret gunner Sergeant Robert D. Mitchell were captured by the Germans only moments after they landed and taken to a POW camp in the Alps, where they remained until the camp was liberated in May 1945.

Larry Pisoni emigrated to America in the 1950s, went to the University of Ohio, married, returned to Italy, and became a successful businessman. He never forgot Brooks and Crutchfield, the first two Americans he had ever seen. In 1995, he determined he would place a memorial—a three-ton block of granite with a plaque—at the site where they had been killed. To his surprise, once word got around of what he was going to do, there was a groundswell of local support and the cause was taken up by the local regional government in the Tyrol. On March 5, 1995, the monument was unveiled in a ceremony attended by several thousand local residents, as well as Jay DeBoer and Brooks's family.

The wording on the monument's plaque is in English and Italian and reads: "At this spot, on Feb. 28, 1945 two American airmen were shot by Nazis—Lieutenant Lucian C. Crutchfield Jr. of San Antonio, Texas, and F/O William F. Brooks of Cohoes, New York. They were two of more than 38,000 Americans who gave their lives on Italian soil during W.W.II to help Europeans of goodwill regain freedom and democracy."

EIGHT

SPROGS, SPORTS, OLD SPORTS, AND WHEELS

As the 57th Bomb Wing continued the attacks on the German transportation and supply system, the bombers were frequently escorted by P-47 Thunderbolts from the veteran 57th Fighter Group, which was also part of the Wing. When the Germans began their retreat from the Cassino battlefield at the end of May, the *Luftwaffe* fighter units that had been deployed to Italy after the Salerno invasion to oppose the Allies were withdrawn back to Germany to defend the homeland against the ever-increasing aerial assault of the Eighth Air Force. The big P-47, armed with eight .50 caliber machine guns and able to carry a five-hundred-pound bomb under each wing, was an even better fighter-bomber than it was a fighter; fighter-bombers were frequently used to attack and suppress German anti-aircraft positions and for dive-bombing attacks against difficult bridge targets and roving hunts across northern Italy in search of trains and road traffic. While aerial combat became less frequent, it did not completely disappear; the Bf-109s of the *Aviazione*

Nationale Repubblica, the reconstituted Italian Fascist air force, continued to take to the air against Allied air formations in infrequent missions through the fall and winter of 1945. Thus the sight of the P-47 Thunderbolts over their formation gave comfort to the crews of the 57th Bomb Wing's three Mitchell groups as they struck the rail lines in the Brenner Pass.

The 57th Fighter Group had been the first Army Air Forces fighter unit to enter combat outside of the Pacific Theater. In July 1942, USS *Ranger* (CV-4) transported forty-eight P-40F Warhawks of the 64th, 65th, and 66th Fighter Squadrons across the South Atlantic, launching them off the coast of Africa to land at Accra, in Ghana. From there the pilots flew their single-engine fighters across sub-Saharan Africa to Khartoum and then on to Cairo, where they provided welcome reinforcement to the RAF's Desert Air Force in the aerial battles before and during the Battle of El Alamein that fall, which saw Rommel's Afrika Korps hurled back from the gates of Egypt.

The group continued flying in support of the British Eighth Army during its westward advance across Libya to Tunisia. On April 18, 1943, a patrolling squadron came across a large formation of *Luftwaffe Junkers Ju-52* trimotor transports and their Bf-109 and Bf-110 escorts over the Mediterranean, headed for the German-held airfields inside the Mareth Line in northern Tunisia. In what became known as the "Palm Sunday Massacre," the P-40 pilots shot down seventy-five German aircraft, some sixty of which were the vulnerable transports, with Bf-110 and a few Bf-109 fighter escorts accounting for the remainder. It was the greatest victory by American fighters in the course of combat in the Mediterranean Theater.

Shortly after the Palm Sunday Massacre, the first replacement pilots arrived. These were young men who were members of Class 43-A, the "bow wave" of fliers who had entered flight training after Pearl Harbor. Among them was Second Lieutenant Michael C. McCarthy, a Boston-Irish nineteen-year-old who would fly with the 64th Fighter Squadron, known as "The Black Scorpions," until the end of the war in May 1945, eventually rising to the rank of major as squadron operations officer before he turned twenty-one and becoming one of very few pilots in the group to survive two complete combat tours. McCarthy retired as a Brigadier General after thirty years in the Air Force. He remembered, "The air-to-ground environment is brutal, life threatening, and consistently dangerous. The fighter pilot population in our squadron changed 400 percent from May 1943 until the end of the war in June 1945. We lost airplanes and pilots on a regular basis. We changed tactics, varied approaches and routes to targets, and emphasized surprise at every opportunity. In the end, we learned that you must fly down the enemy's gun barrel to destroy the target." While many survived their 250-flying hour combat tours to return home, losses in nose-to-nose shootouts with German anti-aircraft gunners across Italy were high.

Alone among American air force fighter units, the 57th Fighter Group followed a command philosophy that required proven ability in combat, not rank or time in the unit, be the basis for selection of element, section, flight, and squadron leaders. As McCarthy recalled, "We followed that policy without exception during my 27 months with the group. In some cases, a captain or major, newly assigned, might fly a complete tour as a wingman and fail every chance to lead an element or a section. It was odd to see a squadron of 16 ships led successfully by a young first lieutenant with a field grade officer riding his wing, but the policy saved lives, put the strongest pilots in lead positions, and produced exceptional combat results." In the group a new pilot was known as a "Sprog." Once he had survived fifteen to twenty missions and demonstrated some ability, he was promoted to "Sport." If he survived half a tour, he became an "Old Sport." Those "Old Sports" who showed skill were promoted into unit leadership as positions opened through completion of tour, transfer, or death. They were the "Wheels" of the group.

The 57th arrived in Italy and transitioned from their worn out P-40Fs and P-40Ls to the P-47 Thunderbolts in December 1943. Their principal targets over the next two years would be the transport system the *Wehrmacht* relied on: marshalling yards, roads, bridges, rail lines, and everything that rolled on them. "We would not ignore airfields, ports, or shipping, but the most lucrative targets would be found on roads and railroads. The Germans were smart and tenacious, took advantage of terrain, used antiaircraft weapons with maximum effect, and gave ground only when it could not be avoided," as McCarthy later described their war.

The 57th Fighter Group transferred to Corsica in March 1944, taking up residence at Alto Airfield near the town of Folleli, north of what would become the three B-25 fields. The scenery was beautiful, and the islands of Pianosa, Monte Cristo, and Elba could be seen plainly in the distance. As McCarthy recalled, "Our squadrons made the transition without incident. Advance parties had been in place long enough to set up tents and prepare mess halls, clubs, and maintenance facilities. Since they had been doing this for most of two years, they knew all the short cuts and problem areas." In fact, the 57th Fighter Group had a well-deserved reputation as the best scroungers in the theater. If they needed something and could not borrow or buy it, they had a team of "midnight requisitioners" who would steal it. "Our road convoys were so diverse that it was difficult to identify the national identity of most of our vehicles. We had more German, Italian, and British rolling stock than American." After the North African desert and the dusty heat of Sicily, Corsica was a big change. As McCarthy remembered, "After a tediously long hot day on the line, ground crews and pilots relaxed in the cool invigorating mountain stream. Improvised diving boards were constructed. Life in the mountains afforded a great many men a chance to rest in quiet and take things easy for a while but for others who craved excitement, the complaint was that life was growing monotonous and dull." Passes were issued to the towns of Bastia, Ajaccio—birthplace of Napoleon—and Corte. Americans and islanders began to get to know each other.

Officers received a regular ration of good old American liquor, and in camp the enlisted men's bar did a thriving business, with cognac, rum, wines, and gin brought in regularly from Naples, Catania, Palermo, Alexandria, Tunis, and Oran. But anywhere a GI traveled on Corsica, he encountered prices on food and drink that were prohibitive on his paycheck. Off-base, the men sopped up the almost lethal Eau de Vie, which many described as containing 180-octane gas. The fiery base of the drink came from the juices of the anise plant.

McCarthy remembered, "In the evening, Special Services supervised a softball league and presented films three times a week. Squadron personnel, sitting on bomb fin crates and tops of trucks, sweated out darkness by playing cards and reading three or four month old newspapers and magazines. Once in a while, a good entertaining film came around the circuit but usually a great many men left the premises before the first reel was over. It was not unusual for the projection machine to cut out a dozen times a night. Sprockets were often torn on the film or the generator would run out of gas."

McCarthy remembered one song that was frequently sung after a few drinks in the Officers' Club (the "little black flowers" it refers to are flak):

> THE DIVE BOMBER'S LAMENT
> I don't mind a dive in a 25
> Till the bombs that I'm carrying smack
> But those little black flowers
> That grow in the sky—
> Oh! My achin' back.
>
> Skimmin' a ridge to plaster a bridge
> Makes you feel as goofy as wine,
> And your heart takes a jolt
> When your Thunderbolt
> Tangles with an Me109.
>
> It's like shootin' ducks
> When you come across trucks
> And I don't mind the rifles that crack
> But those little black flowers
> That grow in the sky—
> Oh! My achin' back!

Once established at Alto, the Thunderbolts' crews had a hectic end of March and April 1944, as momentum built for the final battles at

Cassino. "We were to be a major player in Operation Strangle, the next big air-to-ground operation in the Italian Theater. The plan called for full-scale interdiction of roads, railroads, bridges, marshalling yards, shipping lanes, ports, and airports from the northern Po Valley south through the Apennines, the Arno river cities, and all roads south of Rome used to bring essential supplies to the German army. We would carefully avoid targets near historic sites in Rome, Florence, and Pisa." The Thunderbolts were sent against many heavily defended targets throughout Italy north of the Gustav Line. McCarthy remembered, "We flew several missions a day to destroy German road convoys. Power stations, marshalling yards, and bridges also received close attention. On one mission, I was leading three sections of four. We destroyed a power plant, a factory, two steam locomotives, an electric-powered locomotive on another train, several loaded freight cars, and found and strafed a motor convoy loaded with troops. We destroyed every target on that particular mission." For his leadership of this mission, Lieutenant McCarthy was awarded the Distinguished Flying Cross and was later promoted to captain on the basis of his performance.

"The Jug," as the P-47 was universally known to its pilots throughout the war, was a great dive-bomber because it had excellent stability at all speeds. "It was easy to center the ball, trim, and keep the nose on the target. It was a relief not to stand on the left rudder just to keep the airplane from slipping sideways in a dive (as was the case with the P-40). This natural stability enhanced an excellent gun platform. Strafing a fast-moving train in the Po Valley later in the war, I hit the locomotive with the cone of my eight guns knocking it completely off the tracks while the rest of the train, minus its locomotive, rolled on with no hesitation."

The fact that so many pilots survived in this brutal environment was explained by the toughness of the P-47. McCarthy described the airplane: "It could absorb heavy flak damage and still fly. The big Pratt and Whitney engine was incredibly tough. I flew one from Italy to Corsica taking 45 minutes with zero oil pressure minus two top cylinders that had been blown off by enemy fire. The engine ran until I pulled the throttle back for landing. That was not a fluke. Another squadron pilot repeated this later without three top cylinders and zero oil pressure. The secret was not to change the power setting."

After one air battle with German fighters in May 1944, McCarthy heard a call for help from a fellow pilot of the 65th Squadron.

I found him circling with his wingman in the area just vacated by those involved in the dogfight. One 20-mm shell had knocked out his instrument panel, leaving him without airspeed, altimeter, compass, or engine performance gauges. The second shell hit his right wing ammo compartment, exploding many .50-caliber bullets and forcing the door from its normal horizontal position to a vertical position that disturbed the aerodynamic flow across the wing, making the airplane fly in a severe crab. This was another example of a P-47 defying the principles of flight, flyable despite serious airframe damage.

After examining the airplane from every angle, McCarthy determined it wasn't leaking fluids and had no obvious structural damage other than that to the right wing and the cockpit area.

We decided I would lead back to Corsica with him on my wing. Because of the deformed right wing ammo compartment, we needed to identify the airspeed at which the airplane would stall so we could pick a final approach airspeed for landing. At Alto, we circled the field high enough to permit a safe bailout. In the landing configuration, I slowed from 220 mph calling the airspeed in 5 mph increments. He found the pre-stall shudder began just below 170 mph so we chose that speed for our final approach. I held 185 mph as we turned to line up on final, slowing very smoothly to 170 mph as we crossed the fence. He held excellent position, rotated, and touched down nicely with plenty of room to slow to taxi speed on the available runway.

The P-47 had brought another pilot home safe in conditions no other airplane could have survived.

The summer of 1944 saw the units on Corsica deeply engaged in trying to defeat the Germans who had managed to escape the defeat at Cassino, as P-47s and B-25s concentrated on northern Italy. McCarthy recounted, "We expanded our operations to the Po Valley between Bologna, Turin, Milan, and the main railroad line running through its center along the Po River. German supplies had to transit through this rich, fertile, industrialized part of Italy in order to have any chance to benefit their forces holding the Allies. Activity in the Po area was incredible. Marshalling yards in each city were bustling where the Germans assembled trains during the daylight to make runs to the front at night."

Every part of a fighter-bomber mission was filled with horrible dangers. On one mission in the summer of 1944, McCarthy led his flight in a successful dive-bombing attack against marshalling yards. Since the Thunderbolts still had ammunition after dropping their bombs, he led them on a low-level "armed recce" hunting mission until he found a train in the open on a straight stretch of track. McCarthy deployed two elements to cut the track ahead of and behind the train, then attacked the steam locomotive, bringing the train to a halt. "I set up my section to strafe freight cars immediately behind the disabled locomotive. I told my wingman to take enough space, keep me in sight, pick his own freight car, and do some damage. We were taking some light flak, less intense than usual. My wingman stayed much too close to me on the first strafing pass, so close that his bullets flew over the top of my right wing, shooting at the same freight car." McCarthy ordered the young lieutenant to move out further so he could concentrate on his own target and get some worthwhile results. While the wingman's spacing was better on the next pass, he had managed to line up on the only obstacle within miles—a lone pine tree a hundred feet tall. "Lieutenant Brown, who never saw that tree, hit it dead center with the hub of his four-bladed propeller, which sawed through the pine tree, and filled the engine space full of wood chips and sawdust." The impact of the collision also knocked both wings back, out of alignment. Through a combination of luck and the remarkable resilience of the tough P-47, Lieutenant Brown stayed airborne. "Understandably, he was in total panic. I caught sight of his airplane in a slight climb heading north, and pulled up on his wing."

McCarthy surveyed the damage, amazed any airplane could fly in that condition. Talking calmly on the radio, he told Brown to look at him, that they would keep on climbing and he should not touch his throttle. After a few minutes, McCarthy told Brown they were going to turn left back to Corsica. "If the controls responded well enough and the engine continued to run without drastic overheating, I planned to climb high enough to allow a safe bail out over water in case the engine quit. We had alerted the air rescue guys about that possibility." The P-47's windshield had been cracked in the collision and was covered with oil and debris. "I told him that I would navigate back to base. As minutes passed with the damaged airplane still flying, it was likely we would get home, but that raised a question. How do we get this wreck safely on the ground?"

Once they were back over Alto at six thousand feet, McCarthy told his wingman to drop the gear. The main gear fell out of the gear wells without hydraulic pressure and seemed to lock down. McCarthy sat on Brown's wing as the two P-47s executed a circling descent to turn on final approach. Fortunately, Brown was able to retard his throttle without killing the engine. McCarthy moved forward so Brown could fly formation on him because he couldn't see the runway through his windshield. Brown managed to touch down successfully, at which point McCarthy accelerated back up and came around for his own landing. As he later remembered, "Lieutenant Brown handled himself with courage and skill but decided his luck was gone. He did not fly another mission and neither did that airplane."

On July 1, 1944, the 57th Group marked the end of its second year overseas. While a party in commemoration of the anniversary was planned, pilots of the 66th Fighter Squadron, "The Exterminators," scored a triumph that lived up to their name and pushed subsequent anniversary events into the background. On an early morning mission, a flight from the 66th encountered what was now a rarity: enemy airplanes in the air. Six Bf-109Gs were shot down without a loss for a most appropriate beginning to the group's twenty-fifth month in foreign service.

At the end of June 1944, McCarthy completed his first tour with the 57th Fighter Group. Many pilots considered themselves fortunate to have survived the deadly work of flying a fighter-bomber and welcomed the opportunity to return stateside and get a new assignment. McCarthy listened to the group leaders when they asked him to consider coming back. If he agreed, he would get thirty days' leave at home and return to a position of responsibility in the unit. He took their offer and returned to Boston, where he found his girlfriend had joined the women's division of the Coast Guard, the SPARS. They decided to become engaged but agreed marriage would not happen until the war was over. He returned to Corsica just before the invasion of Southern France on August 15, 1944.

> I came back to flying missions with no drop off in efficiency. We had several new guys who demonstrated the ability to learn, showed leadership potential, and had the courage to endure fierce enemy antiaircraft fire, whose effectiveness continued to be awesome. I was not surprised that my airplane took heavy damage on my first missions to marshalling yards in the Po Valley cities. The Germans were serious about making us pay for the privilege. My reaction to facing lethal antiaircraft fire again startled me. I found my system for dealing with personal fear during my first year in combat needed some "tinkering" to be effective during this last year. The fact that I chose to come back to this dangerous occupation led me to wonder whether God was ready to continue His role in keeping me safe. I finally realized God was very good at His job. He did not need my help. When I left everything in His hands, quit worrying, and slept soundly, I regained my ability to control fear.

Within a few weeks of his return, McCarthy had a very narrow escape. In late August, he led a dive-bombing mission on a marshalling yard. During the dive, he spotted a long train moving out of the yard. "I told Chad Reade, my wingman, to take spacing. We would hit the train with two or three strafing passes. I stopped the double locomotive on our first pass and continued around for another." There had been no defensive fire during that first pass. McCarthy turned over a dry riverbed south of the rail line and dove back at the train. "I was low and very fast, just lining up my firing pass when I saw a huge barn door moving away from a gun emplacement hidden in the riverbed." As he passed directly over the position, the Germans opened up with a Flak-37 gun and fired several rounds, one of which hit McCarthy's airplane in the fuselage behind the cockpit.

"I felt the airplane shudder and the cockpit filled with smoke. As I rolled the canopy back, the smoke cleared. Chad pulled up on my wing and told me there was a large hole over the supercharger on the fuselage, forward of the tail and that the supercharger was smoking. He could see daylight through the fuselage from one side to the other." McCarthy had been ready to bail out but realized he was much too low. "The engine was still running. Chad saw no more smoke so the fire was out. We decided to turn gingerly back to Corsica in a gentle climb." McCarthy suspected the German fire had damaged the control cables for the rudder and elevators. In fact, he had only one elevator and rudder cable each still functioning. On the way back to Corsica, he held a very gentle touch on the controls.

Arriving over the island, McCarthy decided he did not want to bail out since he now felt there was the possibility of a safe landing with his new but badly damaged P-47. He decided not to increase airspeed in the descent for fear that the now fragile tail section of the P-47 might separate from the fuselage. When McCarthy put the gear handle in the down position, the main gear fell out and locked, but the tail wheel remained up. "We let the others land, then, with Chad on my wing, we came around for a smooth no-flap touchdown. Chad told me later there was no sign of structural support that he could identify from his examination of the damaged area." McCarthy held the tail off the runway as long as he could. When the tail finally dropped and touched ground, the fuselage buckled at the point where the 37-mm projectile had hit the P-47. "Chad's comment about no visible means of support was accurate. This airplane had flown for the last time."

After the success of the invasion of Southern France, the campaign in Italy took what would be its final turn. During this period, Captain McCarthy was promoted to Major and became the Operations Officer of the 65th Fighter Squadron. He described the situation at the time: "Offensive pressure by Allied forces pushed the *Wehrmacht* back to the Apennines north of the Arno River where they could again use high terrain to delay the Allied advance despite our greater numbers, excellent weapons, and air superiority. In this final year, the Germans took advantage of bitterly cold winter weather to prevent the Allies from breaking over the Apennines into the Po Valley. Efforts to dislodge German defenses along the east coast also would not succeed until the brutal winter weather loosened its hold on the Italian peninsula."

That fall, the Thunderbolt became an even more formidable weapon than before with the installation of "bazooka" rocket tubes. Each P-47 could carry six rocket tubes, which could be jettisoned in an emergency, three under each wing, in addition to a bomb as big as a thousand-pounder on the pylon under each wing. In subsequent operations the rockets took a heavy toll of enemy installations and supplies. But the tubes the rockets were fired from were made of plastic and inevitably deformed after only a few firings. McCarthy recalled that out of six rockets fired, at least one could be expected to come out of the tube and execute "a looping roll" that could scare the pilot with a near miss on his own plane. The rockets were not particularly accurate, but they were good enough to make flak gunners take cover as the P-47s made their dive-bombing attacks.

Having been the first American fighter unit in combat in the Mediterranean, the 57th Fighter Group set records the other groups couldn't match. In December 1944, its three squadrons became the first and only USAAF fighter squadrons of the war to fly 1000 missions each. The 66th squadron hit that mark on December 13, the 64th on December 22, and the 65th on Christmas Eve. The 57th Group was credited with its 3,000th mission on December 31, 1944, with the 66th Squadron having the honor of flying the mission. The record grew to 4,000 missions by the end of February 1945. And by the end of the war in Italy on May 2, 1945, the group had flown a total of 4,651 missions since August 1942, including 35 missions on May 1 and 2.

It was during this stage of the conflict that First Lieutenant James L. Diers joined the 64th Fighter Squadron in the fall of 1944, after the entire 57th Fighter Group had moved back to the Italian mainland from Corsica to put them closer to the fighting. They were now based at Grosseto on the coast, where they would remain to the end. By this time the pilots of the three fighter groups of the *Aviazione Nationale Repubblica* rarely got airborne; the main enemy were the German and Italian anti-aircraft gunners, who had become very good at their work.

Diers had good reason to remember his first mission over northern Italy. "I was flying tail position in the formation, the last in line. All of a sudden there appeared small puffs of smoke—tiny clouds—right there around me, just a few at first, then many, many more. I was fascinated. I didn't notice that the other seven planes in my flight were weaving, climbing and diving. I heard a shout over the radio, 'Diers, wake up. Get your ass moving, that's flak they're shooting at you!' I complied at once!"

Years later Diers was asked what it was like to make a dive-bombing attack on the German anti-aircraft positions. He recalled, "Once we were over our target and began our dive to release our bombs, all evasive action ceased. We just dove down as fast as possible from about 4,000 feet to a few hundred, pulled the release lever, and dropped the bombs on our target. During those few seconds I felt no sense of danger, no fear of the guns, just concentration on my dive. Bravery was not a factor. Being young and feeling immortal was. But, post dive, I'll admit to a bit of anxiety as I climbed upward out of range and out of the area as fast as possible, full throttle!"

Diers had two particularly memorable missions. One was his ninth, flown on December 15, 1944, with the target a major bridge over the Po River near Piacenza.

We began our bombing run at about 3,000 feet, peeling off to the left in a single file as we dove down. The sky was filled with puffs of smoke from the anti-aircraft guns. As I pulled out of my dive after releasing my bombs, I saw a flash of fire from a gun emplacement on the ground to my left, and swerved left to strafe it. The pilot who preceded me in the bombing run had missed the bridge with his bombs. They had fallen to the left and exploded directly under me and I flew through the fragments! Luckily, the plane seemed to be flying normally. The sturdy P-47 prevailed and I arrived back home safely at Grosseto. The crew chief counted well over a hundred holes in the metal skin of the plane.

Diers's second unforgettable mission came on April 25, 1945, just a week before the war in Europe ended. By now an experienced pilot, Diers had become an element leader. He and his wingman were assigned an "armed reconnaissance" mission near Lake Garda in search of enemy transport. Lake Garda is a beautiful, long, narrow lake in northern Italy, walled in on its eastern bank by steep cliffs rising vertically—a part of the Italian Alps—and pierced by highway tunnels. The main road there ran to the Brenner pass along the lake's eastern edge. Diers described what happened: "Flying over the lake, I noticed a large oil or gasoline tank truck stopped near the mouth of a tunnel through the cliffs." He was out of position to make a run at the truck and called his wingman attack it. "He claimed he couldn't see it, so I got into position and dived to strafe the truck, wondering why it hadn't taken cover in the tunnel opening. I soon found out. It was a trap, using the truck as bait!" Antiaircraft guns opened up at the P-47, firing from the tunnel, from the cliff above the tunnel, and from hillside positions to either side of the road. "I was flying almost at water level over the lake when I was hit. I called on my wingman to come down and help me but he said, 'They're shooting at you!'(As if I didn't know it) so I just radioed back, 'Let's get out of here!'"

Diers pushed the throttle forward to engage the P-47's emergency water injection system, which gave a 20 percent boost in horsepower.

"The system was intended for just such a time as I was having. But it has one negative drawback—when used, it created a dark trail of smoke, which the German gunners saw and interpreted as evidence that they made a hit. They thus assumed that I was really damaged and so concentrated their fire. Black puffs of explosions surrounded me, but that wonderful P-47 roared on." Diers gradually gained altitude, found his wingman, and made it back home safely, "thanking the 'angel on my shoulder' once more."

The aerial battle against the Germans in the Brenner Pass continued until the final weeks of the war. Major McCarthy recalled, "We had learned how to avoid many of the German flak batteries en route to target areas. Over the front lines, the Brenner Pass, and certain parts of the Po Valley, the Germans had become more accurate with 88-mm guns using proximity fuses set to explode as shells came close rather than only on contact. Our world had become more dangerous. Even though the *Wehrmacht* was retreating across all fronts in Europe, German forces were still capable of fighting a defensive battle with ferocious stubbornness that would persist until the final days."

The results of that heavy flak are demonstrated by the experience of one group of sixteen replacement pilots who joined the group on November 4, 1944, as recorded in the diary of Second Lieutenant Ken Lewis who was assigned to the 66th squadron. On February 4, 1945, he wrote,

> Flew my 36th mission this afternoon against Castle Franco, east of Citadella. Quite a hot spot. Pop Heying was leading the show, and was hit on his divebombing run. We completed our runs through heavy flak and joined up with Pop, who was in trouble. His plane was on fire in the fuselage just forward of the tail. The control cables burned through, leaving him only aileron and trim tab control—we headed for home wide open. There was a slight explosion, and the fire then burned itself out, so Pop flew that crippled plane all the way home. It was impossible to land it, so he bailed out just off the field.

Five days later, Lewis wrote,

> Another one of those bad days. Lyth and Matula both got it
> today and bailed out just behind the lines, and Paine had his
> canopy shot off, was wounded in the head, neck and shoul-
> ders, and is in the hospital here now. Matula was hit in a
> strafing run, his plane was a mass of flames. He bailed out
> from low altitude and was either hit himself or hurt on land-
> ing, according to Blackburn who circled over him. Several
> Italians were seen to come from a nearby house and carry him
> over to the house. Lyth was on a two-ship show with Mosites.
> They bombed a train and Lyth got a direct hit. It was an
> ammunition train, and the whole thing blew up right in front
> of him. The huge sheet of flame thrown up covered his plane,
> and set it on fire. He pulled up and bailed out, just short of
> the bomb line. Some son of a bitch was shooting at him with
> 20-mm as he came down in his chute, according to Moe.

On March 6, 1945, only eight weeks before the end of the war, Lewis
sat alone in his room and recorded,

> Just returned from rest leave in France this evening. Bad news
> awaiting me. While I was gone, we lost three more men. Jeep
> Norris killed, Phil Lehman the same, and Kruse bailed out
> over the Brenner Pass. Phil was in France just before I was.
> We spent the first day of my leave and the last day of his
> together. Since I was in France, they just locked up our room,
> so everything is just as he left it. Tomorrow they'll take his
> things away. I sure feel funny tonight—sitting here alone in
> the room, looking at Phil's bed, his clothes and things, know-
> ing he won't be back.

At the end of March Lewis recorded his thoughts about "the big
picture" as he could see it. "During the last weeks of the winter, the

fifteen daily missions the group flies had become somewhat frustrating because there weren't as many juicy targets left to shoot up, but the flak was still intense. Everyone was thinking that the way had been cleared so when does the offensive start? On a few occasions, the group escorted bombers into Austria without losing a single bomber under its control."

The Allied offensive against the Gothic Line began on April 9, 1945, and the 57th Group flew thirty missions a day, hitting enemy command posts and heavy artillery positions in advance of the push by the ground troops. The fight line was a beehive of activity from dawn to dusk every day. The ground crews, as well as the pilots, worked with renewed vigor, stimulated by the tangible results their work was showing; and the men proved they could keep the aircraft operational despite the enemy's tenacious flak defenses. On April 21, the *Wehrmacht* began its retreat into Austria.

Looking back at how he and his unit had survived the war, McCarthy wrote, "One distinguishing characteristic of our performance in the squadron was the willingness to take care of each other. True leadership is unselfish. When you take risks to care for your people, the attitude is contagious and will always pay dividends far beyond your expectations. The fallout in loyalty, respect, dedication, and esprit de corps contributes to the ability of the unit to get tough jobs done with better results." It was a point of view the aircrews of the three bomb groups in the 57th Wing could certainly agree with.

The 57th Fighter Group was so successful that the story of the group's role in Operation Strangle was filmed by famed Hollywood director William Wyler at Alto field on Corsica. The result was the documentary film *Thunderbolt*, which was finally shown around the United States in 1947. For many years it was believed to be lost, until an original print was found at the Air Force Museum in the 1970s. The film has been recently restored and is now available on DVD. It is an excellent documentary on the air war in Italy.

NINE

THE SETTIMO ROAD BRIDGE

August 1944 began on an ambiguous note for the men of the 321st Bomb Group.

August 1 was the second anniversary of the group's activation at Columbia Air Base, so there were no missions or training scheduled. At 1000 hours a formation was called, and Brigadier General Robert Knapp, commander of the 57th Wing and the man who had originally trained the 321st and taken it to war, made awards presentations to several of the aircrew, including awards of the Distinguished Flying Cross to Major Paul Cooper, Lieutenants Frank Vivas and Frank White, and Staff Sergeant Robert Mygrant of the 446th squadron. Tech Sergeant Bill Whittaker of the 447th squadron was presented the Legion of Merit for having been the crew chief of "Idaho Lassie," the oldest B-25 in the group, which had flown 150 missions with no aborts for mechanical problems. Both the Officers' and Enlisted Men's Clubs opened their bars at 1400 hours. War diarist Nickerson recorded that "Cairo Scotch,

Seagram's VO and Schenleys were enjoyed by all," while group flight surgeon Captain "Doc" Smith and his swing band "The Mitchell-Aires," provided entertainment. That night the men enjoyed "Off The Cob," a variety show that had been written, arranged, and staged in just three days by Sergeants Sidney Lestz from the group engineering division, Leonard Lavine and John L. McNevin from the group intelligence section, and aircrew gunner Private John J. Naughton. Within a week, the name of the show was changed to "Cornzapoppin'," and several other officers and enlisted men joined the production, including 445th squadron assistant intelligence officer First Lieutenant Jeffrey Lynn, who at thirty-five was one of the oldest men in the unit. Lynn was a Hollywood actor who had volunteered for active service in the wake of Pearl Harbor after starring in *The Roaring Twenties*; *The Fighting 69th*; *All This, and Heaven Too*; and *Million Dollar Baby*. Later he was remembered for frequently volunteering as bartender in the Officers' Club, where he introduced many young fliers to their first martini. Lynn's previous Broadway experience was put to use in developing the show, and it became such a hit that the troupe were sent to entertain the troops in Naples during September. They put on nine shows in eleven days combining big band music from the "Mitchell-Aires" with comedy routines about their army life inspired by Fred Allen skits.

The 321st Bomb Group was informed that they had been awarded a Presidential Unit Citation for a mission flown to Athens in late 1943, which Knapp had led as a colonel.

But there was bad news too for the 321st that day, when the fifty-mission men were informed that group commander Colonel Richard Smith had ordered the number of missions to complete a tour increased to fifty-five. Captain Nicholson noted that the men's "morale dipped quite a bit" on learning of the increase. Adding missions to the tour was a constant sore spot among the fliers in all three groups; they pointed to the Fifteenth Air Force, whose members only had to complete a "solid" fifty-mission tour in order to be sent home and to the Eighth Air Force, where the required tour had just been increased to thirty-five from twenty-five.

First Lieutenant Joseph Heller in the bombardier's "greenhouse" of a B-25, November 1944. *Wilbur Blume collection*

By the end of the war, "Peggy Lou" had 137 bomb symbols painted on her nose, having never turned back once for a mechanical failure; she was definitely "Lucky 13," her plane-in-squadron number. *Fred Lawrence*

On March 18, 1944, Mount Vesuvius erupted for the first time in 150 years, doing more damage in a week to the nearby Allied air forces than the Germans had in the previous sixteen months of combat. *USAAF via Setzer*

Volcanic ash several feet deep was deposited on the 340th Bomb Group's base at Pompeii Airfield, forcing evacuation to another field. *Setzer collection*

A B-25 of the 321st Bomb Group flies over Mount Vesuvius following the eruption of March 18, 1944. *USAAF via Setzer*

A B-25D of the 340th Bomb Group at Pompeii Airdrome following the eruption of Mount Vesuvius on March 18, 1944. *USAAF via Setzer*

First Lieutenant Sterling Ditchey in his "office." *Sterling Ditchey*

B-25s of the 321st Bomb Group buzz the 340th Bomb Group at Alesani Airfield, Corsica. *Michelle Cahill*

"Sassy Second"
Lieutenant Tom Cahill's
graduation photo from
training. *Michelle Cahill*

When a man panicked during a bombing mission, he would say, "I was so
scared, I was all up inside my flak helmet." *Dan Setzer*

"Position to Assume while over Target"

General Robert Knapp, commanding the 57th Bom Wing, awards Staff Sergean Jerry Rosenthal the Air Medal. *Jerry Rosenthal*

Staff Sergeant George Underwood checks his gun turret. *George Underwood*

The Brenner Pass rail line, seen in August 1944. *USAAF via Setzer*

Captain Dan Bowling of the 445th Bomb Squadron, 321st Bomb Group. In the words of fellow pilot Paul Young, "He was our squadron leader—that's different from the squadron commander." *Dan Bowling*

Robert D. Knapp, commander of the 321st Bomb Group with his crew in North Africa, 1943. Knapp fought to lead the group he had trained into combat on 40 missions, even though he was considered "too old" at forty-five. *USAAF via Setzer*

A bridge in the Po Valley goes down when struck by bombs dropped by the 321st Bomb Group, 1944. *USAAF via Setzer*

In the summer of 1944, the 310th Bomb Group celebrated having flown 500 missions since arrival in North Africa in December 1942. *USAAF via Setzer*

On January 25, 1944, B-25J "9V" from the 489th Bomb Squadron, 340th Bomb Group, attempted to land with one engine. Just short of touchdown, that engine failed and the bomber crashed nose first. *USAAF via Setzer*

The sight no one wanted to see. B-25J "8H" of the 488th Bomb Squadron, 340th Bomb Group, goes down in flames from being hit by flak over the Brenner Pass, January 1944. *USAAF via Setzer*

Second Lieutenant Harry George, co-pilot of "McKinley Jr. High," managed to bail out of the burning B-25 when it was shot down on its thirteenth mission, in July 1944. He was rescued by an Italian farm family, who refused to give him up even when threatened by a German officer at gunpoint, and was able to return to Corsica. *Harry George collection*

Tech Sergeant Fred Lawrence was proud to note in his diary in October 1944 that his B-25J, "Peggy Lou" had flown her 100th mission since arriving in the group back in May. Lawrence was recommended for a Bronze Star for his plane's record, but never received it because the squadron engineering officer, a captain who had been with the unit for a month and a half, refused to sign the necessary paperwork unless he also received an award. *Fred Lawrence*

Fred Lawrence remembered, "Six or eight of the other mechanics would come to your plane and split into teams, and within four to six hours we had that engine off and the replacement on." *USAAF via Setzer*

The first target struck on November 6, 1944, in Operation Bingo was the Trento transformer, which was attacked by the 321st and 340th Bomb Groups. The target was small. With no opposition, the bombardiers were able to hit the target perfectly, completely destroying it. *USAAF via Setzer*

On January 21, 1944, B-25J "8P" of the 488th Bomb Squadron collided over the target with B-25 "8U," which sliced off the starboard vertical fin and horizontal stabilizer and cut tailgunner Staff Sergeant Aubrey Porter out of his turret. "8U" spun in and crashed with no survivors. "8P" pilot W. B. Pelton and co-pilot H. K. Shackelford managed to pull off a miracle and bring their bomber back to Alesani Airfield. *USAAF via Setzer*

Officers of the 321st Bomb Group take time out for an evening poker game in the Officer's Club. *USAAF via Setzer*

Dan Bowling (pilot) and Joe Silnutzer (bombardier) drop anti-personnel fragmentation bombs from B-25J "Lucky 13" in November 1944. *Dan Bowling*

Settimo Bridge before (above) and after (below) the bombing of August 24, 1944. *Juglair collection*

First Lieutenant Joe Heller, playing the role of "Pete, a young replacement bombardier," greets his "new CO," Colonel Chapman, November 1944. *Wilbur Blume collection*

Bombardier First Lieutenant Joe Silnutzer (left) and pilot Captain Dan Bowling (right), February 1944. Dan and Joe were the most effective pilot-bombardier team in the 445th Bomb Squadron and led all the important missions the squadron flew during Operation Bingo. *Dan Bowling*

First Lieutenant Joe Heller (second from right, rear) with his "crew" during the filming of the documentary, *Training in Combat*. *Wilbur Blume collection*

A P-47D Thunderbolt of the 57th Fighter Group moves in close to a 321st Bomb Group B-25. The P-47s defended the bombers against Italian-flown fighters and also attacked flak emplacements. *USAAF via Setzer*

On August 2, the 321st flew its first mission to a target in France, with the 447th and 448th squadrons hitting the Var Road Bridge Number 2 with fifty-six "thousand pounders" dropped by fourteen aircraft. Despite "heavy, intense, accurate flak" which holed sixteen aircraft, a good bomb concentration was scored on the bridge's western approach.

On August 3, the 445th squadron's intelligence officer and war diarist, Captain James E. Nickerson, departed Solenzara to return to the United States on rotation orders. First Lieutenant James O. Locke, his assistant, took over maintenance of the war diary while Jeffrey Lynn moved up to head the intelligence unit. Locke wrote of Nickerson that "Captain Nick, as he was affectionately known in the squadron, was probably the most respected and best liked officer in the outfit. He had time and again gone beyond the ordinary call of duty to aid not only the men in his squadron but also those in the group. His intelligence, common sense, keen sense of humor and magnetic personality will long be remembered by those who were fortunate enough to be closely associated with him." Nickerson, a New York corporate lawyer on Wall Street before the war, was more than an intelligence officer; he became a confidante of both officers and enlisted men as they tried to make sense of the war and their role in it, while also being a strong advocate for the welfare of the men. His advocacy for them was a carryover from his pre-war legal life.

While Nickerson took his leave of Corsica, the 445th and 446th squadrons had their turn with the Var Road bridges outside Laurent, France, with a "100 percent" bombing of the Var Road Bridge Number 3. That same day, B-25D "Idaho Lassie" left Corsica on a return flight to the United States for a war bond tour. The 150-mission veteran airplane was one of the original Mitchells assigned to the group in 1942 and had been in the first formation to fly the South Atlantic. She was flown home by Captain Victor Wilson, who had completed his tour as Squadron Operations Officer; Tech Sergeant Bill Whittaker, her crew chief, was also aboard for the tour of training bases in the states. During her time in the squadron, "Idaho Lassie" had sunk three merchant vessels and a German destroyer, while her gunners had shot down four

German fighters. She had been hit many times by flak, but no crewmember had ever been wounded.

Over the next three days, missions were aborted on account of the weather, which finally cleared on Monday, August 7, sufficiently that an eighteen-plane mission was flown that afternoon to bomb the Pont St. Esprit railroad bridge in southern France. The two morning missions had hit the bridge and reported good to excellent coverage. But because of adverse weather conditions, neither afternoon mission was able to bomb the primary target. The 448th squadron bombed the Var River Road Bridge Number 1 instead, covering it with an 87.5 percent concentration of bombs despite heavy, intense, accurate flak that holed ten planes.

During the bad weather the crews of the 340th group at Alesani were treated to a showing of the hit movie *A Guy Named Joe*, starring Spencer Tracy as "Major Joe Sandidge," a dead World War II bomber pilot who becomes guardian angel to another pilot, Captain Ted Randall, played by Van Johnson. The dead Major Sandidge guides Randall through battle and helps him to romance his old girlfriend, played by Irene Dunne, despite her excessive devotion to Sandidge's memory. The movie may have been a hit back home, where it eventually became the inspiration for director Steven Spielberg's *Always*, but it was a bust at Alesani, where the fliers cat-called the movie for its inaccuracies and began making up their own dialogue, shouted at the screen.

These missions were part of the preparation for Operation Dragoon, the invasion of Southern France. The invasion had originally been planned to take place simultaneously with Normandy, but lack of landing craft and shipping forced a delay until the amphibious forces used at Normandy could be reorganized and re-supplied following Operation Overlord and moved back to the Mediterranean. Both of these invasions were prepared for by extensive use of air power. In the Mediterranean, the final aerial push had begun in a spectacular manner on July 11, 1944. In an operation code-named "Mallroy Mayor" the Twelfth and Fifteenth Air Forces, as well as the Free French Air Force, made attacks on the twenty-three most important bridges over the Po River in order to block German communications between northern Italy and southern France.

Between July 15 and August 10, Twelfth Air Force alone flew 150 bombing missions that dropped eighty thousand tons of explosives, despite the fact that on more than ten days in this period operations were canceled on account of weather—thunderstorms, complete with lightning, on the airfields at Corsica. The rains were so torrential that some men were flooded out of their tents.

On August 8, 1944, the 488th Bomb Squadron of the 340th Bomb Group flew a mission against the Avignon bridges. The flak was deadly, with one B-25 being struck by a direct hit in its bomb bay just before "bombs away." The airplane disintegrated in the explosion, and one tail gunner in another plane reported that the only thing left was one of the rudders, which fluttered through the formation. The pilot and co-pilot were friends of Joseph Heller, who flew the mission in one of the planes immediately behind the shot-down B-25. It was Heller's thirty-third mission; his first had been only sixty-eight days earlier.

On Friday, August 11, the bomb groups of the 57th Wing began hitting beach defenses along the coast between Marseilles and Toulon in preparation for the landings. These missions continued over the next three days as the weather finally cooperated with Allied plans.

On August 14, the 340th's diarist recorded,

> The day before the invasion. Who said so? Well, when returning crews report seeing convoys of several hundred ships moving north, when Group S-2 receives bundles of top secret target charts and photos, when the Group is committed to send up at daybreak 72 ships and 54 more in the afternoon, when all Staff Officers are called into secret session by the Colonel with several ranking visitors who seem to know a good bit more than their appearance would justify, when another secret session is called for all combat crews and when the briefing room with all the top secret drawings brought down from higher HQ is locked and kept under heavy guard should all be at least fair evidence that another tea party is in the air for the Jerries....

The Allies invaded Southern France on August 15, 1944. The B-25 groups on Corsica flew multiple missions all that day, with the first departing at 0200 hours and the last not returning until 1900 hours. Air cover for the invasion was provided by fighter groups of both the Twelfth and Fifteenth Air Forces, though the *Luftwaffe* failed to make an appearance over the invasion beaches.

Lieutenant James Jackson, squadron assistant intelligence officer of the 445th, was able to get a ride on one of these missions, flying as "bombing accuracy photographer" aboard a B-25J named "Babs." He recorded the event in his diary. "We took off at 0205 hours. In all there were 36 planes. Our course led over Ajaccio and then northwest to the French coast which we followed due east past Toulon, Marseilles and the Rhône estuary. At this point we headed inland, weaving and turning to avoid flak positions. None was sent up at us and at 0413 hours we were over the target in good formation and with good visibility. The lead element missed the bridge but plastered the approach. Lying on my stomach over the camera hatch, I watched our bombs leave the ship and lose shape in the sky below."

Anti-aircraft fire opened up as the bombardiers reported "bombs away," and the formation broke up as individual Mitchell bombers took evasive action.

As we came over the water and headed west it seemed to me as if all of southern France was blowing up. I counted six targets that had been hit heavily. One large area of dust and smoke assumed the aspect of land fighting but I could not be certain of that. We were now out of danger from the enemy and began taking off our flak suits. Everyone was relaxed and grinning and felt good. From the time of starting engines I had carefully observed my own reactions by checking my pulse and noting other evidence of emotional strain. I was scarcely nervous the entire trip and was in all pleased with my reaction. There was not the uncertainty in my mind as to whether we would return that there has been on other missions. Of course the raids now are in no degree of comparison as hazardous as they used to be and it seems hardly sporting to fly against so worn an enemy.

At 0500 hours the radioman hooked the crew of "Babs" into a BBC newscast: "The announcer told of the landing in southern France and said the sky was literally filled with aircraft. I looked out of the window at the scores of B-25s, B-26s, B-17s and fighter planes and thought, 'Brother, if you only knew.'" Attacks continued for two more days before the weather closed in again.

The goal of these attacks was to isolate the German forces in Southern France from those stationed in northern Italy. Many bridges had to be bombed more than once, since German engineers, working feverishly to repair them, were often able to restore them to operational capability in an incredibly short time. In just the Piedmont region of northern Italy more than fifty missions were flown to hit bridges in Chivasso, Casale Monferrato, Alessandria, and Asti. In the rest of northern Italy there were strikes against Ventimiglia, Piacenza, and Borgoforte.

On August 18, the 321st Bomb Group flew one of the most dangerous missions they were assigned during the war. The French battleship *Strasbourg* and cruiser *La Gallisoniere* had been spotted in Toulon harbor by aerial reconnaissance; they had been moved to positions where they could fire on the invasion forces. Thirty-six Mitchells were sent to attack them. Weather conditions were so bad that other Corsica-based units turned back from their missions, but the 321st's bombers managed to navigate by dead reckoning over the extensive cloud cover and reach the target. Toulon was defended by eighty-two heavy anti-aircraft guns, which opened fire on the bombers as they turned on the IP to make their run at the vulnerable altitude of thirteen thousand feet. Twenty-seven Mitchells were hit by the intense flak, which wounded twelve crewmen during the bomb run; they dropped their semi–armor-piercing "thousand pounders" with 100 percent accuracy, though, and the battleship and cruiser were sunk, along with a submarine and a destroyer. During the entire war no other medium bomber attack against enemy warships involving a high-altitude horizontal bombing run was as successful. In February 1945, the group would receive their second Presidential Unit Citation for their success in this mission.

On August 20, 1944, the simmering resentment in the groups over the recent increases in the number of required missions flared into the open. Following the increase to fifty-five missions announced at the beginning of the month, another increase, to sixty missions, had been announced in mid-month. And on August 20 General Knapp ordered that men were to fly missions "until they can fly no more." The war diarist of the 340th told the story:

> Something entirely new in the way of disciplinary problems cropped up today. The up-cropping is the result of the recent order of this Wing that the men are to fly till they can fly no more. So many of the men having come into combat with a seeming understanding that at fifty they would be entitled to furloughs or rotation back to the States, and later to have the ante raised to 55, then 60, and now raised indefinitely find themselves grumbling quite loudly. On the morning of the completion of their 55th mission two gunners and several officers turned to the Squadron C.O., telling him that they thought they had done enough flying and hoped to be taken off combat status. The two gunners are now in the guardhouse under charges of misbehaving before the enemy. Actually all that was involved was their telling the C.O. their intentions to no longer fly. It is apparent that the Group Commander and Wing Commander are both interested in having the charges pressed if for no other purpose than to have a test case upon which to base further action. Other combat members of the Group have grievously resented this reaction of the Colonel and have lost much of the respect previously held toward him. The matter is now under investigation.

While the two sergeants were thrown in the stockade, the three officers who had joined the protest were merely put under "hack"—confined to their quarters but still required to fly. One of those officers was Joseph Heller, who was still badly shaken from the events he had experienced on the missions of August 8 and 15. Two days later, Knapp was ordered by General Cannon, commander of Twelfth Air Force, to rescind the order on unlimited missions, and Chapman was ordered to release the sergeants. However, the trouble was not over yet.

On August 22, 1944, the 340th Bombardment Group was given yet another bridge to bomb the next day. The mission was not the kind of raid any of the crews of the 340th had ever felt good about. They thought nothing of bombing railroads, rail bridges, highway bridges, military bases, or any target that could be considered war-related. What they didn't like were the missions where the job was to create "road blocks." These involved bombing towns and villages for the sole purpose of knocking down the buildings and leaving the wreckage in the streets and roads to slow the movement of enemy troops. Everyone knew these missions involved targeting defenseless civilians—the B-25s bombed their targets from eight to twelve thousand feet, which was low enough for any crewman to look outside and see the results of the words "bombs away!"—and no one liked it no matter how much their leaders spoke about military necessity.

In November 1943, for example, the 340th had been ordered to bomb Sofia, the capital of Bulgaria. This was the first time the city was bombed during the war, and the fliers knew that the civilian population was at risk since the raid was sure to be a surprise and those living in the city would not be prepared. Their orders were the source of considerable angst, to the point that the 487th Bomb Squadron's war diarist had written: "It was the first raid which impressed us with the horror of bombing, because it was on a bunch of civilians who must have been surprised by the approach of the planes. Many of the crews have heretofore expressed a dislike of bombing little towns to create road blocks, but most everyone realizes that the citizens should have got out into the hills, and probably had a chance to do so. But this raid was different, and must have cost a lot of lives...." The diarist also had a complaint about the "well-attended blood and guts movie *Sahara*" that was shown for the men's entertainment: "The tragedy of this kind of movie is that the folks back home tend to believe such melodramatic tripe."

On August 23, 1944, the target for the "road block" missions was the town of Ponte San Martino in the Val d'Aosta (Aosta Valley) of northwestern Italy. The town existed because of a bridge that had been built by Julius Caesar's legionaries to span the Aosta River during his invasion of Gaul in 55 BC What was known to the Romans as the Settimo Road ran from the Gran Pass across the Val d'Aosta to the Piccolo San Bernardo pass; it was the most direct route from the Po Valley in Italy to the Rhône Valley in France. Over the two millennia since Caesar's day the farmers of the region had used the Roman bridge, and the town of Ponte San Martino had grown over the centuries into a regional market center.

Napoleon crossed the bridge on his way to the Battle of Marengo in 1800. Fifty years later, a new road was built to better accommodate additional traffic, and a more modern bridge was built across the river just fifty-five feet south of the Roman bridge. But the construction of rail lines in the Brenner Pass through the Alps directly to Austria and on to Germany after the unification of Italy in 1861 meant that commercial traffic bypassed the Val d'Aosta, which became a backwater as the local economy suffered and poverty spread.

The economic decay began to be reversed with the construction of an electrical generation plant outside the town in 1919. In 1931 construction began on a steel production plant nearby that took advantage of the electrical power. The steel plant had a profound economic impact. In 1931–1932 the population of Ponte San Martino jumped from 1,600 to 2,800. In 1939, Mussolini toured the Val d'Aosta to mark the opening of the Fiat plant in Turin. Support for the dictator was not strong in Ponte San Martino because of his pro-German, anti-French policies; members of many families in the village had migrated to France in search of work. Mussolini's local appearance did win him some support, though.

When Italy declared war on June 10, 1940, the proximity of the Val d'Aosta to the French border put it on the front lines. Fortunately, the Battle of the Alps was brief and did not greatly affect the local population. However, the enthusiasm that had been inspired by Mussolini's visit began to fade in the wake of the strong resistance put up by the French and the heavy losses suffered by the Italian Alpine troops.

While work at the steel plant increased, the need for soldiers to help fulfill Mussolini's dream of re-creating the Roman Empire in the Mediterranean meant the young men of the rural farming families were drafted off to war. Many times between the fall of 1940 and the summer of 1943, the sleep of the villagers in Ponte San Martino had been broken by the sound of aircraft overhead as the RAF sent raids across France to bomb Turin, Milan, and Genoa. The raids had increased in the summer of 1944 as the Allied air forces in Italy turned their attention increasingly to southern France and northwestern Italy in preparation for the coming invasion; the rumble of engines had become commonplace by day and night. Nevertheless, the bombers that flew over Ponte San Martino that summer paid the village no mind.

Beginning in late July, Italian partisan units had destroyed many highway and rail bridges in northwestern Italy in preparation for the coming invasion of southern France, leaving the Germans with control of the Piccolo San Bernardo Pass and the Settimo Road. On the day of the invasion, a significant portion of the highway leading to the Piccolo San Bernardo pass was destroyed. In late August, the Allied Command gave orders to redouble efforts to disrupt traffic on the Piccolo San Bernardo pass.

On August 20, 1944, no one in Ponte San Martino paid attention to the lone twin-engine airplane that flew up the valley from the south, so high that the sound of its engines was barely heard on the ground below. Mission completed, the pilot of the Lockheed F-5E Lightning, a photo-reconnaissance version of the famous P-38 fighter, headed back to Borgo Airfield on Corsica, home base of the 5th Photo Reconnaissance Squadron of the 3rd Photo Reconnaissance Group.

At Borgo, photo-interpretation specialists went over the film the F-5 had taken. While the Settimo Road through the Val d'Aosta was no longer a major route, it could be useful for the Germans in southern France to escape the Allies who were now nearing Grenoble in the Rhône Valley, just west of the Piccolo San Bernardo pass at the western end of the Settimo Road, and to feed any available reinforcements into France. The photo interpreters were looking for signs of German movement through the area. They found a German column of trucks and armored vehicles moving up the Settimo Road toward Ponte San Martino.

There was fear that this was the leading unit of what was believed to be two Panzer divisions that could move west across the Piccolo San Bernardo Pass to attack the Allies at Grenoble. "Ultra" intelligence had provided information that two Panzer divisions had been ordered to move from Austria to Southern France to reinforce the resistance to the invasion. The German unit that was seen by the F-5 on August 20 on the Settimo Road was feared to be the leading unit of this formation. Thus the order was given to create a "concrete roadblock" at the bridges across the Aosta to keep the two divisions from entering France.

August 23 began early for the 340th group. Group commander Colonel Chapman had received orders detailing the missions for the day, and he ordered Group Operations Officer Major Joseph E. Ruebel to brief the staff. The target that morning for Mission 521 would be the La Grande Combe railroad bridge at Blanoux, France, not far from Arles.

The crews were up at 0600 hours and headed to the mess tent for breakfast. At 0700 hours pilots of the 488th and 489th Squadrons went to the briefing, where they learned that the mission would be a long one, into France. They were given the codes and radio frequencies to use on this mission and got a report on the weather expected over the target. The mission departed Alesani at 0900 hours.

When the bombers arrived at the target, there was 10/10 cloud coverage, which made a bomb run impossible. The pilots made a wide circle and came back to the target twice in hopes of finding a hole in the clouds, but nothing opened up. Since they had not been assigned an alternate target, they had no choice but to return to Corsica with their bomb loads. On the return trip home they happened to pass by an area that was defended by anti-aircraft guns, and two planes were holed by flak, but the hits were not serious. That the raid was flown without any fighter escort is an indicator of what bad shape the *Luftwaffe* was in. By this point there was not a single German fighter plane stationed in Southern France.

Later that same day, at 1500 hours, another briefing took place for Mission 522. Crews from eighteen planes assembled in the meeting hall. The atmosphere was light, full of the joking and good humor one expects of a group of young men in their twenties. At the front of the room was a large map with a colored ribbon tracing the route of the raid. There were also several aerial photos of the Aosta Valley taken by the Lockheed F-5. The objective of the mission was to bomb the Settimo Road Bridges and also the town of Ponte San Martino in order to create a "road block." The formation was to be made up of twelve aircraft from the 488th Squadron and six from the 489th. They would fly in three "boxes" of six planes each. The eighteen bombers took off at 1600 hours, each armed with four "thousand pounders." Shortly after takeoff, two aircraft in the last box reported mechanical problems and returned to base.

At 1730 hours the formation reached Ponte San Martino. The people in the town heard the roar of the engines. They were alarmed at the sound but also curious as to what was going on. They came out into the streets for a better look. In the distance they could pick out sixteen silvery specks in the sky shimmering in the hot afternoon sun; these were the bombers. Some noticed more silvery specks suddenly appear beneath the first. These were the bombs that soon fell in the center of town, with three distinct impacts followed by a series of explosions that shook the ground and immediately filled the air with a dark suffocating smoke. A few of the bombs did not land in the same area as their fellows. Three overshot the town center and exploded harmlessly in a field.

While in formation, Second Lieutenant Clifton C. Grosskopf, the pilot of bomber "8K," had performed a bizarre maneuver, pulling up out of the formation—a very risky thing given the tightness of the formation during the bomb run—causing his bombs to go astray. In his report following the mission, the pilot justified the move by stating that he was executing an evasive maneuver. This is difficult to believe, considering that the only anti-aircraft gun protecting Ponte San Martino was a single machine gun that could not have reached the bombers' altitude and did not fire a single shot that day.

Although the three bombs of B-25 "8K" had fallen off-target, the loads of the other bombers had landed in a tight pattern and with deadly accuracy. Once the bombs were dropped, the B-25s turned off of the bomb run and flew back to Corsica. The return flight was uneventful except for the situation in "8K." The "evasive maneuver" that had caused three of her four thousand-pounders to fall wide of the target also caused one of the bombs to jam in the bomb bay. The tail-gunner had to climb into the bomb bay, where he was able kick it free.

When Italian historian Roger Juglair began researching this event in 2003, he contacted Robert Burger, who, as a First Lieutenant in the 488th squadron at the time, was the mission lead bombardier in "8T." Burger recalled the mission:

> At the time of the bombing of your town I was 22 years of age. I am now a very active and healthy 83. I was the squadron bombing officer of the 488th bombardment squadron which was part of the 340th Bombardment Group.
>
> The pilot was Saleem Aswad. He was a very good friend of mine. We were briefed for that mission and it was the town itself that was the target. The aircrews were not advised of the reason for the destruction of this town. The mission leader was in contact with our home base by the radio operator using Morse code. The code name of the home base of this mission was Blacktop.
>
> On the approach to the target, as I was just about ready to start sighting in on the target I thought there must be some

mistake. The target was not near a major highway or railroad. There was no antiaircraft fire and the target seemed undefended.

In the military, and I quote from the famous poem "The Charge of the Light Brigade," "Yours not to reason why, yours but to do or die." So I started my bomb run. As my five wingmen saw my bomb bay doors open they in turn opened theirs. When they saw my bombs drop they triggered their load. Each plane carried four one-thousand-pound general purpose bombs.

I ordered the radio operator to send the following signal back to Blacktop. Mike, Sugar, Oboe, King. The phonetic alphabet for Mission Successful and that the weather is OK.

I have always wondered what the casualties were on this mission. Please advise the survivors and the relatives of those causalities that this mission still bothers me to this day and I feel for them.

I did not hear anyone assigned to the mission in question that mentioned anything at all about it not being a military target. When I attacked Ponte San Martino I could easily see that there were no major highways nor railroads in the area. My thoughts were that it was a mistake and I very nearly aborted the mission. In retrospect, my thoughts were that if it were not in error the only other explanation would be old Benito. So, who really knows the real reason?

Burger was referring to the whereabouts of Benito Mussolini, who was known to be hiding in a secure location in northern Italy. In fact, Mussolini was not that far away from Ponte San Martino, being head-quartered with the Ministry of Foreign Affairs of the Italian Social Republic at Salò, a small town on Lake Garda, near Brescia in the Italian Alps.

The radioman in Burger's "8T" had reported the mission a success, but the fact is that in spite of the tight and accurate bomb pattern, while the approach to the new bridge was cratered and the Roman bridge was

hit near the western approach, the bridges, which were obviously legiti-
mate military targets, were not structurally damaged. In spite of the
ferocious attack, both remained intact and passable, with only very light
damage. When post-strike bomb damage assessment photos showed that
the center of the town had been hit, there was major concern in the 340th
Bomb Group about whether the target they had bombed had military
significance. One indication of their concern can be found in a notation
on the debriefing report made by the 489th Bomb Squadron, stating—
unconvincingly—that "the town center is believed to be the command
headquarters of an armored division."

Italian memories of the bombing don't support the notation in the
debriefing report. Most witnesses on the ground told of a quiet, hot
August afternoon, with children playing in the Memorial Plaza by the
monument to the soldiers of the First World War. Some people were on
their doorsteps eating a light snack to hold them over until dinner. There
was no air raid alarm sounded in the village. The steel plant on the edge
of town did get a phone call from the control center in Ivrea informing
them that a formation of bombers was in the area. The employees got
out of the building and assembled in a field nearby. But there was very
little excitement or concern, since it was fairly common for groups of
bombers to pass over the area on their way to bomb targets elsewhere.
The steelworkers' lack of concern evaporated quickly as they saw the
bombs hit the town, raising an immense cloud of black dust and ash;
they began running to see what might have happened to their homes and
loved ones. The workers encountered people running from the town,
blackened by the dust cloud, with many shoeless or half-naked since their
clothes had been blown off them by the concussions. The horror and
despair reached its peak when people realized that the Italo Balbo Ele-
mentary School had been hit. Of the 130 people who died that day,
approximately forty were children.

One important issue about the mission has never been resolved: the
report of "evasive maneuvers" executed by Second Lieutenant Grosskopf,
the pilot of B-25 "8K." No mention of anti-aircraft fire over the target
appears in the reports of Mission 522 in the war diary of the 488th

squadron. And even if there had been anti-aircraft fire, any evasive maneuvers would have been performed before or after the bomb run. From the time the bombers arrived at the Initial Point (IP) and entered their bomb run to the moment the bombs were dropped, all the bombers should have ceased evasive maneuvers and held straight and steady. The pilots following the lead plane, including "8K," should have been holding steady as their bombardiers kept their attention on the leader so they would know when to open bomb doors and then to toggle the bombs when the lead bombardier released his.

No one in the squadron or group ever questioned Grosskopf's statement that he took evasive action in a situation where that was specifically against the rules. There are no statements by any of the other members of the crew of "8K" substantiating or denying Grosskopf's statement. Why did the pilot maneuver away at the last moment? Perhaps because he saw what was happening with the two leading boxes of bombers, which were dropping their bombs on the town. In the aftermath of the raid, as the group discovered the actual results of their mission, Grosskopf's action was swept under the rug because making an example of him would bring unwanted attention from higher authority. Punishing him would also have had an adverse effect on the morale of the other crews.

The August 23 mission, and Grosskopf's action, are the basis for a scene in *Catch-22*. In Heller's novel, at the initial briefing for the mission, Dunbar and the crews in the briefing room balk at dropping bombs on unsuspecting villagers whom they believe will come out of their homes to wave at the American planes as they fly over. Major Danby has explained that "two armored divisions will be coming down from Austria into Italy along this road. The village is on such a steep incline that all the rubble from the houses and other building you destroy will certainly tumble right down and pile up on the road." Dunbar argues that that doesn't matter because "[i]t will only take them a couple days to clear it." The fliers ask if the people in the town can't be warned, but Major Danby tells them that "the Germans might find out and choose another road." The argument continues until Colonel Korn steps into the briefing room. Told that the men believe it cruel to bomb a defenseless village, Korn says, "Would it be any less cruel to let those two German divisions down to fight with our troops? American lives are at stake too, you know. Would you rather see American blood spilled?" Dunbar asks why they can't create the roadblock somewhere else. "Couldn't we bomb the slope of a mountain or the road itself?"

Colonel Korn puts a quick end to their objections:

> "Would you rather go back to Bologna [where the missions were much more dangerous]?" The question, asked quietly, rang out like a shot and created a silence in the room that was awkward and menacing. Yossarian prayed intensely, with shame, that Dunbar would keep his mouth shut. Dunbar dropped his gaze and Colonel Korn knew he had won. "No, I thought not," he continued with undisguised scorn. "You know, Colonel Cathcart and I have to go to a lot of trouble to get you a milk run like this. If you'd sooner fly missions to Bologna, Spezia and Ferrara, we can get those targets with no trouble at all."
>
> Colonel Korn addressed himself to Dunbar and Yossarian in a dry monotone. "You've got my sacred word for it. Nobody is more distressed about those lousy wops up in the hills than Colonel Cathcart and myself."

The three pages of the passage about the bombing of the village are among the most bitter of the entire novel. The helplessness of the men as they silently acquiesce to Colonel Korn is palpable, as is their revulsion at themselves for making such a choice—they are willing to bomb a defenseless village rather than fly more missions into heavily defended targets.

Joseph Heller flew on the Settimo Bridge mission and would have been as aware as anyone else of the response of the group leadership to the event and to Grosskopf's "evasive action." He even has Yossarian's friend Dunbar stand in for Grosskopf at the outset of the next chapter:

"Yossarian no longer gave a damn where his bombs fell, although he did not go as far as Dunbar, who dropped his bombs hundreds of yards past the village and would face a court martial if it could ever be shown he had done it deliberately. Without a word even to Yossarian, Dunbar had washed his hands of the mission."

There is further evidence that the Settimo Bridge mission was a watershed for Heller, the straw that broke the young bombardier's back. Up until that point he shows up regularly in the war diary for the 488th squadron from the time of his arrival on Corsica in late May, flying approximately a mission every other day. He was credited with some forty missions at the time of the Ponte San Martino bombing on August 23, 1944. But after that date his name is listed infrequently in the crew lists for missions. In the five months that he remained with the 488th Bomb Squadron, until January 1945, Heller flew only an additional twenty missions—just one a week on average. He also left his unit at the end of his tour with a total of sixty missions—at a time when the required number of missions to be sent home was seventy.

Was Joseph Heller made an offer: *cooperate with us and let us take care of you*? That's the very same "thoroughly despicable deal" that Yossarian, Heller's stand-in for himself in *Catch-22*, refuses in the book's culminating act of moral courage. Was a similar offer actually made to Heller? Did Heller say "yes" where Yossarian said "no"?

For several months, beginning in mid-September—just about three weeks after the Ponte San Martino bombing—Heller was working with his friend First Lieutenant Wilbur Blume, a bombardier who also held the assignment of group public relations officer and was additionally the officer in charge of the "9th Photo Unit," an unofficial organization in the 340th group. Group commander Colonel Chapman was quite proud of the training program he had established to bring new replacements up to speed before they began flying operational missions, and Blume was assigned to make a documentary film about the program, *Training in Combat*, which Colonel Chapman hoped would impress General Knapp and serve as a model for other groups. Blume and his photographers and team of aircrew "actors" worked on the movie—which Blume termed "a boondoggle for the Colonel," in his own private diary—for five months. Though the film was never completed, portions of it still exist.

One of the actors in the film is Joseph Heller, who plays the role of "Pete," a replacement bombardier. Was this easy duty, which took him away from combat, the payoff for saying nothing to anyone about the events of August 23, 1944? Heller is no longer here to answer such a question, but after the Ponte San Martino bombing the remainder of his tour, as described in the war diaries, is certainly out of the ordinary in comparison to the tours of the rest of the fliers in the group.

Buck Henry, a writer who worked with Heller adapting *Catch-22* into the screenplay for the movie, recalled Heller as "the angriest guy I ever knew." Was he angry at himself? In an interview following the publication of the novel, Heller said that a main theme of the novel is how difficult it is for an individual to make a moral choice in an institution where he has no voice or power. Was Heller angry at himself for being what he considered a moral coward? Did he create an alternative story to the truth as a result? The circumstantial facts support such a theory.

TEN

THE GOTHIC LINE

The Gothic Line (German: *Gotenstellung*; Italian: *Linea Gotica*) was Field Marshal Albert Kesselring's last major line of defense in northern Italy. It had been designed by Erwin Rommel and constructed over the fall of 1943 and spring and summer of 1944, using more than fifteen thousand slave laborers, mostly forced into the German war effort from the countries Germany had occupied in Eastern Europe. The defensive line was ten miles deep, extending from south of La Spezia on the west coast to the Foglia Valley; then on through the natural defensive wall of the Apennines, which ran unbroken almost from coast to coast, fifty miles deep with crests and peaks rising to seven thousand feet and covered with thick forests; then on to the Adriatic Sea between Pesaro and Ravenna on the east coast. The emplacements included numerous concrete-reinforced gun pits and trenches, 2,376 machine-gun pillboxes and nests with interlocking fire, 479 anti-tank, mortar, and assault gun positions, 390,000 feet of barbed wire, and several miles of anti-tank ditches. All of this was positioned on steep hillsides that did not allow the Allies to make use of their superiority in vehicles, reducing combat to a small-unit infantry struggle.

Construction of the Gothic Line was slowed by the poor quality concrete deliberately provided by the local Italian sources. Additionally, captured partisans who were forced into the construction gangs supplemented the natural lethargy of their fellow slave-laborers with clever sabotage. But Kesselring held an inspection of the line in early August of 1944 and declared himself satisfied with what he saw, especially on the Adriatic end of the line, where he "contemplated an assault on the left wing…with a certain confidence."

Throughout the spring and summer of 1944 Hitler worried about the state of preparation of the Gothic Line, and about its name. He was concerned that the Allies would outflank the position with an amphibious operation, and if the Allies broke through they could use the name, with its historical connotations, to magnify their victory claims, creating a political problem for him. To downgrade the line's importance in the eyes of both friend and foe, he ordered its name changed. Kesselring renamed it the "Green Line" (*Grüne Linie*) in June 1944, but regardless of the name change it was known as the Gothic Line by the troops of both sides to the end of the war.

American political and military leaders had always seen Italy as a secondary front. They were willing to fight there to keep the enemy occupied only so long as there was no chance of carrying the war to what they saw as the main front. They were eager for direct confrontation with the German Army in France with the ultimate goal of breaking into and occupying Germany itself. So once the Allies had successfully landed at Normandy and General Mark Clark had let his ego get in the way of ending the war in Italy that same week, the campaign in Italy inevitably became a long slog whose outcome would depend more on events elsewhere in Europe than on the Italian peninsula. Immediately after the victory at Cassino and the fall of Rome, VI Corps and the French Expeditionary Corps—seven experienced divisions—were withdrawn from operations in Italy to participate in Operation Dragoon, the Allied invasion on August 17, 1944, that liberated southern France. The Allied army would be on the German frontier by October.

By early August, the total combined strength of the U.S. Fifth Army and the British Eighth Army had fallen precipitously from 249,000 to 153,000. The veteran units had been replaced by the inexperienced troops of the Brazilian Expeditionary Corps and the American 92nd Infantry Division. There were now only eighteen divisions in Italy to confront the German Tenth and Fourteenth Armies' fourteen front line divisions plus four to seven reserve divisions.

The success of Normandy notwithstanding, Winston Churchill and the British Chiefs of Staff were still keen to break through the Gothic Line and open the route into Austria and Hungary through the "Ljubljana Gap" in northern Yugoslavia. Churchill saw this as a way to forestall the Russian advance into central Europe. The U.S. Chiefs of Staff strongly opposed this strategy as a diversion from the main focus in France, but the Combined Chiefs of Staff agreed at the Second Quebec Conference on September 12, 1944, to support the offensive that had begun in northern Italy three weeks earlier. They planned to break through the Gothic Line that fall.

Operation Olive, as the offensive was known, called for the British Eighth Army to attack up the Adriatic coast toward Pesaro and Rimini and draw in the German reserves from the center of the country. The U.S. Fifth Army would then attack the weakened German forces in the central Apennines north of Florence toward Bologna with British XIII Corps on the right wing fanning toward the east coast to create a pincer with the Eighth Army advance. The offensive began in late August, after the successful invasion of southern France. Operation Olive has been described as the biggest battle ever fought in Italy. Over 1,200,000 men participated in the battle. Rimini, a city that had already been hit hard by previous air raids, had 1,470,000 rounds fired against it by Allied land forces. According to Lieutenant General Sir Oliver Leese, commander of the Eighth Army, "The battle of Rimini was one of the hardest battles of Eighth Army. The fighting was comparable to El Alamein, Mareth, and the Gustav Line (Monte Cassino)."

Fortunately for the Allies, the Italian partisan forces had become very effective in disrupting German preparations in the high mountains. By September 1944, a German general could no longer move freely behind the lines because of partisan activity. Generalleutnant Frido von Senger und Etterlin, commander of *XIV.Panzerkorps*, wrote that he traveled in a Volkswagen "displaying no general's insignia of rank—no peaked cap, no gold or red flags." Brigadier General Wilhelm Crisolli, who commanded *20.Luftwaffefelddivision*, was captured and killed by partisans as he returned from a conference at corps headquarters.

Opposing the British Eighth Army was the Tenth Army's *LXVI. Panzerkorps*. Initially this had only three divisions: *1.Fallschirmjägerdivision* which faced the Polish II Corps, with *71.Infantriedivision* on the Allied paratroopers' right and *278.Infantriedivision* on the Poles' right flank. Five divisions of the German 51st Mountain Corps covered an eighty-mile front to the right of *LXVI.Panzerkorps* with two further divisions, *162.(Turkoman) Infantriedivision* and *98.Infantriedivision* waiting on the Adriatic coast behind *LXVI.Panzerkorps* to confront any Allied amphibious operation. Additionally, Kesselring had *90.Panzergrenadierdivision* and *26.Panzerdivision* in the Army Group Reserve.

The B-25s of the 57th Bomb Wing were intimately involved in the fighting across the Gothic Line, going after German transport routes. The main enemy of the Mitchells would be the weather; the fall rains brought low clouds that covered targets on many days. By late August, Tom Cahill of the 486th squadron had become a First Lieutenant, with his date of rank backdated to the first of the month. His ability as a bombardier had been noticed; just before receiving news of his promotion he had become a designated "lead bombardier." That assignment was a double-edged sword, as he explained to his mother in a letter shortly after his thirty-seventh mission, "It kinda looks like I may not be home for Christmas. When I first got here I was getting twelve to fifteen missions a month, but since I have been leading I am lucky to get in half that many and later when Fall arrives, perhaps less. How many more I'll have to fly I don't know."

In late August, First Lieutenant Dan Bowling arrived on Corsica after traveling across the Atlantic on a Victory ship converted to a hospital ship that took twenty days to get from Norfolk, Virginia, to Naples, Italy. Three weeks after he arrived at Solenzara, Bowling turned twenty-two. A miner's son, he was raised in the hardscrabble mining town of Bisbee, Arizona, which he remembered as "a company town through and through." His father had been a union organizer who was later elected to the Arizona state senate on the Socialist Party ticket. With such a background, Bowling had learned early in life never to back down from a fight; the children of miners whom the Phelps-Dodge Corporation had turned against his father picked on him at school. The Bowling family was finally run out of town and left for Los Angeles when Dan was eleven. He had a reputation for not "taking guff" from anyone he had come across in the Army, regardless of rank.

Bowling's leadership qualities had been recognized during his training: he was made cadet company commander of each of the units he passed through on the way to pinning on his pilot's wings. He was fortunate to have been the beneficiary of extra training before being posted overseas, and held an official "green card" as a fully trained pilot capable of instrument flying, making him unique among all the pilots in the group other than the Group Commander. Shortly after his arrival on Corsica, Bowling was assigned to the 445th Bomb Squadron; on his third training flight he was told by the pilot checking him out that he had more hours as a B-25 first pilot than did his training officer. Within a matter of days he had flown his first combat mission as a first pilot, and after four missions in his first week he was put into training to become a lead pilot. By the end of September Bowling was a flight leader, responsible for two wingmen.

During a September 10 mission to bomb the Guerra ammo and fuel dump in support of the British troops fighting at Rimini, the 310th group got a taste of air combat when the Italian pilots of the *2nd Grupo Caccia* of the *Aviazione del' R.S.I.*, who had recently turned in their Macchi C.205 Veltro fighters for Messerschmitt Bf-109Gs, made an appearance.

First Lieutenant Warren M. Wolfe had been forced to feather one propeller and drop out of formation while approaching the target on account of engine failure; still he continued on and made a successful run over the target. During the withdrawal, six of the Italian-flown Bf-109s spotted the crippled B-25 and made several attacks. Wolfe managed to avoid further damage as he threw his bomber around the sky in evasive action until the arrival of P-47s from the American 57th Fighter Group forced the Messerschmitt pilots to break off their attacks. Wolfe continued on south for two hours before he found a friendly airfield and landed safely.

September 18 saw the 445th squadron suffer their sole loss of the month during an attack on German troop concentrations northwest of Rimini; B-25J 42-27792, flown by First Lieutenant John Richardson, was hit in the wing, which caught fire. Other men in the formation saw "several parachutes" as the bomber steadily lost altitude before diving into the sea.

Eighth Army's initial attack on August 25 had taken the Germans by surprise, to the extent that both corps commander von Vietinghof and the parachute division commander were away on leave. At the time *LXVI.Panzerkorps* was in the process of pulling back its forward units to the Green I fortifications of the Gothic Line proper. Kesselring was unsure if the Allied attack was a major offensive or just Eighth Army advancing to occupy vacated ground with the main attack coming from the U.S. Fifth Army on the Bologna front, and so he didn't bring his reserves forward. It was not until August 28, when he saw a captured copy of Lieutenant General Leese's order of the day to Eighth Army prior to the attack, that Kesselring realized this was a major offensive. At that point he ordered three reinforcement divisions from Bologna, but they would need at least two days to arrive in position—even if the Allied air forces did not destroy the trains or cut the rail lines.

Canadian First and British V Corps reached the Green I main defensive positions running along the ridges on the far side of the Foglia River on August 30. Because of the lack of German manpower, the Canadians were able to punch through; by September 3 they had advanced fifteen miles to the Green II line. Eighth Army was close to breaking through to Rimini and the Romagna plain, but *LXVI.Panzerkorps* had withdrawn in good order behind the line of the Conca river, where fierce resistance from *1.Fallschirmjägerdivision* brought the Canadian advance to a halt.

At the same time the British V Corps' advance was slowed in the difficult mountain terrain with its poor roads. On 3–4 September, while the Canadians attacked along the Romagna plain, V Corps sent armor to dislodge the Coriano Ridge defenses and reach the Marano River, which would open the gate to the Lombardy plain; their advance could then be rapidly exploited by the 1st Armored Division. But after two days of gruesome close-in fighting with heavy losses on both sides, the Allies were forced to call off the assault. An attack to outflank the ridge positions by driving westwards toward Croce and Gemmano to reach the Marano valley, which curved behind the Coriano positions to the coast north of Riccione, was ordered.

The Battle for Gemmano has been called "The Cassino of the Adriatic." Between September 4 and 13 first the 56th Division and then the 46th Division made eleven unsuccessful assaults against Gemmano. On September 15, following a heavy artillery bombardment, the Indian 4th Division made the twelfth attack at 0300 hours and finally carried and secured the German positions on the south side of the Conca Valley. At the same time, on the northern side of the valley, a similarly bloody engagement was taking place at Croce. The *98.Infantriedivision* held out tenaciously over five days of door-to-door and hand-to-hand fighting before 56th Division forced the Germans to withdraw.

With progress at Gemmano slowed, the attack on Coriano was renewed. After a paralyzing bombardment from seven hundred artillery pieces and the bombers of the 12th and Desert Air Forces, the Canadian 5th Armored and British 1st Armored divisions attacked on the night of September 12. The Coriano positions were finally taken on September 14 after two days of continuous combat.

The way to Rimini was once again open. The Germans had taken heavy losses, and the three divisions of reinforcements ordered to the Adriatic front were delayed by Allied air attacks on the railway system.

At this point, the weather intervened. Four days of heavy rain turned the rivers into unbridgeable torrents and halted air operations. Movement slowed to a crawl, giving the German defenders the opportunity to reorganize and reinforce their positions on the Marano river. The open salient to the Lombardy plain was closed. Eighth Army was now confronted by the Rimini Line. But as the weather cleared, the offensive resumed.

In the late afternoon of September 22, an Allied photo reconnaissance flight over the port of La Spezia spotted the Italian light cruiser *Taranto*, which had been previously damaged, in the process of being towed out of drydock. It seemed probable that the Germans intended to tow the ship into the mouth of the harbor and scuttle it there, to prevent Allied use of the harbor after its capture. A mission to sink the ship in drydock was quickly laid on and assigned to the 488th Bomb Squadron for the morning of September 23.

Joe Heller was among the crews who manned their bombers at Alesani that morning; he later recalled this as the last really dangerous mission he would fly before the end of his tour.

Eighteen B-25s took off, formed up over the field, and headed off to the northeast across the Ligurian Sea. An hour later they were west of the port. Heller's plane was assigned to the "chaff flight," dropping strips of aluminum in advance of the attackers in order to confuse the radar-directed anti-aircraft weapons: "Because we carried no bombs, I deduced there was no need for a bombardier. Because we had no bombs, we could go zig-zagging in at top speed and vary our altitude." He took up a position behind the pilots.

The three lead bombers, including Heller's, made their attack from eight thousand feet, dropping chaff as they flew over the target. The sky grew thick with flak as the tail gunner and radioman in the rear of the planes tossed out chaff through the rear hatch. As the planes pulled up and away, turning back toward the sea, Heller saw the twelve B-25s behind them, each carrying six thousand-pound semi–armor-piercing bombs, bracket the cruiser, which turned on its side as it was hit repeatedly.

The bombers flew on to the east, over the hills that surrounded the port. Flak was heavy, but none of the Mitchells was seriously damaged. The attack resulted in a second award of a Presidential Unit Citation to the 340th.

On September 28, eighteen B-25s of the 428th Bomb Squadron of the 310th group were sent to attack a gun and troop area near Rimini. Aboard B-25 Number 771, the crew—pilot First Lieutenant Louis Schovanec, co-pilot Second Lieutenant George Rorer, bombardier Sergeant Edward Stroyke, turret gunner Sergeant Anthony Ruggiero, radio operator Sergeant MacMakin Collier, and tail gunner Sergeant Luis Martinez—were about to discover just how tough a bird the Mitchell was. As Schovanec began to close the bomb doors following Stroyke's shouted "Bombs away!" he remarked to Rorer how lucky they had been that there didn't seem to be any flak. "Suddenly, a burst went off right under us and pitched our tail straight up," Rorer later recounted. Immediately a second burst exploded under the nose of the lead ship in the formation, flown by First Lieutenant Harold Iverson. Rorer recounted what happened next: "When the second shell hit, we were looking down at them through the overhead windows of the cockpit. Iverson's ship was thrown into a steep bank to the left, directly toward us. Louis and I manhandled the ship into a steeper bank and climb, trying to get away. We wrapped the ship around but it was no use—with a terrific crash they slammed into our belly."

Rorer saw Iverson's Mitchell slide away under his plane's right wing. The canopy was caved in, and Iverson and his co-pilot were trying to cover their heads with their arms. The B-25 passed quickly out of sight: "That was the last we ever saw of them." Storer and Schovanec had no time to worry about Iverson's plane; they were fighting to save their own. Iverson's plane had struck their right wing, buckling it at the point between the outer end of the flap and inner end of the aileron, causing the plane to act as if full "up" right aileron had been applied, and forcing the plane into a right bank. The B-25 fell off to its right and entered a spin. According to Rorer, "We both stood on the rudder and forced the control wheel to the left as we pushed the yoke forward, pointing the nose down. The wild gyrations ended as airspeed was restored and we regained a semblance of control. We recovered at 5,000 feet after falling from 13,000 feet in a matter of minutes."

As soon as they had regained control and leveled off, Sergeant Ruggiero, the turret gunner, grabbed his chest 'chute, clipped it on, kicked open the lower forward escape hatch and threw himself through it to bail out. "We never saw Ruggiero's chute open. We were still flying, going straight but the right wing was way down, and we were headed deeper and deeper into enemy territory." It was impossible to turn to the right without entering a spin; but by standing on full left rudder and holding full left up aileron, they were able to make a turn and slide to the left. "It took about ten minutes to get turned around back toward our lines, but it seemed like an eternity."

As they crossed the Allied lines, they considered bailing out, but they knew that if one pilot left his death-grip on the controls the other would not have been able to hold the plane long enough for anyone to get out. "I asked the crew if they wanted to bail out while we held it or ride it down. They all agreed to stick it out." Rorer and Schovanec considered a belly landing at the first flat piece of terrain they could find. As they looked for such a place, they spotted the British airbase at Fano in the distance and decided to try for a wheels-down landing there. "The first thing to find out was would it glide? Back came the power and we slowly lifted the nose; after several tries we found it would only glide at 180 miles an hour, which was fast in any man's book."

They managed to turn to make a long straight-in approach to the field, holding full power and waiting as long as possible to lower the gear. "We touched down at 180 and got on the brakes as soon as the nose wheel was on the ground. The plane swerved from side to side, and threatened to collide with the tower at the last moment, but somehow we got stopped before we ran out of runway."

Everyone had been calm and collected throughout the emergency, but once the plane was on the ground, Rorer found himself shaking as he climbed down the ladder. The men examined the Mitchell and shook their heads in disbelief at what they found. The right rudder was useless and the underside of the fuselage was bashed in at the rear hatch and bent at an angle to the right so that the tail no longer lined up with the rest of the plane. The aft section of the right engine nacelle had been sheared off completely by Iverson's propeller, and, worst of all, about a square foot of rubber had been cut from the right main tire. It was a miracle the tire hadn't come off in the landing. For his Herculean effort in saving his plane and crew, Second Lieutenant Rorer was awarded the Distinguished Flying Cross.

Having secured Croce and Montescudo, the Eighth Army's left wing advanced to the frontier of the city-state of San Marino, which had been occupied by the Germans a week earlier. San Marino fell on September 19 with relatively light cost. But the Marecchia Valley, three miles north, running across the line of advance to Rimini, was a defensible position that the Germans could fall back to.

On the next day the Canadians broke the German positions on the Ausa River and moved onto the Lombardy Plain, and the 3rd Greek Mountain Brigade entered Rimini on the morning of September 21. Then the Germans withdrew from the Rimini Line to new positions on the Marecchia River. At this point the weather changed for the worse with the onset of heavy autumn rains, which came in unexpected torrents. Kesselring's dogged defense had won the day. The Commonwealth forces' advance became very slow, with roads and tracks closed by mudslides creating a logistical nightmare. While the British Eighth Army was now out of the mountains, the Lombardy Plain was waterlogged. They found themselves confronted by swollen rivers that ran across their line of advance and prevented their armor from exploiting the breakthrough, just as had happened the previous autumn. The infantry had to grind their way forward while German Tenth Army commander von Vietinghoff withdrew behind the Uso River a few miles beyond Rimini. These positions were finally forced on September 26, and on September 29 the British reached the Fiumicino River, where four days of torrential rain forced a halt; the British V Corps was fought out and required major reorganization.

Since the beginning of Operation Olive five weeks earlier, Eighth Army had suffered fourteen thousand casualties, which meant a reduction in the strength of British battalions from four to three rifle companies. The Germans had suffered sixteen thousand casualties.

At the outset of the fall offensive, Fifth Army consisted of three corps: U.S. IV Corps on the left included the U.S. 1st Armored Division, the South African 6th Armored Division, and two Regimental Combat Teams (RCT): the 370th RCT of the U.S. 92nd Infantry Division and the Brazilian 6th RCT from the Brazilian Expeditionary Force. U.S. II Corps in the center was composed of the U.S. 34th, 85th, 88th, and 91st Infantry divisions, supported by three tank battalions. The British XIII Corps, which contained the British 1st Infantry Division, British 6th Armored Division, 8th Indian Infantry Division and 1st Canadian Tank Brigade, was on the right. Fifth Army, like Eighth Army, was strong in armor but short on infantry, which put them at a disadvantage vis-à-vis their German opponents, considering the terrain they had to fight in.

Facing Fifth Army were five divisions of General Joachim Lemelsen's Fourteenth Army, which had been badly mauled during the summer retreat and was not of the same quality as the Tenth Army: *20.Luftwaffefelddivision, 16.SS Panzergrenadierdivision, 65. and 362.Infantriedivision*, and *4.Fallschirmjägerdivision*. Both the *20.Luftwaffefelddivision* and *356.Infantriedivision* had been moved to the Adriatic front at the end of the first week in September. And on the western end of the line were two divisions of the Tenth Army: *356.Infantriedivision* and *715. Infantriedivision*.

Of the American units, the most problematic was the 92nd Infantry Division, commanded by Major General Edwin L. "Ned" Almond, who had been specifically chosen in 1942 by Army Chief of Staff General George C. Marshall to form and lead the division, which was composed of African-American troops. The soldiers were called "Eleanor Roosevelt's Running Riflemen" by the Southern white officers Almond had placed in command of every unit from platoons on up; they ran the division like a plantation of the Jim Crow South. The 92nd had participated in the battles around Cassino without success, on account of the racial division and white supremacy that permeated the unit. But Almond himself placed responsibility for the lack of success on the African-American GIs and would, after the war, be one of the few senior Army generals to argue in favor of maintaining segregation in the armed forces. (In July 1950, the formerly segregated 24th Infantry Division—still primarily composed of African-American GIs even after President Truman's order desegregating the Armed forces—would meet disaster when it was fed into Korea to block the invading North Koreans. The men, never properly trained, fought and died in rice paddies opposing hardened troops. Almond, by then chief of staff to General Douglas MacArthur and the man responsible for the training—or rather the lack of training—of the division, would once again blame the men for his own command failures.)

The plan of attack in Operation Olive involved a strike by II Corps along the road from Florence to Firenzuola and Imola through the Il Giogo pass, which would outflank the formidable defenses of the Futa pass on the main Florence-Bologna road, with British XIII Corps advancing on the right through the Gothic Line to cut Route 9 at Faenza—and thus cut Kesselring's lateral communications. The defenses around the Il Giogo pass, which marked the boundary between the Tenth and Fourteenth Armies, were potentially an area of weakness. And that weakness was exacerbated by the transfer of *356.Infateriedivision.*

At the same time that Eighth Army commenced Operation Olive on the Adriatic front, U.S. II Corps and British XIII Corps moved into the mountains to take position for the main assault. German outposts put up fierce resistance, but the Allied advance following the withdrawal of three German divisions to reinforce the Adriatic front forced the Germans to withdraw to the main Gothic Line defenses.

After an artillery bombardment, Fifth Army's main assault commenced at dusk on September 12. The advance at II Giogo Pass was slow, but with British XIII Corps making better progress, General Clark diverted the 337th Infantry, which had been held in reserve to exploit the British success. On September 17 the unit fought its way onto Monte Pratone, three miles east of Il Giogo Pass and a key Gothic Line position.

And II Corps renewed the assault on Monte Altuzzo, which dominated the east side of the pass. Both these positions fell the morning of September 17, after five days' fighting. On September 18, the 8th Indian Division fought through trackless ground to capture the heights of Femina Morta, while the 6th Armored Division took San Godenzo Pass on Route 67 to Forlì. The Germans' formidable Futa Pass defenses were outflanked and on September 22 they were forced to fall back and leave the pass to the British after only light fighting. On the left, the Fifth Army had fought their way to the main Gothic Line. In its sector, the 370th Regimental Combat Team (RCT) of the 92nd Infantry Division had pushed the Germans beyond Highway 12 to Gallicano. And the Brazilian 6th RCT had taken Massarosa, Camaiore, and other small towns. By September 30, the Brazilians had taken Monte Prano and controlled the Serchio Valley region without suffering major casualties. In October the Brazilians also took Fornaci and Barga while the 370th, reinforced by units from the 365th and 371st RCTs, held the left wing sector on the Ligurian Coast.

Although Fifth Army was through the Gothic Line, the troops found the terrain and defenders beyond it even more difficult. Between September 21 and October 3, the U.S. 88th Division fought its way to a standstill on the route to Imola, losing 2,105 men killed and wounded—casualties that equaled the losses of the entire rest of II Corps in breaching the Gothic Line.

U.S. II Corps pushed steadily through Raticosa Pass to reach Monghidoro, 20 miles from Bologna, by October 2. At this point, the weather intervened as it had on the Adriatic front. Air support was impossible because of rain and low clouds, while the rain turned the roads to the ever more distant supply dumps near Florence into morasses. Back on Corsica, the men of the 57th Wing turned in their lightweight summer gear and were issued winter uniforms. Only a few missions were flown by any unit throughout the month of October, and the majority of missions that did get off the ground were recalled on account of bad weather. As Dan Bowling remembered, "A mission that was scrubbed for weather didn't count for your total to finish a tour. But try telling your mind and body that it didn't count!"

At Solenzara, the big event of the month was the completion of the group shower facility by the engineers. The war diarist of the 381st wrote that "The gala opening on October 10, complete with abundant hot water which no one had seen since they arrived on the island, was a rousing success."

On October 3, the weather over the Po Valley cleared enough that the bombers could fly missions against the railroad bringing in German reinforcements. Mission 578 saw the 445th and 446th squadrons put up twelve B-25s each, and the 447th squadron eight planes, to attack the Galliate Railroad Bridge in the northwestern Po Valley. Meanwhile, the 447th and 448th squadrons went after the nearby Giotto fuel dump.

The Galliate Bridge was known with dread throughout the bomb groups as a target that was well-defended by "gunners who knew what in hell they were doing," as Dan Bowling later remembered. Each of the groups had attacked it at various times, but the German repair crews were considered by the men to be among the best in Italy, and it never got completely knocked out. Captain Lawrence "Ace" Russell, one of the most respected pilots in the 445th, flew the lead plane in the October 3 Galliate bridge attack, with his bombardier Danny Galindo as Group Lead bombardier. For both men, this would be mission number 70, after which they would go home.

"Ace" Russell, also known as "Iron Man" for his size and physical prowess, was one of the best-liked men in the 321st, particularly among the enlisted men. Crew Chief Fred Lawrence remembered Russell—who had been the original pilot of the first plane on which Lawrence was crew chief after the move to Italy a year earlier—as a man who "became friends to all and was well-liked and respected." While the line between officers and enlisted men was officially rigidly observed throughout the 57th Wing, Russell frequently went to the Enlisted Men's Club. After being admonished about his fraternization with the troops by the 445th squadron's executive officer, "Captain Russell," Lawrence recalled, "kept coming, without his rank, or with greasy buck sergeant overalls, or a GI uniform with no rank at all." When he was finally threatened with being busted to private, Russell reluctantly stopped showing up at the club, but his friendships out on the flight line with those who did the work without the glory never stopped.

The night before the mission, Dan Bowling recalled, there was a high-stakes poker game in his tent, with Russell and Galindo in attendance. When the game broke up around 2300 hours, Russell commented, "Hey Bowling, I bet you wish you were in my boots. In two weeks I'll be home and a war hero because I survived seventy missions." For Bowling the morrow's mission would be only number eighteen—in the thirty days since his first.

The morning of October 3, the crews climbed aboard trucks to ride out to the revetments where their Mitchells waited. Galindo was seated next to Bowling, who remembered his friend commenting that in two weeks he would be back in their mutual hometown of Los Angeles. "I am the only green-eyed Mexican hero in the Air Force!"

The crews manned their planes. Bowling was second element lead in "Pistol Packin' Mama," right behind the three B-25s led by Russell and Galindo in "Scrap Iron."

What the crews hadn't been told at the briefing was that the Galliate bridge was at the moment the most important railroad bridge in the Brenner Pass. Fighter bombers had taken out the rail line north of the bridge, blocking troop trains on their way to Bologna with reinforcements. And the Germans were working overtime with extra crews to repair the track; photo recon flights had revealed they had brought in several new 88-mm guns to defend the vital bridge, in addition to those already on site. On the morning of October 3, 1944, the Galliate railroad bridge was the most heavily defended target in northern Italy.

There was three-tenths cloud cover over the Po Valley as the B-25s droned north-northeast at an altitude of ten thousand feet. The target came into sight, and Russell led the formation in a turn at the IP. Bowling remembered, "Russell and Galindo always had long bomb runs, straight and level for three to four minutes." This type of approach gave the Germans time to put at least six or seven volleys into the air, and the black clouds of flak explosions ahead of the formation of Mitchells were thick.

"Two minutes into the bomb run, my left wingman—Lieutenant Robert Frank—exploded and I could see his co-pilot trying to get out," Bowling remembered. "With thirty seconds to go, Russell's plane pulled up and to the right. I could see their right wingman smoking and also pulling to the right. I told my bombardier Joe Silnutz we were taking lead, and just then Russell radioed they were all bailing out."

Lieutenant Frank's B-25, "Evora," had taken a direct hit by an "88" in the left engine, which exploded and set the gas tanks in the wing on fire. Sergeant Gerald M. Bertling, tail gunner in aircraft 44-28948, the right wing plane of the fourth element of the formation, later reported, "After we began our bomb run we encountered heavy, intense, and accurate flak. A few seconds before the bombs were released, I saw two large pieces of metal fly past our element. I turned in time to see the left wing plane of the first element on fire sliding under the formation and losing altitude quickly. It began to spin and after it lost 3,000 feet, one wing fell away and it began to spin faster. I saw the plane crash and burn a few miles from the target. I did not see any parachutes."

Staff Sergeant William A. Smith, tail gunner of aircraft 43-4008, which was the right wingman in the rear formation, reported, "Just before the bomb release point, I noticed a trail of flame coming from behind our left rudder. The next instant the aircraft came into view. The entire left side of it seemed to be engulfed in flames. Then the plane rolled over on its left side and started downward out of control leaving a trail of burning fragments. I did not observe any parachutes. We then went into a steep bank and I was unable to see the plane in question after we leveled off."

The German graves registration unit reported the crash the following day, noting that one crewman had been seen to attempt to bail out, but his parachute was already on fire. The six Americans were buried in the village cemetery at Novara on October 5.

Russell's B-25 had received a direct hit in the right engine, which burst into flames. He managed to keep his bomber on the run until Galindo could make the bomb drop, after which the plane fell out of formation and began to lose altitude quickly. Bowling's co-pilot, Second Lieutenant Harold L. Cox, later reported,

> Approximately five seconds before the bomb release point, Captain Russell's bomber received a flak hit in the right engine. There was a burst of flame which went out immediately, followed by gray smoke. The plane jerked sharply to the right and left formation several times, but he kept it under control until the bombs were away. As we broke away from the target, Captain Russell completed a 180 degree turn and went off to our right. At this time he had not feathered the right engine. After making our 180 degree turn, I observed Captain Russell's plane under control and holding altitude well, but the right engine was still smoking. As we turned to the left, it appeared as if Captain Russell was turning to follow. He was in the vicinity of Novara. Approximately 30 seconds after we completed our turn on course, Captain Russell called, saying "Anyone in the Drybeef formation. This is 740. I'm going down." I was on VHF at the time and heard his call loud and clear. Immediately I asked for his position. His only reply was "This is 740 going down." I called again for his position but received no answer.

Bowling and his bombardier Joe Silnutzer made an accurate drop on the bridge. "We pulled up and broke right and I noticed solid flak at our previous position. There were two close explosions I could hear over the engines, followed by the sound of hail on a tin roof as we were showered with shrapnel." The shrapnel damaged the rudder controls, leaving only the trim tabs for directional control, and the hydraulic system was hit and lost all pressure. There were several large holes in the wings. When he arrived back at Solenzara, Bowling orbited to allow the other damaged aircraft, with wounded aboard, to land first. After he landed, Bowling and his crew counted sixty-four holes in "Pistol Packin' Mama." "She was reconditioned with patches everywhere, so many in fact that her new nickname was 'Patches.'"

Of the twelve B-25s from the 445th squadron, two were lost, seven were hit by flak, and four aircrewmen on two different planes were wounded. The survivors had made a 100 percent drop with the squadrons following them making accurate drops, knocking out the bridge. It was the toughest mission the squadron had flown yet.

The loss of Russell and Galindo, as well as of Captain Robert Casaburi, the squadron lead navigator, Sergeants William Hickey and John Plott, and Corporal Joseph Tronolone—a mechanic who had volunteered as a gunner to get the chance to go home—affected the rest of the squadron deeply, since all were "old hands" in the unit. On November 11, 1944, Second Lieutenant John Martin, Russell's co-pilot, returned to the squadron after evading capture to report that Russell, Galindo, and the rest had all survived and been taken prisoner by the Germans after they narrowly escaped being lynched by a mob of Italian Fascists.

U.S. II Corps renewed the offensive toward Bologna on October 5, supported by the British XIII Corps. Progress was gradual, against stiffening opposition. On October 9, II Corps attacked the massive fifteen-hundred-foot-high sheer escarpment behind Livergnano. It was finally secured five days later.

Following the Galliate mission, rain closed down air operations for fourteen days. Crew Chief Fred Lawrence recorded in his diary that he learned to play pinochle during the long confinement to tents: "The bad weather confined us to our tents, playing cards, writing letters, much reading was done, as the heavy rains made a mud hole of our tent area. The club would open at night, but the drinkers tired of that, and were content to sit by the fireplace, swapping stories, listening to our jukebox, playing ping-pong or shooting craps."

By the second half of October, it was clear that despite the determined battles in the waterlogged Romagna Plain and the mountains of the central Apennines, exhaustion and combat losses were increasingly affecting the Allied ground forces' ability to continue the offensive. No breakthrough was going to happen before the winter weather returned. Generals Alexander and Clark decided to make a last push for Bologna before winter gripped the Apennines.

On the Adriatic front, the 10th Indian Infantry Division crossed the Fiumicino River (believed to be the river known to the Romans as the Rubicon) and turned the German defensive line, forcing a pullback by the Tenth Army units downstream towards Bologna. This actually helped Kesselring, since it shortened his defensive front and reduced the distance between his two armies, giving him a better opportunity to switch units between the two fronts.

British V Corps crossed the Savio River on October 9. By the end of October, Eighth Army's advance reached Forlì, halfway between Rimini and Bologna. On October 16, Fifth Army made a last effort to take Bologna. The Allies in Italy were now short of artillery shells because of a global reduction in ammunition production in anticipation of imminent German defeat. Fifth Army's artillery batteries were rationed so strictly that the total rounds fired in the last week of October were less than the total fired during one eight-hour period on October 2. U.S. II Corps and British XIII Corps fought on for the next eleven days, making little progress along the main road to Bologna. But there was better progress on the right. On October 20, the U.S. 88th Division took Monte Grande, four miles from Route 9; three days later the British 78th Division was atop Monte Spaduro. Unfortunately, the last four miles to Bologna were over difficult terrain and were defended by three of the best German Divisions in Italy: *29.Panzergrenadierdivision*, *90.Panzergrenadierdivision*, and *1.Fallschirmjägerdivision*, which Kesselring had withdrawn from the Romagna. On October 29, the advance of the Brazilian 6th RCT was halted at Barga.

Just over a week earlier, on October 20, the 321st group had been ordered to attack the Galliate railroad bridge again. The Germans had made a determined effort to repair the bridge and were close to making it operational, so that troop trains could get through to give needed reinforcements to the Fourteenth Army defending Bologna. The announcement of the target by Group Operations Officer Captain Jeffrey Lynn was met with shock by the assembled crews, many of whom had been on the devastating mission of October 3 to the same target. As members of the group who would participate in the Battle of the Brenner Pass later observed, their battle was a struggle between the bombers and the German engineers responsible for repairs, so that repeat bombings of the same targets were necessary. Dan Bowling remembered that many planes were full of shrapnel holes from flak on their return to Solenzara from this second mission against the bridge, but there were no losses and all crews returned unharmed. Again the bridge was reported knocked out. The good weather that followed the raid allowed the bombers, along with the P-47 fighter-bombers of the 57th Fighter Group, to go after the troop trains in the pass the next day.

The buildup of the 1st Brazilian Division to full strength and the reinforcement of the 92nd Division had not nearly compensated Fifth Army for the units sent to France. The situation in the Eighth Army was worse: replacements were now diverted to northern Europe, while the Canadian Corps had been ordered to prepare for shipment to the Netherlands in February 1945.

While Fifth Army continued its attempt to dislodge the Germans from the well-placed artillery positions that had been key in preventing the Allied advance towards Bologna and the Po Valley, they had only limited success. The German defenses around Monte Castello, Monte Belvedere, Della Toraccia, Castelnuovo di Vergato, Torre di Nerone, La Serra, Soprassasso, and Castel D'Aiano still held.

For the crews of the 57th Wing, their targets throughout the campaign of the previous six months had primarily been road and railroad bridges, which presented the smallest of pinpoint targets and demanded the highest results in precision bombing. In the 445th squadron, bombing results in September, October, and November during the Gothic Line campaign were 94.5 percent over the three months, the best in the wing. The results in all three groups were over 92 percent for the period. The Corsica B-25s were the most accurate bomber units in the Mediterranean Theater.

The main factor behind the steady increase in bombing accuracy could be summed up by the old line, "practice makes perfect." Whenever pilots and bombardiers were not flying missions, bombardiers were involved in training on the ground with the Norden bombsight simulator, while pilots put in time in the Link trainer to increase their ability to fly on instruments. On clear days, formations of B-25s bombed the small nearby islands with practice bombs to get the simultaneous "drop on lead" perfected. The 57th Wing's *nom de guerre* "The Bridgebusters" was now backed by a demonstrated record of achievement.

At the end of October, the fall rains in the Alps turned to snow, heralding the arrival of the coldest European winter in a century. It was clear the Allied armies were not strong enough to overcome the well-supplied Germans, who were receiving 24,000 tons—600 percent of their minimum daily requirements—shipped from Munich and Augsburg by rail through the Brenner Pass to Bologna, the main German supply center. Even after the bombing missions that had been flown against the rail line over the summer, a train from Augsburg still took less than twelve hours to arrive in Bologna on most days. Large-scale offensive operations were impossible until the spring thaw that would not come to the Alps until April 1945; during the intervening winter months, some way had to be found to reduce the enemy's strength.

ELEVEN

KEEP 'EM FLYING

Throughout the 57th Wing, all maintenance was performed outdoors at the individual aircraft revetments. When it wasn't raining on Corsica, it was dry and blowing dust got into everything, most particularly engines; eventually there was only so much repair work that could be done to an engine before it had to be changed. When a crew chief faced an engine change, he never lacked for help. As Tech Sergeant Fred Lawrence remembered, "Six or eight of the other mechanics would come to your plane and split into teams, and within four to six hours we had that engine off and the replacement on, and we were ready for a test hop. We shared our time and talent with whoever needed it."

Following the *Luftwaffe*'s visit to Alesani, all the groups took camouflage more seriously. While many of the new silver Mitchells that began arriving in the groups around the time of the move to Corsica were given a coat of camouflage paint over their upper surfaces following that event, there was not enough paint on Corsica to meet the demand.

Unpainted airplanes still needed to be camouflaged; thus the arrival of camouflage netting. Crew chief Frank Dean of the 310th group remembered well the effort expended on these nets:

> My crew, Harry Drake and Sid Honing, welcomed their new plane with its practically-new engines and low-time airframe, thinking it would not require the maintenance that the old one had. With each new ship, there came camouflage nets and a lot of back-breaking work, for it took four nets to cover one plane: one for the tail, one for each wing, and one for the fuselage. They were especially difficult to drape over two propellers and the vertical stabilizers that were sixteen feet off the ground. Teetering on our single six-foot wooden stepladder, while trying to muscle an armload of awkward, heavy netting to another mechanic who was trying to keep from being pulled from the slippery aluminum surface of the airplane led to the development of new and unusual curse words.
>
> Because of the need to cover the shining aircraft, each night we looked upon the painted planes with envy and longing. We resented the nets, the time required to cover the bomber, the time to remove them, to fold them and stack them out of the way. They lay beside the dispersal area as a hated reminder they would have to be put back on again in the evening. Hated still more were the times when the dew and rains made them heavier, muddy, and more difficult to handle. We would finish our chores and arrive late at the mess kitchen along with other wet, muddy, angry mechanics who shared our misfortune, and all too often arrived after the squadron's allotment of steak or fresh hamburger ran out. Our hatred for the nets fell on deaf ears and it was not until the last few months of the war that it was safe to leave our planes uncovered. We called down wrath and wished the most unspeakable punishment on those who had advocated unpainted bombers.

While the aircrews were eligible to return home after a tour defined by the number of missions flown, and could get sent to Capri for relief after tough missions, there was no "tour" or other relief for the ground staff, who might get a few days off here and there, primarily limited to the island of Corsica. By the late summer of 1944, obvious morale problems led to ground crews members' getting the chance for a day or two in Rome or Naples when they won a lottery for passes, with the men flown to and from their vacation by a B-25. Eventually, when the group had been together for eighteen months, with air crews rotating home while ground crews remained, a lottery system was established that sent one ground crew member home on rotation each month, while another got a week at a rest camp.

Dan Bowling had cause to remember a trip to Rome in February 1945 to pick up crewmen from their leave.

> We took the squadron rum runner, which was devoid of armor and armament, along with the rum runner from the 446th squadron. We were supposed to meet the guys at 1400 hours for the flight back to Corsica, but at the allotted time, no one showed up. At 1630, it was getting late and we were not supposed to return to Corsica after dark since the strips weren't lighted for night landings. The plane from the 446th finally left. I knew those ground crews were going to be in real trouble if they weren't at muster in the morning, with guys getting busted for overstaying their pass. We decided to wait. Finally, as the sun was setting around 1715 hours, fifteen drunks showed up. We stuffed them in the airplane, which made us dangerously overloaded, and cranked up. I gave it full throttle on takeoff, and we took nearly the entire runway to get off the ground, and then we were tail-heavy and I had to get some of them to climb over the bomb bay and get in the nose for weight distribution, while we were trying to climb out over Rome. I could see Saint Peter's right in front of the nose. We were absolutely forbidden to fly over the Holy

City, but I was too low to turn away. So there we were, flying right over the Pope and everyone. I knew we were going to be in trouble.

They arrived at Solenzara two hours later in the darkness. Fortunately, the sky was clear and the moon was full. "I was able to pick out the field in the moonlight, and we got down safe." Bowling convinced his superiors not to punish the sergeants from the 445th, but he learned the next day that the sergeants of the 446th were going to be brought up on charges for overstaying their leaves. "I went over to the Operations Office for the 446th and managed to convince them that we all were alive because of the dedication of the ground crews, and that punishing them like this was only going to harm morale for no purpose." Bowling's argument carried the day.

The most difficult event for any ground crewman was the loss of his airplane and the crew. Over the time they spent together, aircrew and ground crew grew close, knowing that the lives of the aircrews were in the hands of the mechanics and armorers who ensured that their airplane worked. Ground crew chief Fred Lawrence lost his first aircrew in the fall of 1943 when they failed to return from the mission to Athens for which the 321st group would later receive their first Presidential Unit Citation. After that, as four crews came, served their tour flying his airplane, and rotated home, "I never made friends with combat crews, as I had my first crew, who were shot down and killed. I had a great deal of respect for them, but I didn't want the hurt and sadness of another lost or killed crewmember affecting me, as it had before."

When a formation returned from a mission, those on the ground would count the number of planes and search intently for their plane. Lawrence felt that the toughest thing he experienced after the loss of his first crew was seeing an empty space in a returning formation and thinking of the ground crew and what they would go through over the loss. "Then there was the equal sense of helplessness when one of our planes came bellying in, skidding, sliding, twisting, as the pilot tried desperately to control the plane, to insure no injuries to his crew. We prayed there would be no fire. All would dash to the plane, emergency crews, fire, ambulance, jeeps, would make a rush to the crashed plane to pull wounded or other crewmen from the wreckage."

Ground crews never knew when what appeared to be a standard operation could turn into a full-out emergency in an instant. That summer of 1944, one B-25 landed on the uneven PSP runway at Solenzara, with fuel sloshing inside the plane from flak damage. As the plane bounced on the runway, the fuel sloshed against an electrical wire and exploded in fire before the Mitchell came to a stop. Armorer Bernard Seegmiller recorded in his diary what happened:

> About 1000 hours today as a group of us were busy working on my plane we heard a sliding crash and explosion. We knew it was a plane and we started running for the runway, which was obscured from us by a narrow belt of brush.... I emerged from the brush to see the plane just bursting into flames.... At first there was no sign of survivors and I began to slacken my pace because the ammunition on the plane had commenced exploding. Then I saw a man fall from the pilot's escape hatch and roll frantically upon the ground very near the flames that were coming from the left engine. He appeared to be only semi-conscious as his efforts to save himself were rather undirected. By that time I was running again and only Sergeant Art Hanna was ahead of me. I could see the man's clothes were on fire and began encouraging Hanna, who was carrying a coat on his arm, to hurry and attempt to smother the fire with his coat. I had left my shirt at the plane and was quite empty-handed. An ack-ack battery was set up nearer to the crash than we were and one of the boys had arrived on the scene and was trying uselessly to put the fire out with his hands while the poor fellow staggered and rolled, screaming for someone to put the fire out. I called to the ack-ack boy to use his coat, but he was too excited to hear me. All the while I was running as fast as I could and had overtaken Hanna. I

could see now that it was the pilot's Mae West that was burning and as soon as I reached the spot I told the other boy to give me his coat, which I practically jerked off him. I used my pocket knife to cut off what was left of the burning Mae West. It was no time until the fire was out but the fellow was severely burned. His hair, eyes and nose were a white crisp. Soon the ambulance arrived and took him away. He was conscious and rational and I thought perhaps he would live, but I have heard several rumors that he died.

By the time we had finished, the plane was almost entirely in flames. However if others had arrived the same time we did I think someone could have been gotten out of the radio compartment. After it was all over it occurred to me that there might have been bombs in the plane. I do not feel that what I did was in any sense heroic or other than anyone else would have done, but I am pleased to think I had presence of mind enough to be of some assistance. There were some who did not go near because of the ammunition that was exploding. I went back this afternoon and saw a great many projectiles and cases that could have given one a nasty wound. The corpses of the other five men were lumped among the still burning ashes, all burned beyond recognition.

Sergeants Seegmiller and Hanna were both awarded the Bronze Star for their brave acts.

Tech Sergeant John Sikora, an original member of the 310th group who was there to the end of the war, described the workaday life of the ground crews:

When our plane landed from a mission we always assumed it would be required again just as soon as we could get it ready. In Africa, we never flew more than one mission a day, but it was different on Corsica; you had to assume it would be going out very soon. We started looking over the aircraft as it was taxying into the parking place and usually had a pretty good idea of what damage had been sustained, and how the engines were operating before it stopped rolling. A good mechanic can tell a lot just by listening to an engine run, and the B-25 was so loud it announced to the world if anything was wrong. We jumped on the plane, completed our work as quickly as possible, and reported to the engineering officer that it was ready. We had a friendly competition between the squadrons to see who could maintain the highest in-commission rate, and we worked our tails off to keep our squadron on top. We worked out the problems, and I tell you this, we never let a plane go that we wouldn't have got on and gone along.

And then there were the times when "things just happened." Just because he wasn't flying missions didn't mean a man was safe. As the work tempo increased during the Fourth Battle of Cassino in May, the inherent danger of working with aircraft designed to carry and drop explosives made life even more difficult. Loading bombs was an exercise in "handling eggs," particularly if a bomber had returned from the previous mission with ordnance that hadn't been dropped.

On May 24, 1944, B-25J 43-27483, a Mitchell so new in the squadron she didn't have a name, was being loaded by four privates and two noncoms. Four thousand-pound high-explosive bombs lay in their cart a few feet from the airplane. Weather had forced an abort of the day's mission, and the bomb bay was still filled with bomb clusters: six twenty-pound fragmentation bombs wired together on a steel pipe, three on each end, designed to separate and scatter when dropped. As the men worked to unload the clusters, one of the bands that held three bombs broke loose and the bomblets armed themselves as they tumbled toward the ground. One of the loaders was seen to catch two of them in his arms, but the third hit the runway. The explosion scythed the loading crew, killing five outright and badly wounding the sixth, and the bomber caught fire in its fully fueled wing gas tanks.

As the alarm siren wailed across the field, the squadron ambulance sped toward the fire. Corporal Charlie C. Parker, the driver, and Private John Palsma, the medic, jumped out as the ambulance screeched to a halt and rushed to the injured loader. Bystanders who had taken cover screamed at them to get away because the cart holding the four bombs had just caught fire. Parker and Palsma loaded the wounded man onto their stretcher and ran away as fast as they could. They had gone less than a hundred feet when the four bombs detonated in an earth-shattering explosion that disintegrated what was left of the burning airplane, throwing them and their load to the ground and showering them with pieces of molten shrapnel. The body of the ambulance was blown completely off its frame, leaving only the chassis and steering wheel column. One fourteen-cylinder R-2600 Twin Cyclone engine was later found three hundred yards from the explosion. Somehow, though badly wounded, the medic and driver grabbed the man they had come to rescue and dragged him to safety—only to discover he had been killed in the blast. Six men were dead, with Parker and Palsma badly wounded. The injuries were so extensive that only three of the six dead could be identified. For their courageous disregard of their own safety, Parker and Palsma were each awarded the Soldier's Medal; most men in the group believed they deserved far more than the lowest award that could be given. Armorer Robert Silliman remembered that "there was never a loading operation you did where you didn't know that the slightest mistake would likely be fatal."

The rule in the 310th group was that when an engine was changed one of the men who had participated in the change had to go along on the test flight. This was a way of ensuring that everyone on the crew paid attention to his assignment, since one of them would be required to stake his life on his work. Tech Sergeant Maurice Guichard was in charge of engine changes in the 381st squadron and had reason to recall one test flight in particular in August 1944 at Ghisonaccia. "I performed the preflight and when the crew came out, there was the Squadron Commander. This man was a high time B-25 pilot, so there was no question as to his ability." The pilot, co-pilot, radio operator, and Sergeant Guichard climbed aboard. "The engines were checked and, as before, they were smooth as silk." Guichard took position just behind the pilots, where he could hear the engines and monitor the gauges. They taxied out to the strip, checked the magnetos on each engine, and with all indications good, proceeded to take off. "We started our climb and everything was OK. The pilot instructed the co-pilot to pull up the gear. Down came his left hand to unlatch the down locks but before he even touched the latch, the aircraft swerved to the left violently." The B-25 was just over the treetops. Guichard glanced at the instruments and saw the fuel pressure on the left engine was falling off. In an instant it was at zero. He shouted to the pilot "feather the left engine!" The squadron commander was too busy trying to keep the airplane under control, but the co-pilot hit the feathering button. The left engine came back to life with a roar, and the Mitchell leveled off. The pilot immediately pulled back both throttles and put the plane back on the ground. With both pilots standing on the brakes, it took all the available runway to stop, but they made it.

"I was scared more than I had ever been before and thought for sure we bought the farm. We taxied back in almost complete silence, the pilot saying only what had to be said in the operation of the plane." When they climbed out, the squadron commander told Guichard "In all the flying I've done, that's as close as I've come to a crash." When Guichard went to check the engine, he found that the carburetor bleed plug had come off, causing the fuel starvation.

In an incident in December 1944, the ground crews were reminded once again that the smallest mistake could have enormous consequences. Armorer Sergeant Richard Dexter and an assistant were bore sighting the turret guns of a B-25, with Dexter standing on the plane's wing while the assistant worked inside the turret. A .50 caliber round that had been left in one of the guns accidentally discharged when the assistant touched the trigger with his elbow. The bullet hit Dexter in his abdomen, and he was dead before he hit the ground. Dexter had been very popular among his fellows, and his death was taken hard by all.

Sergeant Lawrence had one unnerving experience in February 1945. Walking down the flight line to his B-25, he passed an aircrew boarding an airplane. Shortly after he arrived at his own revetment, "I saw a big column of black smoke, coming from somewhere in the vicinity of the revetments I had just passed." Lawrence ran toward the smoke, only to be met by the flight crew he had seen boarding the plane running in the opposite direction, yelling about fire and bombs going to explode. "I flagged down an armament jeep just coming down the taxi strip, and hollered to them to hit the deck. At that instant, a terrific blast shattered my eardrums as I hit the ground. Debris rained all around us as we covered our heads with our hands."

It was later learned that the fire had been started by a discarded cigarette, which had ignited a small pool of avgas (aviation gasoline) that was left on the ground where a ground crewman had been washing parts. The flightline chief, Sergeant Wendell Bell, climbed into the bomber, which was loaded with four thousand-pound bombs, full fuel, and ammunition for the eight guns, which had already caught fire. Bell started it up and taxied the plane across the strip—then extinguished the onboard fire. Other bombs that had been rolled to the side of the revetment after an order to change loads did catch fire and cause an explosion. Lawrence described the aftermath: "Damage wasn't that bad, one man was slightly injured from a piece of shrapnel, though he was some distance away."

The ground crews were particularly proud when their airplanes set operation records for flying missions without mechanical aborts. While the operational life of many B-25s might not be more than five to ten missions before they fell prey to German flak or the horrid weather in the Alps, there were bombers like the old B-25D "Idaho Lassie," which led a charmed existence through a South Atlantic crossing and 150 missions without an abort. Another "original" B-25D, "Poopsie," made it to 125 missions, flying her last against the Gothic Line defenses in September 1944, after which the bomber was flown back to the states for a bond tour, with visits to training bases to inspire trainee mechanics. Sergeant Lawrence was proud to note in his diary in October of the same year that his B-25J, "Peggy Lou," had flown her hundredth mission since arriving in the group back in May. Tech Sergeant Lawrence was recommended for a Bronze Star for his plane's record, but he never received it because the squadron engineering officer, a captain who had been with the unit for a month and a half, refused to sign the necessary paperwork unless he also received an award. "It would have been nice to show the medal to my folks," Lawrence remembered, "but let's face it, there were more deserving men at the front, who had risked a hell of a lot more than I. At least that pipsqueak Captain didn't get it." By the end of the war, after surviving the worst the Germans could throw at her, "Peggy Lou" would have 137 bomb symbols painted on her nose, never having turned back for a mechanical failure; she was definitely "Lucky 13," her plane-in-squadron number.

The all-time record for operational survival in the 445th squadron was held by Dan Bowling's B-25J "Pistol Packin' Mama," appropriately known to the ground crews as "Patches." By the time she was taken off operations in March 1945, "Patches" had flown more than two hundred missions, had bellied in four times, and bore the scars of four hundred flak hits. The airplane had been bent so many times that it flew with eight degrees of left aileron trim and six degrees of right rudder. When trimmed, "Patches" flew with a profound bias that eventually led to her retirement since it was deemed "unsightly" for the first six planes of a formation to be flying straight and true while the remainder flying behind "Patches" were trimmed up in a crab and practically flying sideways. That the plane survived as she did was a tribute to the inherent toughness of the B-25 as a design—and to the dedication of the ground crews to "keep 'em flying."

While aircrews had a mission "tour," after which they would be rotated home, the ground personnel were originally considered to be there for the duration. When the monthly lottery for ground crew members to go home was instituted to build morale, the crews would each contribute a dollar to the "pot" for the lucky winner and the squadron executive officer would draw a name from a hat. When operations went into "high gear," as during the Gothic Line offensive when the ground crews put in twenty-hour days, the lotteries were held twice a month if the arrival of replacements made that possible.

In addition to keeping the planes in good working order, there was another duty of the ground support echelon that was crucial to the maintenance of morale on Corsica. Napoleon put it well when he said, "An army marches on its stomach." While there was not much that could be done about living situations on the bases beyond the individual efforts of tent mates to scrounge wood for floors and walls, the leadership of the 57th Wing did do their best to apply Napoleon's adage; B-25s from all three bomb groups were sent out across the Mediterranean, from Cairo to Palermo to Tunis to Oran, in search of deals to be made for food and drink, even during periods of heavy operations such as those that preceded the invasion of southern France. On August 13, the 340th group war diarist recorded, "The Catania Mission returned partially successful with a total of 200 Litres of assorted beverages for the Enlisted Men's Club and an endless assortment of fresh vegetables including some 1800 eggs for headquarters' mess."

Each squadron had an older B-25 that had seen better days and had been taken off operations. These airplanes were stripped of unnecessary operational gear and used as transports, flown by men going on rest leave to Naples or Sicily or as far afield as Cairo, and then they were flown back to Corsica by crews returning from leave. Eventually the planes came to be known as "rum runners." It was the assignment of each crew going on leave to take the opportunity to buy whatever they could of alcoholic beverages, foodstuffs, and so forth to fill the "rum runner" on their return flight.

These operations were strictly "off the books," though everyone in authority from General Knapp on down knew of and supported them. Any crew that might run into trouble with some hard-headed rear area supply officer or military policeman had only to put in a call to 57th Wing HQ, where if necessary Knapp himself would vouch for the orders the men were operating under. In the 445th squadron, supply Master Sergeant Gene Graf was in charge of coordinating the "rum running." The monthly dues men paid for membership in the Enlisted and Officers' Clubs were pooled and given to the senior man of the leave crew for use in his "shopping trip." There was a similar system in each squadron. In the 340th Bomb Group, 1st Lieutenant Ben Kanowski, a pilot with the additional assignment of mess officer, gained a solid reputation for coming up with items for trades, for an encyclopedic knowledge of where markets for such trades were to be found, and for knowing whom to deal with throughout the Mediterranean Theater.

Recalling the flights of the "rum runners," 380th squadron bombardier Sterling Ditchey explained, "Being a member of an overseas Army Air Corps flying organization, there seemed to always be old 'war weary' aircraft on station, and with pilots available to fly them. So people like myself, during an R-and-R (Rest and Recuperation), were treated with trips to places that we never had dreamed we would see: Cannes, France; Tripoli and Benghazi, Libya; Rome, Naples and Catania, Italy; Cairo, Egypt; and Tel Aviv, Jerusalem and Bethlehem, Palestine. I returned home at the end of my tour with a very genuine sense of just how big the world was, that I had not had before." Like many young Americans in Rome, Ditchey visited Saint Peter's to receive communion from Pope Pius XII, who performed the ceremony daily for the Allied troops. Ditchey was one of the few who climbed the stairs in the dome of Saint Peter's to stand in the cupola atop the famous dome.

Radioman-gunner Jerry Rosenthal recalled one young private who came into the 381st squadron in the spring of 1945 as a replacement in the ground echelon. When asked what his aptitude and abilities were, the private mentioned that he had a brother in the Navy who was currently a lieutenant commander in charge of the Navy Supply Depot in Naples. "That kid was promptly promoted to Sergeant and given an assignment that required him to fly down to Naples at least every other week if not more often and remain overnight. Our rum-runner always came back fully loaded with proof the Navy really did have the best chow." Milo Minderbinder was an exaggeration of how the wing supported itself, but the ability of some to "make deals" made the work of the rest easier than it might have been.

TWELVE

OPERATION BINGO

Most famous of the passes through the Alps that separate Austria from northern Italy, the Brenner Pass is also the lowest, at 4,511 feet. Its possession has long been coveted since it can be kept open in the winter without undue hardship. Before there were roads, the Brenner was the primary invasion route from the north into Italy. Hannibal's elephants passed through in 218 BC. In 268 AD the Alemanni used the pass to cross into Italy, where they were stopped at the Battle of Lake Benacus. The road through the Brenner Pass was just a track for mule trains and carts until a carriage road was constructed in 1777 at the behest of Hapsburg empress Maria Theresa. The railway was completed in 1867—the only transalpine rail route without a major tunnel.

During World War II the pass was the main supply route for German forces in Italy. With the best Allied units withdrawn for service in France, the remaining force had proven too weak to crack the Gothic Line before the onset of winter. If there was to be a breakthrough, German supplies and reserves had to be greatly reduced. Twenty-four thousand tons of supplies were flowing through the Brenner each day, six times the minimum daily requirement for the Germans. Even after bombing missions against the railway over the summer, the trip from Munich to Bologna took only eight to twelve hours.

With the Allied armies unable to operate effectively on the Italian mainland during the winter, only airpower would be able to reduce the German supplies. General Knapp put his planning section to work devising a plan of attack.

Three main rail lines from Munich and Augsburg fed down to Innsbruck, Austria, the northern end of the pass, then south through the pass to Verona, where they branched out east, west, and south into the Po Valley, with the main lateral line from Verona east to Vicenza and west to Milan and Turin, while three single-track lines ran south to end at Bologna, the main supply point for the forces in the Gothic Line facing Fifth and Eighth armies. The electrified double-track Brenner Pass rail line meant the Germans did not have to use their coal-fired trains or divert dwindling coal supplies to the southern front. Seventy-two trains a day ran through the route. If their electrical power supply could be destroyed, the Germans would be forced to replace the electric locomotives with steam locomotives, requiring diversion of locomotives and crews from elsewhere in German-controlled Europe at a time when the entire German rail system was under attack. And shipping space in the trains would have to be diverted to bringing coal to power the replacement trains.

The Allied planners believed that if the electric power could be cut, the carrying capacity of the line would drop to ten thousand tons a day. While the elimination of the electrical power supply would only bring the supplies the Germans were receiving down to 250 percent of the minimum requirement, there would be little margin for error on the German side. And once the number of trains was reduced, the bombers would be sent against the marshalling yards, the stations along the line, all twenty-four bridges, the storage areas, and the repair depots. Such a campaign would require multiple missions to each target: once it had been hit hard enough to knock it out, it would have to be hit again (and again) in order to keep it knocked out in a race with German repair units. If German repairs were delayed or prevented, the Gothic Line could be cut off over the course of the winter.

The codename for the campaign was Operation Bingo. The four Twelfth Air Force B-25 Bomb Groups based in Corsica would carry out the bulk of the operation, supported by fighter bombers of XII Fighter Command, which would soon become XXII Tactical Air Command. Knapp presented his plan to his old friend General Ira Eaker, with whom he had served on the Mexican border in the years immediately following the First World War. Eaker, now commander of the Mediterranean Allied Air Forces, saw the promise in Knapp's proposal: that the Air Force could actually do such a good job that the ground forces would be able to smash through the remains of the Gothic Line after the thaw in the Alps the next spring and bring the war in Italy to a rapid end.

Second Lieutenant Paul Young arrived on Corsica in early October 1944. A farm boy from Indiana, he had joined the Air Force in 1942 and originally trained as a glider pilot. "However, fortunately for me, they decided in the spring of 1944 that they had enough glider pilots, and I was sent on to powered flight training instead of to the infantry, since I had demonstrated some aptitude as a pilot." On his arrival in Corsica he was assigned to the 445th squadron of the 321st group at Solenzara. "The weather was bad most of that month, but fortunately there was enough clear weather over Corsica that I was able to get in some training and demonstrate to them that I was good at flying the B-25. I was assigned as a co-pilot with the understanding that if I showed I had what it took on operations, I'd be moving up to first pilot pretty quickly."

The opening mission of Operation Bingo would be Paul Young's first mission. "There was no 'sunny Italy' that I ever saw. It was cold and damp on Corsica, which made it hard to sleep through the night in our tents without waking up shivering. Coupled with the fact I had the jitters for my first mission, I had no trouble getting up when they woke us at 0500 hours to get ready."

The 310th Bomb Group was assigned to hit the transformers at San Ambroglio, while the 340th and 321st Bomb Groups would hit those at

Trento and Ala respectively. If these missions were successful, electrical power would be denied to trains as far north as Balzano.

The mission to Ala on Monday, November 6, 1944, was the six hundredth flown by the 321st since their arrival in the Mediterranean Theater twenty months earlier. Captain Gerald Wagner led the nine B-25s of the 445th squadron in B-25J 43-27742, "Vicious Vera," while Paul Young flew his first mission as co-pilot for Second Lieutenant Max Poteete in 43-27741, "Val," which had led "Vicious Vera" down the North American production line at Kansas City the previous spring. The 446th squadron commander, Lieutenant Colonel Paul Cooper, led the nine planes of his squadron, while First Lieutenant Marion Walker led nine from the 447th in "Cover Girl," a B-25 that had arrived in Solenzara shortly before the battle of Cassino in May. Captain Harold Farwell led the nine Mitchells from the 448th squadron in "Out of Bounds," another veteran bomber. All planes were loaded with eight five-hundred-pound high explosive bombs. The transformer itself was a small target; taking it out would call for real skill. But with no flak or fighters over the target, each squadron's lead bombardier was able to zero in on the buildings perfectly. The group war diarist recorded afterwards that the bombing concentrations were so good that it was "pickle barrel bombing," with 100 percent of all bombs falling on the target. The Ala transformer was knocked out completely and not replaced until after the war, when an entirely new one was built.

The 340th reported equally good results at Trento, as did the 310th at San Ambroglio. As predicted, the power outage did affect trains as far north as Balzano, and within days Ultra had picked up reports of a drop in supply delivery to the predicted ten thousand tons, as well as orders to divert coal-fired locomotives. Operation Bingo was off to a roaring start.

The next day, November 7, the campaign against the bridges began. The 321st hit the Sacile Railroad bridge, putting a string of "thousand-pounders" right through its center to chalk up a 97.2 percent bombing concentration for the mission; the center span of the Motta di Livenza Railroad bridge broke away to fall into the river, despite the fact that

5/10 cloud cover prevented six Mitchells of the eighteen sent from dropping their bombs.

Tuesday, November 7, was election day in the United States, with Franklin Delano Roosevelt running for his fourth term against New York Governor Thomas E. Dewey. All the GIs had voted a month previously. While many were concerned at the thought of a president remaining in office for four terms, reluctance to "change horses in mid-stream" in the midst of a world war convinced most men to vote for FDR. For the overwhelming majority of those in the 57th Wing old enough to vote, this vote for FDR was their first. The outcome would not be official until the next day, when Dewey conceded defeat to the president, who had won thirty-six of forty-eight states in the Electoral College.

That Wednesday on Corsica saw all missions canceled because of high winds that blew down several tents at Solenzara. Sergeant Seegmiller wrote in his diary,

> The election is over and everyone seems pretty well satisfied. For my part, I believe it is best for the war effort and especially for the peace settlements to follow, that Roosevelt was re-elected. Otherwise, much hard-earned political ground would have been lost among the United Nations.
>
> For the past several days a terrific wind has annoyed us almost constantly. One night I hardly closed my eyes until 0300 hours for fear the tent would come down on us. At the present time it is rattling and flapping like a loose sail. Oh, for a solid roof once more! Despite the wind, a westerly from off the mountains, the weather is very warm. I did not put on a coat all day today. A huge pine tree blew down on the Swede's tent the other day while everyone was at chow. If he had been in his sack it would have got him for sure.

On Thursday, the winds died down sufficiently to allow missions to take off, but cloud cover over Italy forced the bombers to abort short of their targets. Second Lieutenant Jay DeBoer flew his first mission as co-pilot to Dan Bowling in "Pistol Packin' Mama," while Paul Young flew his second mission as co-pilot for Bowling's wingman, First Lieutenant Sam Monger, in "Miss Belle Fontaine." With fifty-mile-an-hour crosswinds at Solenzara when they returned, the planes were forced to land at the 310th group's base at Ghisonaccia. Sergeant Seegmiller led a group of armorers up to the field to unload bombs, driving the two big trucks in the high winds, a trip he recorded was dangerous.

Friday, November 10, was a tough day for the 321st. Forty-four Mitchells were sent to Ostiglia to bomb the temporary rail bridge and a ferry terminal the Germans had recently completed. Once again, Dan Bowling was the second group lead with Jay DeBoer in the right seat, and Joe Silnutzer working the Norden sight while Phil Starczewski navigated. Paul Young was once again on Bowling's wing with Sam Monger as his first pilot. The bridge was fiercely defended by anti-aircraft guns that shot down the bombers flown by two formation leaders and two other B-25s and holed a total of thirty planes. The 446th squadron lost the second element lead ship, B-25J 43-27732, known as "Leydale," when it was hit in the right engine over the target moments before "bombs away." Pilot First Lieutenant Walton Ligon was hit by a piece of flak that nearly amputated his left arm above the elbow. Co-pilot Captain Gale Dickson took over while Bombardier First Lieutenant Lawrence Clausen applied a tourniquet to Ligon and tried to help him with his parachute after the plane took a second hit. Dickson ordered the crew to bail out. Clausen, navigator First Lieutenant John Chapman, radioman Tech Sergeant Julius Nagy, and tail gunner Staff Sergeant George Glendening managed to bail out, but Ligon and Dickson both went down with the bomber. Turret gunner Staff Sergeant Vernon Bender also jumped, but his parachute failed to open. Despite being wounded, Sergeant Nagy managed to evade capture and link up with Lieutenant Clausen. They were both rescued by partisans while Chapman and Glendening were picked up and became prisoners of war. All the other eleven bombers from the 446th were holed by the intense flak, with crewmen in each plane wounded.

The 447th squadron took heavy losses. First Lieutenant Gorden Ramey's B-25 "Traveling Comedy" was hit by flak and lost an engine. Ramey attempted an emergency landing at Pisa. When the first attempt to land failed, he attempted a go-around. The remaining engine cut out, and the Mitchell crashed into a canal beyond the field. A moment before the crash, three crewmembers bailed out from approximately three hundred feet; only Tech Sergeant Alvin L. Simberg survived when his parachute opened less than fifty feet above ground. Ramey, Lieutenant Albert K. Condit, Lieutenant Edmond E. Bardy Jr., and Corporal Robert Kipp were killed. Navigator Flight Officer Lester Volkmann survived the crash and was rushed to the hospital in serious condition.

"Ready Teddie," the B-25 flown by mission lead pilot Captain Maurice "Wigs" Wiginton, was hit by flak in both main gas tanks, but only one sealed. Flak knocked out the electrical system, preventing the plane from dropping, while avgas fumes from the ruptured tank overcame bombardier First Lieutenant Leeland Messna and prevented a manual bomb drop. Wiginton was able to land "Ready Teddie" on return to Solenzara despite a full bomb load and the fumes filling the plane.

Four additional B-25s, two from the second echelon and one each from the third and fourth echelons, were also lost. All the other B-25s in the formation were holed by flak; four crewmen were killed and twelve others injured.

First Lieutenant Douglas Anderson led eleven Mitchells from the 448th squadron in B-25J 43-27805, "Desirable." Just as he reached the IP, Anderson's B-25 was hit by flak that shot out the left engine. Anderson continued on to the bomb release point as other flak bursts knocked out his hydraulic system, lowering both wheels and flaps and destroying the compass, covering the pilots with shattered plexiglass, and cutting one of the rudder control cables. Douglas and his crew managed to remain airborne for over twenty minutes until tall mountains ahead forced them to abandon ship, with all seven men parachuting safely. Douglas was captured, but the other six managed to find the partisans and were returned to Corsica a month later.

Veteran B-25J 43-4068, "The Duchess," flown by First Lieutenant Milford Kruse, received many hits, one of which knocked out the right engine. Turret gunner Sergeant Nico Pined, bombardier Staff Sergeant Woodward Pealer, and radioman Staff Sergeant Irving Schaffer were wounded, and a burst of flak shot out the hydraulic system, lowering the main gear halfway. Kruse was able to make a successful belly landing back at the 310th group's field at Ghisonaccia.

The 321st had knocked out seven spans of the pontoon bridge. A total of thirty-two aircrewmen were wounded—one of the heaviest losses on any single mission. Paul Young remembered it well. "It was my first mission where the Germans made a serious attempt to kill me. It wasn't easy to sit there as co-pilot and take it as all that flak exploded around us, but in retrospect it was better I had that first experience as a co-pilot where I wasn't responsible for a crew while I put everything I'd heard people say about how to control fear to work."

Sergeant Schaffer had noted in his diary that morning that the weather was "very cold." Throughout the winter of 1944–1945, cold was one of the big factors the men dealt with. Paul Young remembered, "We boarded up the tents as best we could, and we would supplement the coal ration by going out in search parties to cut down trees for fuel. A lot of the guys made stoves that burned avgas. We were cold on the ground, we were cold in the planes. I was just cold all the time."

The B-25 had only limited heating, and the oxygen systems had all been removed because of the fire danger from flak hits. Radioman Staff Sergeant Jerry Rosenthal, who joined the 488th squadron in late November, remembered,

> Anoxia was a big problem, since the missions into the Brenner Pass were generally flown at 11,500 to 15,000 feet. We would take our gloves off to check our finger nails for signs of anoxia even though we couldn't do anything about it. We also got to know all about Aerotitis Media, the inflammation of the inner ear from changes in altitude. The air temperature in the airplane at my station as radioman was around 25 below, and

if you took off your glove and touched anything, you could freeze your skin to whatever it was. The pilots and bombardier and turret gunner in the nose had a couple heaters there that probably got the temperature up to 10 below, as did the tail gunner. But the radioman's position was unheated and drafty since it was right behind the bomb bay.

Rosenthal learned from a veteran he shared a tent with at Alesani how to prepare to face the cold. "I acquired a blue wool electric flight suit, even though there was no electricity available for it in the airplane, but I wore it over my GI long johns, then a wool shirt over that followed by my A2 jacket with a super heavy sheepskin coat over that! Wool socks, then GI shoes with the wonderful sheep lined flying boots over them. I had sheepskin overalls to cover the wool GI pants, and with all that, I was able to prevent frostbite!" He also remembered that in all that gear, movement inside the constricted space of the fuselage "wasn't all that easy."

In addition to the cold, the men in the Mitchells were forced to fight the forces of nature. Turbulent winds swept down from the high Alps at speeds of up to fifty and sixty miles an hour, making accurate bombing more difficult. The mountains on either side of the Brenner Pass were anywhere from eight to ten thousand feet. Second Lieutenant Victor Hanson, 445th squadron co-pilot, recalled a mission when his plane got hit and dropped out of the formation. The pilot turned away from the flak into a box canyon that he discovered was too narrow to turn around in. "We were climbing against the downslope winds that were going down only a little bit slower than we were going up. We were holding maximum power and just barely climbing. All those rocks out in front definitely had my attention as we got closer and closer. In the end, we cleared the ridge by maybe 20 feet. That was my scariest mission and it didn't have anything to do with the Germans."

On January 21, 1945, Jerry Rosenthal lost his friend and tentmate Staff Sergeant Aubrey Porter to a freak accident due to the harsh conditions of mountain flying:

Our mission was to Ora-San Michelle Railroad Diversion. Porter was flying as tail gunner in '8P' which was in the second box flying number three. There was very rough air over the target, the planes were bouncing around very violently with great fluctuations in altitude by each. We made three runs over the target because the bombardiers couldn't get lined up and the flight leader was gung ho. On the third run there was heavy, accurate flak. '8U' was in number six position, directly below '8P.' Just before bombs away, '8U' bounced up and struck the right tail section of '8P' with its left propeller, which cut away the rudder and stabilizer and continued into the tail gunner's compartment and part of the left stabilizer. Porter was actually cut out of the tail! '8U' lost its left wing, fell into a flat spin and went down.

Gil Hartwell, tail gunner of the lead ship, saw the whole thing and reported that "Porter fell through space without a 'chute. I saw his 'chute and 8U's wing fall past us. There were no 'chutes from 8U."

The war diary of the 340th reported, "Second Lieutenant William B. Pelton and his co-pilot, Flight Officer Harry K. Shackelford, of the 488th pulled an aerodynamic miracle this afternoon when they brought their B-25 back from the mission to Ora-San Michelle without its right stabilizer or right elevator. How they landed the plane safely is still bewildering our operations officer and the hundreds of men who saw the damaged craft come in." "8P" was later rebuilt and continued to fly. Porter's body was found and buried by partisans; it was exhumed and re-buried in the American Cemetery at Naples-Anzio after the war.

The Germans were well aware of what the bombers were attempting to accomplish with their missions against the railroad. The last *Luftwaffe* fighter unit had departed Italy following the fall of Rome, leaving the Italian ANR pilots behind with responsibility for air defense. Between October 1944 and February 1945, *2° Gruppo Caccia "Gigi Tre Osei"* was the only ANR fighter unit active in the defense of northern Italy; *1°*

Gruppo Caccia "Asso di Bastoni" had suffered such heavy losses in the Cassino campaign that the unit was withdrawn for training in Germany from October 1944 to February 1945, when it returned to Italy. Throughout the Brenner campaign, the ANR squadrons never had more than forty fighters available at any given time and spent long periods without sufficient fuel available to make an effective defensive effort. This was due to the success of the Eighth Air Force's campaign against the German synthetic oil industry after the surrender of Romania denied the Germans access to the Ploesti oil fields, which had largely been destroyed by the Fifteenth Air Force during the Oil Campaign in the spring and summer of 1944. The last interception missions were carried out on 19 April 1945 when 22 Bf-109s took off to attack the bombers in the Brenner Pass. They were blocked by two squadrons of the Fifteenth Air Force's 322nd Fighter Group, the "Tuskeegee Airmen," and never got close enough to the B-25s for anyone in them to be aware of their presence.

The anti-aircraft artillery never let up. The primary defense was provided by *IV Flakkorps*, with 366 88-mm anti-aircraft guns that had been stationed from Verona to Innsbruck on November 1. The "88" could fire a 9.24 kg (20.34 pound) shell to over forty-nine thousand feet. The Flak-37, a rapid-fire 37-mm weapon, could hit targets at fifteen thousand feet, well above the usual bombing altitude of the B-25s. The batteries used radar tracking for range and optical tracking for direction. German observers were placed on the high mountain peaks to either side of the pass and equipped with transits that allowed them to determine an attacking formation's altitude within five feet. The guns could thus be fired with great accuracy.

Italian forces fought alongside the Germans, equipped with a 90-mm cannon that could hit targets at altitudes up to twenty-six thousand feet, and a 105-mm weapon that reached to forty thousand feet. The Italians had a 37-mm weapon with similar range to the German Flak-37, and a 75-mm cannon that could hit an airplane at twenty-seven thousand feet.

At the end of November, the Germans moved sixty-nine more "88s" into the pass, giving them a total of 435 heavy weapons. By January

1945, batteries were located as far north as Bressanone. In February of that year a flak map with flak positions shown as red dots had a solid red line half an inch wide running from Verona to Innsbruck.

The guns were mobile, and the Germans adopted the tactic of moving them around. Paul Young recalled,

> You'd approach a place where you'd been shot at on a previous mission, and begin to tighten up in expectation of running the gantlet. Only there wouldn't be a single shot! Then, just as you relaxed, two or three would open up from a completely different position and scare the bejesus out of you worse than you'd been anticipating. It got to the point where I was just drum tight from the minute we crossed the bomb line till we flew back into Allied territory.
>
> That anticipation, the fear that built up, took a lot out of you over the long run.

By January 1945, flak positions at altitudes up to three thousand feet had been identified in the mountains to either side of the pass. One battery west of Ala was at forty-one hundred feet, three thousand feet higher than the target. At Rovereto, known as the worst flak trap in Italy, where the bombers could only attack from one direction, the Germans put concrete gun pits halfway up mountainsides in the narrow pass to either side of the town, almost at the bombers' altitude.

In answer to these defenses, antiflak operations became standard, with three antiflak planes leading each formation to drop strips of aluminum foil called "window" to confuse the radar. In January 1945 another weapon was added: white phosphorus. When flak positions were spotted, the anti-flak ships would attack with hundred-pound white phosphorous bombs to burn the gunners, damage the guns, and blow up the unused ammunition. The Germans considered use of white phosphorus to be chemical warfare and announced that any captured bomber crews identified as having used white phosphorus would be summarily executed as war criminals—something that happened to shot-down crews on at least three occasions between February 1945 and the end of the war.

While the leaders of the groups ordered the crews to fly straight and level bomb runs of at least four minutes from the Initial Point to "bombs away," the crews were reluctant to do so because this was enough time for the German gunners to loose several volleys. The bomb run was the time when most shoot-downs and flak hits happened.

Dan Bowling and his bombardier Joe Silnutzer decided to find a way to avoid this exposure to the enemy and still hit the target with an accurate drop. As Bowling recalled, "Joe and I decided that the only way to survive our missions was by performing evasive action. We practiced many times on the bomb range. We would fly a certain compass heading to the practice target circle, then turn ten to fifteen degrees right or left, then change again to a different compass heading and immediately change to the exact course to target. Joe's timing with that Norden sight was so accurate that we would only be thirty to forty seconds straight and level to the target." Shortly after they worked out their evasion tactic, Bowling was made a squadron lead pilot and Silnutzer a squadron lead bombardier. "When I was out front ahead of everyone else, they had to do what I did, so they followed me. I could look out just after we changed course and see a barrage of flak go off right where we would have been had we continued on. Then we'd turn and there would be another barrage go off where we would have been. When we turned on to the bomb run, the gunners were so confused they didn't have the time to put up that last volley before we dropped and broke formation."

Joe Silnutzer was probably the best bombardier in the 57th Wing, and Bowling was one of the top pilots. Only a few other lead crew pilot-bombardier teams tried to emulate their bombing tactic. After 321st group commander Colonel Smith—who was quite open that "I want a star when I leave," and held bombing accuracy to be the key to that event—would give the order at a pre-mission briefing for the crews to fly straight and level for four minutes, Bowling would tell the other pilots in his formation to follow him. "I was proud of two things about the missions I led. One was that we had the highest bombing accuracy of anybody in the group, and the other was that I had the lowest losses on my missions. We got the target and we didn't lose our friends." Eventually 445th squadron commander Colonel Cassidy ceased arguing with Bowling about his tactics. Instead, Bowling received the highest unspoken praise possible: he was the pilot picked to lead the 445th on every tough mission during the worst period of the Battle of the Brenner toward the end of the war.

December saw Twelfth Air Force tactical bombing power reduced to the three groups in the 57th Wing, as the 17th and 320th Bomb Groups moved their eight squadrons of Martin B-26 Marauders to France, while the 319th Bomb Group, which had converted from B-26s to B-25s at the end of October, was notified it would return from Corsica to the States at the end of December to transition to the new Douglas A-26 Invader, which it would take to the Pacific in May 1945. Not only was the 57th Wing left alone on Corsica, but so few replacements had arrived since October that the mission tour had been raised from sixty in October to sixty-five in November and finally to seventy in December. At one point in November the 340th group had forty-five crews qualified to go home, which would leave only twenty-two crews, with no replacements. While many of the men grumbled about this and the war diarist for the 340th Bomb Group wrote about "a severe loss of morale" among the fliers of the group, they gradually became resigned to their fate. Paul Young, who had been made a first pilot in early December, told the 445th's operations officer that he was willing to fly any pilot assignment—first pilot or co-pilot—that came up. "It was the only way I could think of to get all the way to 70 missions and get home." As winter weather reduced the days on which missions could be flown, the strain on the men of trying to get enough missions to go home grew worse.

Interestingly, Joseph Heller, who had been a "loud voice" on the subject of increasing mission total before, is nowhere mentioned in the extensive discussion of aircrew reaction to the increase in missions one finds in the war diary of the 340th group at this time. A review of the mission records shows that Heller flew a mission in the first week of

November and then disappeared from the operational record of the group. Other researchers have speculated that he must have spent the month in his tent. In fact, he did not.

Lieutenant Wilbur Blume, a bombardier with an extensive background in photography, had the previous summer been put in charge of the group photographers, the unofficial "9th Photographic Unit." They accompanied missions to obtain photographs of the results. In all three bomb groups, many of the radiomen were given K-20 cameras and told to "record the results," but the men of Blume's group show up in the records as "photographers" in the crew lists. Blume was also detailed to perform some of the work of group public relations officer as regarded photography. Colonel Chapman, the Group Commander, was very aware of his public image, and Blume made several short documentaries with his group for the colonel, before receiving a new and important assignment.

In his diary, which has never before been available to a researcher, Blume recorded that in September 1944 he was detailed to make a documentary about the training program that Chapman had instituted for new replacement crews. Blume spent most of September and much of October putting *Training in Combat* together, creating a shooting list and shooting schedule, writing a script, and so forth. And in the latter part of September he chose his actors—including Joseph Heller for the role of "Pete," a replacement bombardier. Bad weather in October limited the amount of outdoor shooting that could be done. More work on the documentary was accomplished in November, and "Pete" is in several scenes of what is left of the documentary, which has recently been pieced together at the National Archives.

Heller's name isn't found in the operational record, and he was not heard from in the general grousing about mission totals, because he wasn't flying; when he did fly after the Ponte San Martino attack in September, he flew what he later termed "milk runs." If a bargain was indeed offered to him in the aftermath of that mission, the *quid pro quo* would undoubtedly have been these safer duties in exchange for his silence about that mission. Heller's writing and interviews demonstrate that he was a man with a strong moral conscience; in retrospect, a bargain like this would certainly gnaw at a man like that over the years.

On December 10, "Haulin' Ass," the B-25J flown by First Lieutenant Fred Ritger of the 446th squadron, was shot down on a mission to bomb a troop assembly area in heavily defended Bologna. Though he was hit by flak on the bomb run, Ritger held "Haulin' Ass" in formation until "bombs away." As he commenced evasion action, the bomber began to lose altitude. By the time they got to Modena, "Haulin' Ass" was down to four thousand feet and unable to climb over the mountains between there and Corsica. Ritger passed the word to bail out. Co-pilot Second Lieutenant Albert Rondel, bombardier Second Lieutenant Charles Kaenzig, and radioman Corporal Emmitt Allen successfully bailed out but were captured and made prisoners of war. Turret gunner Sergeant Ingwal Hermanson and tail gunner Staff Sergeant Stuart Huntoon were killed when their parachutes failed to open. Ritger managed to connect with the local partisans and evaded capture until he got through the lines on December 22. Following his return to Corsica on December 23, Fred Ritger was ordered home as a successful evader.

December 10 was Jerry Rosenthal's first mission, and he remembered it well. The 340th group sent thirty-six planes from the four squadrons to hit the Rovereto railroad bridge, the most deadly target in northern Italy; there was no "guessing" about the Rovereto flak gunners.

With the briefing set for 0800 hours and takeoff for 0900 hours, Rosenthal and the rest of the crews were awakened at 0600 hours for a breakfast of fried eggs, bacon, and hot cakes. The briefing officer informed them that there was a possibility of enemy air activity, and that ten P-47s from the 57th Fighter Group were assigned as escort. Rosenthal's plane for the mission was "8K," 43-27916, which would fly number four in the third six-plane box with First Lieutenant J. H. Kroening, pilot; Second Lieutenant V. Fortuna as co-pilot; Second Lieutenant Norman Rosenthal, bombardier; Sergeant H. Lisby, turret gunner; and Sergeant P. Sims as tail gunner.

The eighteen B-25s from the 488th squadron crossed into Italy just north of La Spezia. Rosenthal and the others donned their flak vests and started to watch for strangers as the escorts joined up and took position. "We were at 12,000 over Lake Garda and climbed to 13,400 on the bomb run. No Oxygen. On the bomb run I pulled my helmet down around my ankles and picked up the K20 camera to shoot the bombs away and maybe the bomb strike of the leading boxes. The first box caught heavy, intense and inaccurate flak at the beginning of the bomb run and we got heavy, intense and accurate flak just before bombs away. My camera got jerked out of my hands when a flak burst came up through the floor and hit it."

As the bombers broke away after "bombs away," Rosenthal saw six Bf-109s jump the lead squadron from 9 o'clock high, while three others attacked the 488th's formation, two from left low and one left high. Other enemy fighters hit a B-25 that exploded and another that spun in with both engines on fire. One Messerschmitt flew through the formation; Rosenthal saw it coming but wasn't able to track it. Gunners in the formation got one of the German fighters, and the P-47 fighter-bombers knocked down four. The result of the mission was 64 thousand-pound bombs dropped in good pattern on the bridge. But the Rovereto gunners holed ten Mitchells and wounded one crewman. "It was a rough four hours."

Throughout the rest of December many missions were canceled as winter delivered rain and wet snow on Corsica; on half the days where the weather was good enough to launch a mission from the island, the weather over the mainland was so bad that the missions were called back or aborted when their leaders found the targets cloud-covered. Each group began to send weather reconnaissance flights in the morning to see the mainland weather for themselves in an attempt to get in missions wherever possible. The week before Christmas, each squadron of each group saw Christmas trees arrive in the Enlisted and Officers' Clubs, where they were decorated with the long aluminum strips of chaff used to bluff German radars. The end of 1944 saw the weather in Italy improve, and it continued to do so through most of the month of January, as it became clear and very cold. January and February would see a total of forty-six operational days of fifty-nine total.

In January 1945, the three groups flew forty-eight missions, 1,250 sorties, over the Brenner. Thirty-nine missions drew flak, with 224 aircraft hit and damaged and five lost. Even in the face of this opposition, the bombers closed the pass to through traffic on five separate days.

The 340th group's war diarist recorded that "milk runs are getting few and far between in northern Italy." The weather was such that there were several days of "severe clear" on Corsica when no missions could be flown because of storms in the Alps. Such days were given over to training missions. On January 10, the 340th's Captain Saleem Aswad led five Mitchells for formation flight training. As they finished the flight, Aswad noticed the formation had grown by one, with the addition of a B-25 carrying the markings of the 321st group. With Solenzara Field in sight not far away, Aswad gave a momentary thought to doing a mass "buzz job" of the 321st's base, to see what the newcomer might do. But as he turned toward Solenzara, something told him it was a bad idea and he turned away before reaching the field. As the formation passed over at a proper altitude, the sixth bomber peeled off and was observed to enter the landing pattern. On his return to Alesani, Aswad discovered just how lucky he had been. The B-25 that had joined up was being flown by Brigadier General Knapp, the wing commander, with the commanding officer of the 321st group in the right seat!

The success of the Soviet winter offensive of 1945 riveted the men on Corsica. The 340th's war diarist noted, "The Russian drive into Brandenburg has assumed spectacular proportions. Troops are now reliably reported within 40 miles of Berlin and a great massing of Russian troops on the Oder River in the vicinity of Frankfurt threatens the Nazis with a final smash into the capital city once the river is crossed in that sector." The war was moving out of range for the bombers on Corsica, and advance parties for all three groups were checking over the airfields on the mainland that they had been informed they would move to when the weather allowed.

With replacements few and far between as the higher Army leadership looked to a final defeat of the Nazis in Germany itself, the mission total was changed yet again. The men were informed in late February that the tour of duty was now "for the duration." Some men tried to turn in their wings, willing to accept transfer to the infantry as an escape from the repeated "charges of the light brigade" into the Brenner Pass, but they were refused. Paul Young remembered that "It really was like what was in the novel: you had to be crazy to continue, but if you tried to get out that meant you were sane and you had to stay. It wasn't called Catch-22 or anything, but the policy was there." Three weeks before the new policy was announced, Joseph Heller climbed aboard a C-47 at Alesani that took him to Naples, where he boarded a ship bound for New York; he had flown a total of only sixty missions. How he left when he did, when the rigidly enforced tour required at that time was seventy missions, has never been explained.

During February the bombers went as far north as Innsbruck, Austria. Fortunately the *Luftwaffe* was now so depleted even in Austria that they did not run into fighter opposition. German gun batteries were shifted north to Trento and Bressasone. New batteries appeared at Laves. The number of guns in the pass rose to 482. It was a rare mission now that did not draw flak. The German early warning system had been refined. When the incoming formation got within two hundred kilometers of a defended area, the gun batteries were alerted. When the formation passed within eighty kilometers, the guns were manned. Course and altitude were given by the mountaintop observers. There were no surprise attacks.

February 1945 was the worst month of the war for the 340th Bomb Group in terms of losses. Enemy defenses were stronger than ever before along the Brenner Pass. Aircrews described the flak as "murderous." Over the course of the month, six Mitchells were shot down, with thirty-seven aircrew members listed as missing in action and eleven others wounded.

On February 5 First Lieutenant Tom Cahill, now the senior bombardier in the 486th squadron and the acting Squadron Bombing Officer, flew his sixty-fifth mission. Each of the eight missions he had flown in January had been against targets heavily defended with flak. With luck, he would hit the magic "70" in a few weeks and receive orders home. On January 23 he had been awarded the Distinguished Flying Cross for his work as a lead bombardier in the same awards ceremony at which the 340th Group received their second Presidential Unit Citation for the September 1944 mission that Joe Heller had flown in and that sank the Italian cruiser *Taranto*. On this February 5 mission, Cahill would fly as navigator rather than bombardier with First Lieutenant Charles R. Ross, a different pilot and crew from the lead crew he normally flew with. Cahill's job was to navigate for the three anti-flak bombers that would go in ahead of the main formation of twelve B-25s of the 486th squadron. The targets for the anti-flak bombers were the guns at deadly Rovereto, while the main formation would head four miles north to hit the railroad bridge at Calliano. As the anti-flak planes dove on the gunners, the Germans opened up with 88-mm and 37-mm weapons. Cahill's B-25 was in the lead, and the bomb doors had just come open to drop the plane's load of white phosphorus on the gun positions when it took a solid hit in an engine. Flames quickly spread to the wing, and the bomber fell off to the side. A gunner in one of the other planes reported seeing one parachute, but there was never any other word of a possible survivor. The B-25 exploded as it hit the snowy hillside and burned out completely. Tom Cahill was two months short of his twenty-fourth birthday at the time of his death in action. The other two bombers in the formation pulled away in the face of the murderous gunfire, and no drop was made.

Five days after Tom Cahill went down, Sterling Ditchey, who had flown across the Caribbean and South America in the same formation with Cahill, reached the magic "70." Fortunately, a few replacements had been received in the 380th squadron and Ditchey received his orders to return stateside via ship. When he arrived in New York in early March, he was five weeks short of his twenty-second birthday.

The three groups flew eighty-two missions, 1,771 sorties during February. Sixty-two missions drew flak. Fourteen aircraft were lost and 305 were damaged, despite the introduction of white phosphorus for anti-flak operations. From January 30 through March 26, 1945, the rail line was cut somewhere every single day. But the fact that the line was out did not mean that no traffic was going through. Out of necessity, the Germans were running separate trains through different sectors, so that they had to unload and reload supplies, with delay in delivery. The trip from Munich to Bologna had taken anywhere from eight to twelve hours in October 1944; by March 1945 a delivery could take four to five days.

German NCO Werner Mork returned to northern Italy from Germany in late February 1945. Writing after the war, he recalled,

> Once we got to the Brenner in Northern Italy, it was the train itself that suddenly became the target. From this point on there were many disrupted stretches of track and in particular damaged bridges. At those points we had to exit the train and make our way across the rickety rail bridges by foot to where another train waited on the other side. The Brenner train was no longer a reliable means of transportation; I frequently had to get out and walk. Sometimes, on the other side of a damaged bridge there wouldn't even be a train, but rather a line of trucks that would take us to the next rail station that was still intact. All this sure raised our confidence that we would win the war.

In March 1945, the number of flak batteries increased yet again, especially in the northern Brenner Pass. Forty-three new guns were added for a total of 525. Ninety-six missions were flown during the month. Fifty-eight took flak, with fourteen B-25s lost and 207 damaged.

On March 10, the crew of "Puss and Boots," the B-25 Sterling Ditchey and his crew had brought to Corsica the previous May, flew her last mission, perhaps the toughest the 310th group flew in the Brenner Pass campaign.

The main Brenner Pass rail line ran through the town of Ora. A nearby bridge that had been previously knocked out had been repaired so that a single track was operational. A new line had also been constructed around a previously bombed area and was also now usable. Two missions were planned to hit both targets. Forty-eight B-25s from the 379th, 380th, 381st, and 428th squadrons of the 310th would each carry four thousand-pound bombs. Seven more would carry hundred-pound white phosphorus bombs and twenty-pound fragmentation bombs. Six others would fly as anti-flak suppression, while one anti-flak and six regular spares would follow the formation. Group Operations Officer Major Royal Allison and 379th Squadron Operations Officer Major Carl E. Rice decided to lead the two flights themselves.

The plan of attack was for the six anti-flak bombers from the 381st squadron to precede the main formation and hit gun positions. Thirty-two enemy guns were reported to be clustered in the area, with both German "88s" and Italian "105s." Twenty-four of the bombers in the main force from the 379th and 380th squadrons would bomb the railroad bridge, while eighteen B-25s from the 428th squadron would bomb the diversion line.

The bombers crossed the Italian coast north of La Spezia and climbed to cross the snowy peaks. Ahead of the main formation, the six anti-flak ships ran into heavy flak before they had a chance to drop their bombs. The Germans had lit smoke pots that obscured the targets. Box after box of the B-25s flew into the worst flak the crews had ever seen. Three of the bombers were shot down on the bomb run while a fourth crashed after dropping its bombs and attempting to turn away, and ten more were crippled by flak hits. Major Rice remembered, "Never have I heard so many flak bursts as on the bomb run that day." Major Allison reported, "The flak was everywhere—intense, heavy and accurate. Going into it seemed like a suicidal act. The first box was badly shot up and their plight could be seen by the others. The succeeding boxes went right in regardless."

In the first box was "Puss and Boots," now flown by First Lieutenant George F. Tilley Jr. The B-25 was severely damaged and forced out of the formation. Bombardier Second Lieutenant Russell Grigsby recalled, "We had broken away from the main formation a few minutes away from the

IP, when wham-wham-wham-wham, four bursts of flak exploded right below us." The flak riddled "Puss and Boots" and tore gaping holes in the wings, both engine nacelles, the cockpit—where large fragments smashed all but three instruments—and the radioman's station. The main hydraulic lines were completely severed and the emergency system was shot away; the landing gear and flaps were inoperable. "The right engine was smoking," Grigsby later wrote, "and several gas lines had been cut so that fuel began to pour into the turret gunner's and radioman's compartments."

Miraculously, none of the crew had been hit, though daylight poured through the fuselage. Tilley feathered the right engine, extinguishing the flames. With the bomber going down, the choice was bailing out or attempting to restart the engine with the chance it might explode. After several failed attempts, Tilley managed to get the engine running again. Realizing he had no airspeed indicator, the pilot called for help. First Lieutenant Victor Irons brought his Mitchell alongside the wounded "Puss and Boots."

Once the bomber was over Corsica, bombardier Grigsby and engineer-gunner Staff Sergeant George McTavey attempted to crank open the bomb doors to get rid of the plane's explosives, but it was impossible. They then tried unsuccessfully to crank down the landing gear. "By this time the fuel was ankle deep in both forward and rear compartments, and with the fumes we had to fight nausea as well as broken controls and flames."

A second attempt was made to lower the wheels; when it failed, Tilley pulled up and told the crew to prepare to bail out. Grigsby went out the lower forward hatch, followed by the navigator and co-pilot, while the radioman and tail gunner came out the rear lower hatch. Tilley trimmed the bomber and headed it out to sea, then bailed out successfully. He was awarded the Distinguished Flying Cross for saving his crew. Lieutenant Irons, who had escorted "Puss and Boots" home despite heavy damage to his own plane, was also awarded the DFC.

The B-25 flown by First Lieutenant George Rorer, who had survived a mid-air collision the previous September, was badly hit and caught fire in the right engine nacelle. With his co-pilot too seriously injured to bail out, Rorer attempted a crash landing. As he touched down, the right wingtip caught a tree. The Mitchell cartwheeled, burst into flames and broke in two. There were no survivors.

The 428th squadron B-25 flown by First Lieutenant Jordan Keister was hit and the right engine and nacelle burst into flames as the bomber fell behind the formation. As Keister fought to control his stricken plane, men in the other Mitchells saw four parachutes blossom when the crew bailed out. Moments later, the right wing tore off and the Mitchell spun in and exploded on impact.

Five pilots of the 379th squadron—Lieutenants George Parry, Richard McEldery, Andrew Dennis, Noah T. Shirley, and Gordon M. Jacobs—were awarded the DFC for bringing their badly shot-up bombers back successfully to save their crews.

Amazingly, despite the deadly flak that badly damaged eighteen bombers of the forty-eight and destroyed four, there were few men wounded. Multiple holes in areas occupied by crewmen should have caused wounds but didn't. Several planes returned with plexiglass hanging in pieces in the bombardiers' greenhouses, yet all the bombardiers had escaped uninjured. Ruptured gas lines and fuel tanks sprayed gasoline into fuselages, yet no one was burned.

Despite everything that the bombers had encountered on the mission, the railroad was cut in several places and the bridge so badly damaged that it could not be repaired before the end of the war. The 310th Bomb Group was awarded a second Distinguished Unit Citation for the Ora Bridge mission.

Paul Young would long remember his thirty-seventh mission, flown on March 24, 1945:

> As we flew away from the target, the guys in back called on the intercom to ask if we had taken a hit up front, since things were "very windy back here." We checked everywhere, but there was no damage. Our radioman then crawled into the space over the bomb bay and opened the inspection hatch to

discover that one of our thousand pounders had hung up by its tail shackles. It was hanging out the bomb bay, preventing the doors from closing. Not only that, but the arming propeller on the nose was spinning. I looked over at my co-pilot. Our first reaction was to bail out before the bomb was fully armed. But we were still thirty miles behind the lines, over enemy territory. There was a quick crew conference on the intercom and the radioman said he'd try something first before we bailed out. He then shucked his gear and lowered himself through that small inspection hatch in the roof of the bomb bay to hang by his arms while he repeatedly kicked the bomb. After what seemed an eternity, the tail gunner reported the bomb had fallen free. He then pulled the radioman out of the bomb bay. When we got back to our base, the first thing I did was write up a recommendation for a Distinguished Flying Cross for our radioman.

The squadron's war diary took no special notice of the event, noting only that three thousand-pound bombs were jettisoned after the mission: two at sea, one "over enemy territory."

On March 23, 1945, the 310th group suffered their last loss due to enemy air action. On a mission to bomb the Pordenone Railroad Bridge, the formation was attacked by an estimated twenty Italian-flown Bf-109s just as they broke from their bomb drop. Five of the fighters went after the B-25 flown by Second Lieutenant James J. Summers of the 380th squadron, the trailing aircraft of the box of six. Cannon fire struck the left engine and wing; white smoke began to trail as the oil system was knocked out. The hydraulic system had also been hit, with the result that the landing gear dropped down. With the extra drag of the gear, the bomber couldn't keep up with the others and dropped out of formation to the left. Inside, Summers and his co-pilot First Lieutenant Alex Zebelian Jr. fought to maintain control as the Mitchell headed toward the mountains below. The tail gunner and radioman went out the rear hatch while the bombardier kicked open the forward hatch and threw himself out. Parachutes blossomed quickly. Several Messerschmitts pressed a second attack, setting the damaged engine on fire; flames quickly spread to the wing. The Spitfire escort finally arrived and drove the enemy fighters off as the pilot, co-pilot, and turret gunner made their exit. By the end of the month, the co-pilot, turret gunner, and bombardier were back on Corsica, having been rescued by partisans. The others had been captured and made prisoner.

Captain Everett Robinson flew the lead plane of the formation from the 380th squadron. The second attack by the Italian fighters hit his B-25 in the engine before they were driven off by the escorts. Robinson managed to hold the badly damaged bomber in the air to return to Ghisonaccia, where he made a successful emergency landing; he was awarded a DFC for bringing his crew home uninjured.

The last formation of the 310th to attack the bridge were the twelve B-25s from the 379th squadron. Flying lead for the third box of six was First Lieutenant John M. Ford with his co-pilot, First Lieutenant William Poole. Two 109s hit the B-25 in its right engine and set it afire. Ford held formation until his bombardier could drop on the bridge before diving to put out the flames, then brought the bomber home.

First Lieutenant Walter E. Grauman's B-25 was on Ford's wing. The turret gunner opened fire as the Bf-109s flashed past, and one was seen to be smoking as it turned away. Altogether the bombers and their escort accounted for four enemy fighters shot down and three damaged.

The rains that came for the first time in two months at the end of March gave the crews of the 57th a five-day respite from operations, which was considered a mixed blessing. While the crews got needed rest, the Germans had five bomb-free days for their repair crews to work on a railroad system that had been made practically impassable.

March saw the operational use of SHORAN (SHOrt Range Aerial Navigation). The SHORAN system employed two radio transmitting stations, one high frequency and one low frequency. The equipment in the aircraft being guided included a transmitter, a receiver, an operator's console, and a K1A model bombing computer. The transmitter sent radio pulses to one of the ground stations, then to another, and the distance in miles to the station was calculated by clocking the elapsed time between the transmitter pulse and the returned signal. As the aircraft faced the target, the low-frequency station was on the left, and the high-frequency station was on the right, allowing the computer to triangulate the two stations and the target, whose location is known. Unlike the similar British "Oboe" blind bombing system, which could guide only one airplane at a time, SHORAN could guide multiple aircraft simultaneously. Thus, with the lead bombers equipped with the gear, the lead bombardier dropped his bombs when the computer placed the airplane over the target, with the bombardiers in the other planes "dropping on lead." SHORAN allowed the bombers to go after fixed targets regardless of the weather, increasing the missions flown.

The major limitation of SHORAN was that the system was limited to line-of-sight radio communication, which required the transmitting airplane to fly at altitudes above as much as fourteen thousand feet, depending on local geography, a difficult feat in a loaded B-25 without an oxygen system.

The SHORAN gear had first arrived in the 310th Group in late December 1944. Once the lead navigators and bombardiers were trained in its use, they taught their skills to the 321st and 340th groups during February, and the first missions were flown against Brenner targets in March. With SHORAN, the mission rate nearly doubled; the only limiting factor was if the cloud cover extended above the maximum altitude the Mitchells could fly at, fifteen thousand feet. Jerry Rosenthal recalled that by early March he had thirty missions and by the end of April his mission total was seventy. The last month of the war was the worst.

On April 6, 1945, the Quartermaster General of the German Fourteenth Army reported that it took four to five days for a shipment of supplies to get through the Brenner Pass. During the month of March, an average of eighteen hundred tons of supplies arrived each day, less than half the daily minimum necessary to sustain operations.

FINALE

THIRTEEN

FINALE

As the 57th Bomb Wing continued its engagement in the Battle of the Brenner Pass at the end of 1944, change came to the Italian Theater. In December, vainglorious Fifth Army commander General Mark W. Clark was appointed to command the Fifteenth Army Group as successor to British Army General Sir Harold Alexander, who was promoted to command of all Allied ground troops in Italy. More important for the aircrews was the officer who replaced Clark. Lieutenant General Lucian K. Truscott Jr.'s appointment to commanding general of Fifth Army was the most significant assignment of senior leadership in the entire Italian campaign.

Truscott was the American senior commander most successful in dealing effectively with the armed forces of other nations—a skill Mark Clark totally lacked. Truscott was gruff, intent on getting things done efficiently; he was no posing prima donna like Patton or Clark. His personality was free of the indecisiveness and incompetence that bedeviled so many of his contemporaries in North Africa and Italy, and he never, ever treated his soldiers or officers with the contempt for which Douglas MacArthur was so well known. He respected his men, and he demanded a lot from them. After Truscott was promoted to general, his troops were required to cover ground at the speed of the Roman Legions; this standard speed of advance was known throughout the army as "the Truscott Trot."

A more complete contrast to Clark could not be imagined. Though Truscott still had to suffer General Clark's repeated show-pony performances, the morale of the whole Army benefitted from his command. Even on Corsica, Dan Bowling recalled that "things changed for the better after Christmas. There was a different attitude everywhere." Truscott was now in command of the most international of Allied forces. Fifth Army had more British, South African, Brazilian, Polish, and Italian troops than Americans. This had been a constant problem for Clark, whose decision that beating the British to Rome was more important than defeating the *Wehrmacht* in Italy had been the final straw for many of the foreign officers who served under him.

Truscott took immediate action to help the units that were failing. The 92nd Division had performed poorly in combat with Italian Fascist units in late December; he rebuilt it by a thorough housecleaning of the worst of the Southern white supremacists, combined the best troops into a single regiment, and brought in the 442nd Regimental Combat Team, the Nisei (Japanese-American) unit recognized as the best combat regiment in the Army. The 92nd would redeem itself in the coming fight.

Truscott faced a difficult situation: on top of the massive losses suffered during the battles of the previous autumn, bad winter weather and difficult mountain terrain negated the ground forces' power of armored maneuver and made it nearly possible for the Allies to exploit their overwhelming air superiority. The manpower shortage was compounded by the need to transfer some British troops to Greece following the German evacuation of that country in December and to withdraw the British 5th Division and the Canadian Corps for transfer to northwest Europe.

Fortunately Truscott was able to convince Army Chief of Staff General George C. Marshall that now was the time to commit the Army's most unique combat unit, the Tenth Mountain Division, to combat.

Inspired by the humiliation that the Finnish ski troops had imposed on Soviet armored units during the Winter War of 1939–40, the Army had in 1942 created a regiment to train for winter warfare in mountain environments, with a full division formed by the end of that year. Trained at Camp Hale, Colorado, eight thousand feet high in the Rocky Mountains, the unit had within its ranks lumberjacks, cowboys, Olympians who would have competed in the Helsinki Winter Games of 1940, members of the National Ski Patrol, and All-American athletes. Marshall had deliberately held back committing the unit to combat until there was a situation that only they could handle. War high in the Tyrolean Alps in the coldest winter Europe had experienced in a century qualified as just such a situation. The Tenth Mountain Division arrived in Italy in December 1944 and entered combat in late January. They would remain in combat for the 110 days left of the war in Europe, though as Sergeant Tony Sileo recalled, "they took our skis away from us after our first couple weeks of patrols."

The division entered combat on January 28, 1945. At the end of the fall 1944 offensive against the Gothic Line, Allied troops had failed to take the commanding heights of Monte Belvedere, the key to Bologna, despite making three assaults. To get to Monte Belvedere, the ridge line known as Riva Ridge had to be taken. The Germans, considering the ridge impossible to climb, had manned it with only one battalion of mountain troops. On the night of February 18, 1945, the 86th Mountain Infantry's 1st Battalion and Fox Company of the 2nd Battalion made the fifteen-hundred-foot vertical assault in a snowstorm. By dawn, the GIs held the ridge. That day the 85th and 87th Regiments made a bayonet attack on Monte Belvedere itself without covering artillery fire. Again the surprise assault was successful; after a hard fight, the peak was captured. The men withstood seven German counterattacks over the next two days. In three days of fighting in conditions that no other

American unit had ever fought in, the division suffered 850 casualties, including 195 dead. They were now in position to breach the Gothic Line, take Highway 65 and open the way to the Po Valley.

The Allied offensive now awaited the spring thaw.

The war's finale saw the bombers of the 57th Wing leave Corsica in early April 1945 after having been in residence for a year. As the front lines in northern Italy moved and new targets in Austria and northern Yugoslavia were brought onto the list, the bases on Corsica were too distant from the action to allow the Mitchells to operate with full bomb loads.

The 340th group began its move to Rimini, a base south of Venice on the Adriatic coast of the Italian mainland, on April 4, 1945. The men were happy to discover that their quarters at the new base would be in Miramare and Riccione, towns which had been popular before the war as fashionable summer resorts. At last they would be living indoors. The group's war diarist noted, "The rooms have running water, are wired for lights, and have suffered no bomb or shell damage. Everybody is blinking with amazement at finding himself plunked down in this pleasant little town with fairly well dressed people, attractive girls, and small shops."

On April 6 the group flew its last missions from Alesani; the B-25s attacked the Poggio Rusco rail bridge and a ship in La Spezia harbor, both of which were missed, and also bombed a coastal gun near La Spezia that was holding up the 92nd Division's advance on the town of Massa, with good results. The Mitchells then flew on to the new field outside Rimini to take up permanent residence there.

The 321st had begun their move from Solenzara to Falconara a week earlier. On April 5, they flew their first mission from the Italian mainland. While missions were still being flown into the Brenner Pass, the emphasis had changed to missions in direct support of the coming Allied ground offensive. Dan Bowling, now promoted to captain, led twenty bombers of the 445th as part of an eighty-plane strike against German Defense Area "Harry," with the bombers dropping fragmentation bombs against gun positions and troop emplacements.

Sergeant Bernard Seegmiller arrived at Falconara on April 7 and recorded his impressions in his diary two days later.

We arrived here the afternoon of the 7th by C-47. The weather was quite bad and we flew blind most of the way. Some of our B-25s were forced to turn back on account of icing conditions. We are quartered inside a huge compound which accommodates the entire group. Each squadron occupies a barracks that is complete with showers, kitchen, administration and latrines. The construction is brick with tile floors and a great deal of marble. Some improvising has been done to convert the squat-down latrines into showers. I am told this place was built as a cavalry base by the Mussolini gang. It is very elaborate and well laid out. The field is very well laid out and steel planking covers the runway and taxi strips and hard stands. A British outfit built the landing facility and are still operating with Spits, Beaufighters, Mosquitos and PBYs. Fifteenth Air Force heavies frequently land here on emergency returns from targets in Germany and Austria. Several have come in badly shot up since we came over.

The ground crews of the 321st were happiest about the large hangars at Falconara. Finally, difficult jobs like engine changes could be done inside, with proper equipment for removing and replacing engines and performing other major repairs of shot-up airplanes.

On March 30, the 310th group commenced their move from Ghisonaccia to Fano, Italy, also on the Adriatic coast. The move to Fano was accomplished over the first ten days of April, with the main group arriving by April 6. The men were impressed to find that Fano was a neat, well-built seaside town at the end of the old Roman *Via Flaminia*, and that it had largely escaped the ravages of war as the Allies advanced up the Adriatic coast. The airfield was a mile south of town. Line personnel were quartered in several long, single-story masonry structures that had been divided into three-room apartments, and there were hangar facilities for maintenance. The Mitchells shared the field with Royal Air Force and South African Air Force tactical squadrons, composed of Spitfires, P-40 Kittyhawk dive-bombers, Beaufighters, Mosquitos, and B-26 Marauders.

One thing the men of all three groups noticed quickly was the wide-spread presence of military police. Gone were the days of not worrying overmuch about a shave, whether clothes were oil stained, whether all officers were properly saluted by the men, and, for the junior officers, whether their seniors were shown proper "military courtesy." As Tech Sergeant Fred Lawrence put it, "people are complaining about having rejoined the Army."

The Allies' final offensive commenced with massive aerial and artillery bombardments on April 9, 1945. Sergeant Seegmiller recorded his memories at the end of the day: "Today has been a big one. Every available aircraft in the theater operated in preparing a push-off for the Eighth and Fifth Armies. It began about 1500 hours and we watched every type of plane in the American Air Force go over like great flocks of geese as our own were taking off. It was an impressive sight and I could not help thinking, 'Those poor damn Germans.'"

From April 9, the 57th Wing was flying a "maximum effort" in support of the Allied armies, with each group and each squadron flying multiple missions. The 340th's war diarist, First Lieutenant Glenn Pierre, wrote of the day: "A terrific air pounding of German positions northeast and east of Bologna by 600 bombers and hundreds of fighters started shortly after one o'clock. 340th group put up 76 aircraft, almost half the B-25 wing effort. Our targets were two artillery concentration areas near Imola. Photo Interpreter says most of the 13 boxes of six aircraft each bombed very accurately. After the air attacks had ceased—about 1800 hours—the artillery got going and the Polish corps and the 10th British Corps, whom we were supporting, jumped off over the Senio river, bound for the banks of the Santerno river, the first pause point."

On April 11 Captain Jackson, the 321st group's war diarist, wrote,

> With the new Italian offensive rolling along, the target for today was the Argenta Reserve Area. Wing called for another maximum-effort day and we came through with 48 Mitchells taking off at 0758 hours and 24 more taking off at 0853 hours. The past three days, briefings have begun in the early

morning darkness; but no one seems to mind it, just so the offensive keeps going. The combined frag-load this morning was 8,520 fragmentation bombs and it forebodes another bad day for German GIs. The first formation over ran into heavy, moderate, accurate flak and one plane received a hit in the tail while on the bomb-run. It was last seen turning east and losing altitude rapidly. The second formation also ran into heavy flak and returned with three aircraft holed. The consolation was a 99 percent accuracy. After a hurried noon chow and darn little sack time, 24 planes went out for the San Ambrogio Rail Culvert at 1430 hours, and 18 more headed for the Volargne Rail Fill at 1540 hours.

Mission 846, to bomb the German troop assembly area at Argenta in front of the Australian division of the Eighth Army, was Dan Bowling's sixtieth and most memorable mission of the war. The newly promoted Captain Bowling led eighteen Mitchells at the forefront of a formation of forty-eight B-25s from all four squadrons in B-25J 43-27899, "Flo," one of the newest aircraft in the squadron, with Second Lieutenant Paul Riggenbach in the right seat, navigator First Lieutenant Robert Mitchell guiding the formation to the target, bombardier First Lieutenant Joe Silnutzer as group lead on whose aim the bombardiers in all the other planes in the group would depend, turret gunner Sergeant Antonio Palermo, radioman Sergeant Charles Eberhardt, and tail gunner Sergeant Philip Hieronimus. Fourteen Mitchells from the 446th squadron, led by Major Robert Smedley in "Merrily We Bomb Along," followed Bowling's formation. Six B-25s of the 447th Squadron led by First Lieutenant Norman Rose in "Number 62" were right behind Smedley's formation, while First Lieutenant W. F. Autrey in B-25J "Number 86," led ten 448th squadron planes in the rear formation.

The pre-mission briefing emphasized that timing was of the essence. There were two German divisions at Argenta that it was feared were ready to attempt a counterattack. Bowling, bombardier Silnutzer, and navigator Mitchell were told that the Allied troops would light smoke pots to mark the lines since the target was very close to the Allied positions. "If the white smoke changes to yellow, do not bomb," was the order. Yellow smoke would signify that the Allied troops had begun their attack. Considering the numerous occasions throughout the war when Allied bombers had hit their own side at places like Cassino and St. Lo, it was crucial for the bombers to arrive over the target on time, ahead of the attack. The thousands of twenty-pound fragmentation bombs they would shower over the enemy troops would give the Allied troops the cover they needed at the moment they started their advance. At the last minute, Bowling asked for information on the defenses and was informed there were over two hundred anti-aircraft weapons. "We were to bomb at 10,500 feet and 200 miles per hour. This was the most heavily-defended target we had gone against. I knew it was going to be tough."

Takeoff was at 0758 hours. Both Silnutzer and Mitchell had argued with Bowling about taking a new airplane on its first mission. It was a preview of things to come this day when the right engine took three tries to turn over properly and start. At the runway, there was a sharp drop on the right engine magnetos when Bowling checked them before takeoff.

After a turn over the field for join-up, Bowling led the forty-eight Mitchells on the forty-minute flight north over the Adriatic to Ravenna, where they would turn inland and head for Argenta. "When we were climbing to 10,500 feet, I realized the plane was very sluggish. When we got to altitude, I had to set the engines at nearly full-throttle to maintain 200 miles an hour, and the cylinder head temperatures on both engines were nearly at the red line." This meant severe problems for Bowling.

"I had to do something to save the engines, so I notified the formation I was reducing speed 20 miles an hour and climbing 500 feet. Three minutes from the target, we would dive back down to the correct altitude and pick up the right speed." It was crucially important that the formation have the right speed and altitude when they dropped their loads, since those were the settings in the Norden bombsights and any variance would mean they could not make an accurate drop.

The bombers arrived over the target three minutes early and Bowling increased power and dove back to 10,500 feet as he picked up speed back to two hundred miles per hour. "Suddenly all hell broke loose with black flak puffs right where we would have been had I not dived and picked up speed. Those flak gunners were right on us. Joe opened the bomb bay." As the bombers turned onto their bomb run, navigator Mitchell called out that he saw yellow smoke on the ground. Silnutzer replied "bomb doors closing." Bowling sensed something wrong and screamed at his bombardier to re-open the doors. "Roll forward six or seven hundred feet and bomb! I'll take the blame!"

Mitchell kept arguing they had to abort, that they were too late. "Then the flak was all around us. The plane on our right was hit twice and gone. I pulled to the right and had both engines past the red line, waiting for the explosion." As the formation followed Bowling's evasive action, the German gunners put a solid field of exploding flak where they would have been. "They were ten seconds too late to get us." The planes turned back left and forty-five seconds later Silnutzer announced "bombs away!"

Bowling immediately rolled left and reduced power. "The engines sounded ready to blow, so I got us headed back to the Adriatic, where at least we'd have a chance of being picked up. Moments later, the cylinder head temperatures came back down to red line. Still dangerous, but now with the bomber in a dive for the coast, cooler air was circulating through the cowling."

Forty minutes later, the bombers were back at Ancona. Bowling taxied to the hardstand, where two jeeps with four officers were waiting. "I thought we'd done it, hit our own troops." He shut down the engines while Silnutzer and Mitchell climbed out. "I saw it was the intel officer, ops officer, group bombardier and the deputy group CO. I figured we'd had it." And then the four were grabbing Silnutzer and Mitchell and shaking their hands." When Bowling crawled out, Colonel Camara, the deputy group CO, told him the mission had been perfect, that they had hit the Germans directly on target with a 100 percent drop.

The next day, the Line Chief Master Sergeant told Bowling that the engines on "Flo" had not been reset after her arrival in the group. When planes were flown across the South Atlantic, the engine power setting were adjusted for the long-range cruise power settings needed for the delivery flight across the South Atlantic. As a result, it had been a very near thing that Bowling had not lost both engines in his attack run.

The success at Argenta was marred by the loss of "Maggie," the B-25 flown by First Lieutenant Lewis Dentoni. It had been hit and forced out of formation from Bowling's right wing as the planes entered the bomb run. Flak hit the tail of the bomber and shattered it; everyone who saw that believed it likely killed tail gunner Staff Sergeant David Morisi immediately since they saw him blown out of the tail. Other crews reported seeing the bomber at six thousand feet over Lake Comacchio as it tipped over into a spin. One gunner thought he saw two parachutes pop open before the bomber crashed just behind Allied lines and caught fire, but no survivors were ever found. First Lieutenant Max Lewis, normally a first pilot, had flown the mission when his tentmate, Dentoni's co-pilot, reported an ear infection. Bowling's bombardier Joe Silnutzer was hit hard by the loss; he had shared his tent with Dentoni and Lewis since he arrived on Corsica and the three were close friends who had gone to Rome and Capri together on leaves.

Amazingly, Morisi, who had flown several previous missions with Bowling, had survived the hit on "Maggie"; the impact of the flak had knocked him unconscious and blown him out of the airplane still in his seat with all equipment still attached. The young sergeant came to and unhooked his seatbelt so that his seat and armor plate fell to the ground below and then pulled his ripcord and came down just north of the battle line, where he was captured by the Germans and spent the final weeks of the war as a prisoner.

The next day, the group was informed that an officer on the ground had mistakenly fired the flare that meant the yellow smoke pots were to be lit, rather than the correct white pots. The troops reported that the Germans were in shock from the bombing when they went over to the attack. Several thousand were killed and wounded, and the Australians took over thirty-five hundred prisoners.

Bad weather soon returned, and after an April 12 mission to Yugoslavia the 321st had to stand down. Sergeant Seegmiller discovered that there was a downside to living inside a barracks and wrote in his diary,

> It's cold and noisy in these brick barracks. Today I asked Captain Johnson if something couldn't be done for us armorers so we could get some sleep at night. He arranged to move us all to a single bay in the far end and partition it off from the rest which was quite decent of him. The first several days after we got here we worked almost constantly and all of us were completely worn out. Things have sort of slacked off since then. Yesterday a bomb fell on Bob Long and injured his back and foot. He was taken to the hospital and the report we have so far says he has a fractured spine and will be in a cast several months.

On the morning of Friday, April 13, the men in the three groups learned of the death of President Franklin D. Roosevelt as they stood in line for breakfast. For many, he was the only president they could remember.

On Saturday, April 14, 1945, the American Fifth Army offensive toward Bologna got underway. The attack was preceded by a thirty-minute wave of bombing from B-25s dropping fragmentation bombs and P-47s rocketing and strafing the German positions, all following a thirty-minute artillery barrage. Sergeant Hugh Evans of Item Company, 85th Mountain Infantry, remembered that "I had never seen anything like that, seen so many airplanes. You couldn't believe anyone could survive that."

The Morning Report of the 86th Infantry recorded,

> Promptly at 0830 the airplanes began to circle lazily over the front lines, to be greeted with shouts and waves from the troops below. The planes moved over the valley and let loose

with firebombs over Rocca di Roffeno. Great geysers of flame and heavy black smoke rose up to 200 feet in the air, and the concussion could be felt 3000 yards away.

When the planes had finished, the artillery opened up, seemingly pounding every spot that the Air Corps had missed. In a few moments the valley was almost completely obscured by a fog of gray, black, and white smoke. The bursting shells started rockslides on the shale slopes of Rocca di Roffeno, and buildings were reduced to irregular piles of rubble.

Unfortunately, the barrage was not as effective as at Argenta because of hazy weather that prevented fully accurate bombing. When the 85th and 87th Regiments attacked Hills 903 and 913 near Castel d'Aiano, the fighting was fierce, and 553 men were killed, wounded, or missing that first day. Among the wounded was a twenty-one-year-old Kansan, platoon leader Second Lieutenant Robert J. Dole of Item Company, who was badly wounded by machine gun fire that hit his upper back and right arm. When fellow soldiers saw how bad his injuries were, all they could do was give him the largest dose of morphine they dared and write an "M" for "morphine" on his forehead with his own blood, so that no one who found him would give him a second, fatal dose. They had to leave him behind as they continued the advance.

As the Tenth Mountain Division fought at Castel d'Aiano, the first two flights of the 445th squadron successfully attacked Argenta again, using SHORAN to bomb through the clouds (though the third flight did not drop due to malfunction of the SHORAN gear). That afternoon, Dan Bowling was rolling down the runway on takeoff for another mission to hit German artillery outside Bologna when he was surprised to see a Messerschmitt Bf-109 flash past as the pilot dropped his landing gear and put the fighter down on the runway. He barely missed Bowling, who managed to get airborne despite the near collision. As he turned over the field and looked down, Bowling could see the enemy fighter parked beside the runway, with the pilot out of the cockpit surrounded by ground personnel. "It turned out he was in the Croatian Air Force fighting for the Germans, and had decided today was a good day to end his war, so he flew over from Yugoslavia and landed at the first field he found, which happened to be ours."

With the success of the Battle of the Brenner, the end of the war in Italy came quickly. On April 18, Eighth Army units in the east broke through the Argenta Gap and sent armor forward to encircle the Tenth Army and meet the American IV Corps, which advanced from the Apennines in Central Italy. The remaining defenders of Bologna were trapped.

On April 19, Dan Bowling flew what would turn out to be his final mission of the war. The Vignola Road Bridge between Bologna and Modena separated the headquarters of *90.Panzergrenadierdivision* from the unit's vehicle storage park. Bowling led six bombers from the 445th, while seven bombers of the 446th followed. Flight operations that day were so heavy that the usual eighteen-plane formation could not be put together. Despite flak from two six-gun 88-mm flak batteries, they hit the target in two extremely close bomb patterns over the entire length of the three-hundred-foot bridge, with four spans destroyed and one seriously damaged. The mission went into the 321st record book as "Mission of the Month." When Bowling returned to Falconara, he learned he was being taken off flying duties. He was offered a promotion to major if he remained with the unit but declined the honor and took the orders that arrived two weeks later to send him home.

On April 21, the Polish Third Carpathian Division and the *Italian Grupo Friuli*, both from Eighth Army, and the U.S. 34th Infantry Division from Fifth Army entered Bologna. Meanwhile, bypassing Bologna, the Tenth Mountain Division reached the Po River on April 22, and the Eighth Army's 8th Indian Infantry Division arrived on the river the next day. The 340th's war diarist, Lieutenant Pierre, wrote, "Bologna has fallen to the Fifth and Eighth armies, it was announced today. Air support undoubtedly was a big key in making the Germans release their iron grip of last autumn and winter. With their supplies cut off by bombing and communications badly slashed, the Germans could only fall back under the tremendous armored drive of our Allied 15th Army Group."

The bombers of the 57th continued flying missions to hit bridges and block the German retreat until the weather closed in on April 25. Captain Jackson of the 445th squadron wrote, "'Going home' is the topic of the day. Everyone constantly talks or makes a ready listener for such talk. The war from this group's point of view is over. Targets change so fast that missions are uncertain from day to day."

As much as everyone expected the end, there was still time for fighting and dying. The 321st group flew its 895th mission to bomb the Cavarzere Road Bridge on April 25, led by Captain Wayne Kendall of the 445th in "Spirit of Portchester," a SHORAN-equipped B-25, with nine other Mitchells, including 43-335955, "06," flown by Paul Young. The nine B-25s from the 446th squadron included the veteran 43-4074, "27," flown by First Lieutenant Roland Jackson. Three bombers from the 447th rounded out the formation. The mission proved "hot" with German flak again reaching for the planes.

The veteran Mitchell 43-4074, which had survived the battle of Cassino, the invasion of Southern France, the first assault on the Gothic Line, and the entire Battle of the Brenner Pass, was hit by flak that knocked out an engine and set her afire. Shrapnel from several explosions flew through the thin aluminum skin of the plane, wounding bombardier Sergeant Robert Lattin, turret gunner Staff Sergeant Joseph Dalpos, radioman Sergeant Henry Nichols, and tail gunner Sergeant George W. Darnielle. Nichols, Dapos, and Darnielle bailed out, but Darnielle's parachute failed to open and he fell to his death. Lieutenant Jackson was able to keep the plane aloft until they had crossed the Allied lines, where he crash-landed at the first airfield he spotted. Pilot and co-pilot managed to pull the wounded bombardier out of the nose and ran from the burning bomber, which exploded minutes later.

Sergeant Darnielle was the last member of the 57th Bomb Wing to be killed in action. Two other missions were flown that day by the 321st, but they were "milk runs," and Mission 897 proved to be the group's last mission of the war.

On April 25 the Italian Committee of National Liberation called for a general uprising by the partisans in the remaining German-held towns and cities across northern Italy. By April 27, Genoa, Milan, and Turin were liberated.

Units of the Eighth Army advanced towards Venice and Trieste on April 25, while units of the U.S. Fifth Army drove north toward Austria and northwest to Milan. On the left flank, the 92nd Infantry Division moved along the coast to Genoa. A rapid advance towards Turin by the Brazilian division took the German–Italian Army of Liguria by surprise, leading to its collapse and surrender.

On April 27, Benito Mussolini and his mistress Clara Petacci were stopped by communist partisans near the village of Dongo, on Lake Como, as they headed for Switzerland to board a plane and escape to Spain. They were identified by Urbano Lazzaro, the Political Commissar of the 52nd Garibaldi Brigade. The next day they were both summarily shot, along with fifteen ministers and officials of the Italian Social Republic, in the village of Giulino di Mezzegra. On April 29, the bodies were trucked south to Milan where they were dumped on the old Piazzale Loreto which had been renamed "Piazza Quindici Martiri" in honor of fifteen anti-Fascists recently executed there. After being shot, kicked, and spat upon, the bodies were hung upside down on meat hooks from the roof of an Esso gas station and stoned by civilians.

On April 28, Captain Jackson of the 445th squadron wrote,

> Well, it looks like the inevitable has happened, because without doubt, we have run out of targets. Today was a good flying day, but wing did not assign any targets and approved local transition flights. The battle lines are more fluid than ever before, and wherever our troops haven't entered, reports are that the Partisans are holding the towns. Milan, Turin and Venice were taken over by the Partisans and our forces moved up to make conjunction with them. It seems that the Allied command is reluctant to assign targets to us because of the possibility of assigned objectives already taken by

rapidly moving ground forces. The day was climaxed with an announcement from Gen. Clark that "German resistance in Italy has virtually been eliminated."

By April 29 the German Army Group C had retreated on all fronts, having lost most of its fighting strength. General Heinrich von Vietinghoff, who had stymied the Allied armies from Salerno to the Gothic Line, was left with little option but surrender. That day, he signed the instrument of surrender on behalf of the German armies in Italy, with hostilities to come to a formal end on May 2, 1945. On hearing the news of the German surrender, Captain Jackson wrote, "After almost two-and-a-half years of slugging, bombing, mud and mountains, the enemy collapsed practically overnight and the Italian campaign closed in a blast of superlatives. We've made greater gains than any other theatre; we've taken the biggest bag of prisoners on all fronts; we're the first theatre to wind up; and we're the first theatre to receive an unconditional surrender from an army group. As for the group, we just wound up our busiest month in existence and set a lot of records for future operations to aim at."

During the Battle of the Brenner Pass between November 6, 1944 and April 6, 1945, the 57th Bomb Wing flew 6,839 individual sorties. They dropped 10,267 tons of bombs on the rail targets. Forty-six B-25s were lost, while 532 were damaged. Over five hundred aircrew members were killed or wounded.

On Memorial Day, May 30, 1945, General Lucian Truscott came to Nettuno, Italy, to dedicate the Sicily-Rome American Cemetery on behalf of America and president Harry Truman. There is unfortunately no recording of his speech, but famed GI cartoonist Bill Mauldin, who had chronicled the Italian campaign through his characters "Willie and Joe," was present. He wrote about the experience in his memoir, *The Brass Ring*:

> The general's remarks were brief and extemporaneous. He apologized to the dead men for their presence here. He said

everybody tells leaders it is not their fault that men get killed in war, but that every leader knows in his heart this is not altogether true. He said he hoped anybody here through any mistake of his would forgive him, but he realized that was asking a hell of a lot under the circumstances. He would not speak about the glorious dead because he didn't see much glory in getting killed if you were in your late teens or early twenties. He promised that if in the future he ran into anybody, especially old men, who thought death in battle was glorious, he would straighten them out. He said he thought that was the least he could do.

Today, if one travels from Innsbruck to Bologna on the Brenner Pass train, the rails run some three to five hundred yards west of the tracks bombed by the 57th Wing seventy years ago. The destruction was so complete that there was no attempt at post-war repair; a new line was constructed. Italy is a land where armies have left ruins for two and a half thousand years, and the traveler who knows what to look for can see the ruins of the old rail line to the east. At Rovereto, once known as the deadliest flak target in Italy, the concrete positions of the German anti-aircraft artillery batteries can still be seen high on the mountains on either side of the narrow pass through which young men rode aluminum steeds, "Cannon to the right of them, / Cannon to left of them, / Cannon in front of them," "Into the valley of Death."

NOTES ON SOURCES

The primary source of information for this book is the collection of war diaries of the three bomb groups and twelve bomb squadrons of the 57th Bomb Wing, maintained by Dan Setzer at the 57th Bomb Wing Association website. These war diaries have been digitized by volunteers, often sons of wing members. They are interspersed with other material contributed to the site by original members of the wing and by family members. These include quotations from diaries and letters of wing members. Included in this material is the diary of Sergeant Bernard Seegmiller, an armorer of the 445th Bomb Squadron of the 321st Bomb Group, and a prolific and insightful diarist. Other items that have been added into the war diaries include official correspondence regarding loss reports, statements by returned aircrew who successfully evaded capture after being shot down, and so forth.

The diaries themselves vary widely in quality, depending on the depth of responsibility felt by the individuals who were assigned to maintain them. In the 321st Bomb Group, Captain William Nickerson, the squadron intelligence officer for the 445th Bomb Squadron, is the standout war diarist. He was a Wall Street lawyer by profession before the war, and he understood the importance of maintaining thorough records. Additionally, he had a strong sense of history, which is revealed throughout his commentaries. He trained his replacement, First Lieutenant James O. Locke, well, and the 445th's war diaries remain the gold standard for the wing throughout the war. In contrast, the war diarists for the other three squadrons in the 321st did nothing more than list the daily missions and the aircraft and aircrew assigned for each mission, without additional commentary.

The next-best war diarist is Lieutenant Glenn Pierre, who maintained the war diaries for the 340th Bomb Group. Whereas Captain Nickerson stuck to documentary history, Lieutenant Pierre seems to be a frustrated novelist. He writes with a lighter tone and finds time to refer to attitudes and outlooks and personal conflicts, to which Nickerson paid no attention. This approach was of great assistance to me in identifying the source of the conflict that I believe shaped the writing of Joseph Heller, who flew as a bombardier in the 488th Bomb Squadron of the 340th.

The website also contains many personal accounts that have been provided over the years by members of the wing. Many of these were originally published in *Men of the 57th Bomb Wing*, the official journal of the 57th Bomb Wing Association.

The 310th Bomb Group has the least-preserved war diaries. In fact, the documents on the website stop well before the events of 1944–45. Fortunately, Charles Arthur Hair privately wrote and published *The Saga of '54 And More* and *Bullets, Bombs and Bridges*, a two-volume history of the 310th that covers the unit from its initial formation in 1942 through the end of the war. *Bullets, Bombs and Bridges* covers the period from Cassino through the Battle of the Brenner to the end of the war. This history was written for the members of the group and their families and has not been generally available to the public. I am indebted to Sterling Ditchey for providing me with his copies. The books are based on material gathered by Sergeant Frank B. Dean, who became the unofficial group historian after the war and collected many records and remembrances by members of the group in the years after the war. This has been as close a substitute to the war diaries for the 310th as I could find. George Underwood is also to be praised for having kept every piece of paper that referred to him and his friends—orders, reports, and so forth—which helped to flesh out the story of the group.

Sergeant Frederick H. Lawrence, 445th Bomb Squadron crew chief, who was a "plank owner" of the group and served in it to the end of the war, also wrote two books about the 321st: *Mediterranean Mitchells*, a history of the group from its formation in August 1942 to the end of the war, and *Untold and Unsung*, a personal memoir of being a mechanic in the group. Too often the voice of the enlisted man is passed over in writing military history unless an individual happens to have some writing ability and leaves behind work such as these two books. Both were privately published, and I am in debt to Dan Bowling for giving me his copies to study.

Dan Bowling, who was described by his fellow 445th Bomb Squadron pilot Paul Young as "our squadron leader—that's different from the squadron commander," sat down over the six months immediately after his discharge in 1945 and wrote an account of his experiences in the 445th Bomb Squadron during the Battle of the Brenner Pass. Dan didn't have to search his memories to produce the manuscript, which was his way of dealing with what had happened to him and what he had done during the war. It is the only first-person account of the campaign other than Tom Cahill's letters and is as close as one can get to climbing in a time machine and going back to interview one of these men at the age of twenty-two. Dan put the manuscript in a box that sat in his garage for nearly fifty years, until his son Lance Bowling discovered it. Lance, who is a successful record producer, immediately understood the historical value of his discovery and had his father's account privately published as *Follow P.D.I.: My Experiences as an AAF B-25 Pilot During World War II*. I'm indebted to Lance for giving me a copy for my research.

Tom Cahill's letters remain with us because of the efforts of his niece, Michelle Cahill, to gather them from her grandmother's home and publish them as an e-book: *Dear Mom: A Family Finds Its Past in World War II Letters Home.* The book is available POD on Amazon. Like Dan's book, Tom's letters open a door into time and provide an immediacy no interview today could convey.

Patricia Chapman Meder, daughter of the commander of the 340th Bomb Group, wrote *The True Story of Catch-22—the Real Men And Missions of Joseph Heller's 340th Bomb Group in World War II.* Fortunately, in her research she gathered many of the interviews Heller gave in the years after publication of the novel, which provided the first insights for me into finding out what experiences might have motivated his writing it. Heller's characters are different from the men on whose lives he based them, but there is also a closeness to the real people that he never admitted.

Dan Setzer put me in touch with Italian historian Roger Juglair, whose work on the bombing of the Settimo Bridges and the town of Ponte San Martino on August 24, 1944, was crucial to understanding Heller's state of mind during the war. Armed with Roger's detailed account of the event, I suddenly saw the vital truth of *Catch-22* when I read chapters 29 and 30 and found within them all the events of the August 24 mission, complete with all the arguments noted by the group war diarist after the fact.

By chance, I happened on the blog kept by Burton Blume, which revealed the existence of the documentary *Training in Combat.* The stills Burton had put up of Joseph Heller in the role of "Pete, a young bombardier," were the first photos I found of Heller during the war—when over the years he was asked for photos, Heller often said that he was not very photogenic then. Once I was in contact with Burton, I discovered the existence of his father's diary, to which he gave me access and where I found the crucial information about the documentary project being "the Colonel's boondoggle." All of this, along with a long conversation with Buck Henry about his memories of working with Heller, led to my educated guess about why the novel was written. Other researchers had made note of the fact that Heller "shut up" after late August, but no one else had knowledge of the existence of the documentary project. The only way to confirm the accuracy of my educated guess would be for Joe Heller himself to return from the dead and answer questions, but the facts and the circumstances certainly support my hypothesis.

The chapter about the 57th Fighter Group is based on the memoirs of Brigadier General Michael C. McCarthy's memoir, *Air to Ground Battle For Italy*, published by the Air University Press at Maxwell Air Force Base as part of the Air Force University's series of oral history monographs. Additional material on the group came from former pilot Harmon Dier's private account, *957 Days in the AAF in World War II*, a personal history of his time in the 66th Fighter Squadron of the 57th Group written for his family and donated by his son to the 57th Fighter Group Association, where it was published on the group's website.

Interviews with pilots Paul Young, Dan Bowling, and Victor Hanson of the 445th Bomb Squadron, radioman-gunner Jerry Rosenthal of the 488th Bomb Squadron, and bombardier Sterling Ditchey and gunner George Underwood of the 310th Bomb Group provided personal insight into the events in question.

ONE: THE AVIGNON MISSION

Chapter One is a dramatization of the mission of August 8, 1944, which Joseph Heller described in his 1973 *Playboy* interview, extensively quoted in Patricia Chapman Meder's *The True Story of Catch-22*.

TWO: WELCOME ABOARD THE "USS CORSICA"

The quotations describing the eruption of Mount Vesuvius come from "The Mount Vesuvius Eruption of March 1944," which can be found in the war diaries of the 340th Bomb Group for March 1944 at the 57th Bomb Wing Association website

Descriptions of the missions covered in this chapter are found in the war diaries of the 340th Bomb Group and 321st Bomb Group for March–April 1944.

The quotations from the diary of Sergeant Bernard Seegmiller are found in the April 1944 war diary for the 445th Bomb Squadron of the 321st Bomb Group, as are the diary quotations describing the trip to view Vesuvius by the four sergeants who made the trip.

The descriptions of the move to Corsica are found in the war diaries of the 340th and 321st Bomb Groups for April 1944.

The background history of Corsica in the Second World War is based on Edwin A. Hoyt's *Backwater War: The Allied Campaign In Italy, 1943–45*, published in New York in 2006 by Stackpole.

The description of the *Lehregeschwader 1/Kampfgeschwader 76* raid on Corsica is based on the description in *The German Air Raid on the 340th Bomb Group Stationed at Alesani Airfield, Corsica*, published at the 57th Bomb Wing Association website.

THREE: THE WAR NO ONE WANTED TO FIGHT

Discussion of Allied disagreement over the proposed Italian campaign is also found in Hoyt's *Backwater War*.

The difficulties of the Salerno invasion are dealt with in depth in volume 3 of Martin Blumenson's *Salerno to Cassino: United States Army in World War II, Mediterranean Theater of Operations*, published in 1969 in Washington, D.C., by the Office of the Chief of Military History, U.S. Army.

My account of the German response to the Italian surrender and the development of a strategic response to the Allied landings is based upon material presented in Ralph S. Mavrogordato's "Chapter 12: Hitler's Decision on the Defense of Italy" in *Command Decisions*, edited by Kent

Roberts Greenfield and published in 1960 by the United States Army Center of Military History.

FOUR: POINT OF NO RETURN

The account of the development of the South Atlantic air route is based on William R. Stanley's "The Trans-South Atlantic Air Link in World War II" in *Geo Journal* 33, no. 4 (August 1994), pp. 459–63, and "The Army Air Forces in World War II: The Early Development of Air Transport and Ferrying," AFHRA Document 00180144, Air Force Historical Research Agency.

Material on Sterling Ditchey's training, his meeting his future wife, and his flight to Africa come from *What Grandpa Did In The War*, a personal memoir Sterling wrote for his family, and from personal interviews.

Tom Cahill's story comes from his letters in *Dear Mom: A Family Finds Its Past In World War II Letters Home.*

FIVE: THE CRUCIAL MONTH

The discussion of the four battles of Cassino is based on material from the following sources: Rudolf Bohmler, *Monte Cassino: a German View* (London: Cassell, 1964); Gregory Blaxland, *Alexander's Generals: the Italian Campaign 1944–1945* (London: William Kimber, 1979); and John Keegan: *The Second World War* (London: Penguin, 1989).

Mark Clark's decision to liberate Rome rather than capture the German Army is discussed in Sidney T. Matthews's "Chapter 14: General Clark's Decision to Drive to Rome" in Greenfield's *Command Decisions.*

Material regarding the 57th Bomb Wing comes from the May 1944 war diaries of the 340th and 321st Bomb Groups and Charles A. Hale's

Bullets, Bombs and Bridges: *The Story of the 310th Bombardment Group*, Part II, and in Frederick H. Lawrence's *Untold and Unsung*, both published privately.

SIX: THE WORST DAY

The information on the June 22, 1944, mission comes from Hale's *Bullets, Bombs and Bridges*, Part II.

George Underwood's story is based on personal interviews with me and on *My Experience of World War II*, the personal memoir George created for his family.

SEVEN: SHOT DOWN

The stories of shot-down airmen come from Hale's *Bullets, Bombs, and Bridges*, Part II.

The story of the DeBoer crew's experience comes from Dan Bowling's *Follow P.D.I.: My Experience As An AAF B-25 Pilot in World War II*; from information provided by Paul Young; and from answers to questions I posed to Jay DeBoer via his son William.

Information on the Italian Resistance comes from Tom Behan's *The Italian Resistance: Fascists, Guerrillas and the Allies* (London: Pluto, 2009).

Information on the B-25 "McKinley Jr. High" is from an account by Harry George recorded by his son and posted at the 57th Bomb Wing Association website.

EIGHT: SPROGS, SPORTS, OLD SPORTS, AND WHEELS

This chapter is based on the memoir of Brigadier General Michael C. McCarthy, *Air To Ground Battle For Italy*, published by the Air University Press at Maxwell Air Force Base as part of the Air Force University's series of oral history monographs, and on former pilot Harmon Dier's private account, *957 Days in the AAF in World War II*, a personal history of his time in the 66th Fighter Squadron of the 57th Group written for his family and donated by his son to the 57th Fighter Group Association.

NINE: THE SETTIMO BRIDGE

Information about the missions flown by the 340th Bomb Group and the controversy over mission requirements is in the August 1944 war diaries of the 340th group and the 445th Bomb Squadron.

The 310th's missions in August and the mission to Toulon to attack the French ships is detailed in Charles A. Hale's *Bullets, Bombs and Bridges*, Part II.

The information about the Italian experience of the bombing of Ponte San Martino on August 23 comes from materials provided by Roger Juglair.

The final scene of Chapter 29 and the first scene of Chapter 30 of *Catch-22* are Heller's fictionalization of the Ponte San Martino–Settimo Bridge mission. The two long quotations from *Catch-22* come from page 327 and page 330 in the 50th anniversary edition of Heller's novel.

Information on the documentary project comes from the diary of Wilbur Blume.

TEN: THE GOTHIC LINE

The battle to break the Gothic Line is detailed in Douglas Orgill's *The Gothic Line: The Autumn Campaign in Italy 1944* (London: Heinemann, 1967).

Information on the participation of 57th Bomb Wing units and diary quotes are found in the 321st and 340th Bomb Group war diaries for September–October 1944. Information on the participation of the 310th Bomb Group is from Charles A. Hale's *Bullets, Bombs and Bridges*, Part II.

Dan Bowling's recollections of the Gothic Line campaign are taken from *Follow P.D.I.* and a personal interview.

Captain "Ace" Russell and the bad weather are detailed in Lawrence's *Untold and Unsung.*

ELEVEN: KEEP 'EM FLYING

This chapter is based on stories from original crewmen collected by Frederick H. Lawrence and told in *Untold and Unsung.*

Quotations from Sergeant Seegmiller were found in the May, June, July, August, and September war diaries of the 321st Bomb Group.

Dan Bowling's account of his Rome flight is in his *Follow P.D.I.*

TWELVE: OPERATION BINGO

The 321st and 340th Bomb Groups war diaries for November 1944–April 1945 and Hale's *Bullets, Bombs and Bridges* provide the detail for this chapter.

Additional material is from interviews with Sterling Ditchey, Jerry Rosenthal, Bernie Peters, Victor Hanson, and Paul Young and from Tom Cahill's letters in *Dear Mom.*

My account of the making of *Training During Combat* is based on the diary of Wilbur Blume, provided to me by his son, Burton Blume.

The explanation of the operation of SHOTAN is found in Hale's *Bullets, Bombs and Bridges.*

THIRTEEN: FINALE

Operational material and quotations come from the war diaries of the 321st and 340th Bomb Groups and from Charles A. Hale's *Bullets, Bombs and Bridges.*

The account of Dan Bowling's experience is from a personal interview and from his account in *Follow P.D.I.*

Information about the 10th Mountain Division was developed from personal interviews conducted with former division members Albert G. Field, Anthony Sileo, Bob Whitman, Gene Evans, and Hugh Evans.

INDEX

B